"Many are the ways in which women *de facto* exercise transformative and prophetic leadership throughout the world. Such ways, however, often remain ignored and insufficiently affirmed in many corners of church and society. We have an obligation, ethical and religious, to learn more from how, where, and why Christian women lead. Reading the voices gathered in Ahida Pilarski's *Daughters of Wisdom* is a solid step in fulfilling such an obligation."

—HOSFFMAN OSPINO, Boston College

"*Daughters of Wisdom* offers a paradigm for every conversation about women and the church in the third millennium, drawing from the tradition, the academy, and the apostolate. Readers learn of the ways women integrate faith, family, and communal life in prophetic ways in spaces within the church and the world."

—SUSAN M. TIMONEY, The Catholic University of America

"If the Catholic Church across the world is going to walk together in synodality, then, as this inspiring volume makes clear, its men and male leadership are going to have to catch up. The essays here reiterate that the wisdom of women, who have long sustained the church as the Blessed Virgin sustained the Christ child, lights a vibrant way ahead and their lead offers a guide to the path of faithfulness in this third millennium."

—DANIEL P. RHODES, Loyola University Chicago

"*Daughters of Wisdom* vibrantly reveals the steadfast living Spirit moving among us through the creative and adaptive leadership of women on the peripheries, amidst great obstacles with great love. Indeed, hidden treasures for the church and world, we must heed their prophetic invitation to risk creating living structures of and for the earth and the gospel. This hope-filled book will inspire us to do so, together as church."

—JOANNE DOI, Catholic Theological Union

Daughters of Wisdom

†

# STUDIES IN WORLD CATHOLICISM

*Michael L. Budde and William T. Cavanaugh, Series Editors*

*Karen M. Kraft, Managing Editor*

## Other Titles in This Series

*Beyond the Borders of Baptism: Catholicity, Allegiances, and Lived Identities.* Edited by Michael L. Budde. Vol. 1, 2016. ISBN 9781498204736

*New World Pope: Pope Francis and the Future of the Church.* Edited by Michael L. Budde. Vol. 2, 2017. ISBN 9781498283717

*Scattered and Gathered: Catholics in Diaspora.* Edited by Michael L. Budde. Vol. 3, 2017. ISBN 9781532607097.

*A Living Tradition: Catholic Social Doctrine and Holy See Diplomacy.* A. Alexander Stummvoll. Vol. 4, 2018. ISBN 9781532605116.

*Fragile World: Ecology and the Church.* Edited by William T. Cavanaugh. Vol. 5, 2018. ISBN 9781498283403.

*Love, Joy, and Sex: African Conversation on Pope Francis's* Amoris Laetitia *and the Gospel of Family in a Divided World.* Edited by Stan Chu Ilo. Vol. 6, 2017. ISBN 9781532618956.

*The Church and Indigenous Peoples in the Americas: In between Reconciliation and Decolonization.* Edited by Michel Andraos. Vol. 7, 2019. ISBN 9781532631115.

*Pentecostalism, Catholicism, and the Spirit in the World.* Edited by Stan Chu Ilo. Vol. 8, 2019. ISBN 9781532650352.

*Gathered in My Name: Ecumenism in the World Church.* Edited by William T. Cavanaugh. Vol. 9, 2020. ISBN 9781532685583.

*For God and My Country: Catholic Leadership in Modern Uganda.* J. J. Carney. Vol. 10, 2020. ISBN 9781532682520.

*African Ecological Ethics and Spirituality for Cosmic Flourishing: An African Commentary on* Laudato Si'. Edited by Stan Chu Ilo. Vol. 11, 2022. ISBN 9781666738711.

## Forthcoming Titles in This Series

*Fratelli Tutti: A Global Commentary.* Edited by William T. Cavanaugh, Carlos Mendoza-Álvarez, OP, Ikenna U. Okafor, and Daniel Franklin Pilario, CM.

# Daughters of Wisdom

Women and Leadership in the Global Church

EDITED BY

*Ahida Calderón Pilarski*

FOREWORD BY

*Teresa Maya, CCVI*

CONTRIBUTORS

*J. J. Carney*
*Neomi De Anda*
*Wendy M. Louis*
*MarySylvia Nwachukwu, DDL*
*Jeane Caña Peracullo*

*Ahida Calderón Pilarski*
*Barbara E. Reid, OP*
*Melinda A. Roper, MM*
*María del Pilar Silveira*
*Niceta M. Vargas, OSA*

CASCADE *Books* · Eugene, Oregon

DAUGHTERS OF WISDOM
Women and Leadership in the Global Church

Studies in World Catholicism 12

Cascade Books
An Imprint of Wipf and Stock Publishers
199 W. 8th Ave., Suite 3
Eugene, OR 97401

www.wipfandstock.com

PAPERBACK ISBN: 978-1-7252-9033-4
HARDCOVER ISBN: 978-1-7252-9018-1
EBOOK ISBN: 978-1-7252-9032-7

*Cataloguing-in-Publication data:*

Names: Pilarski, Ahida Calderón, editor. | Maya, Teresa, foreword.

Title: Daughters of wisdom : women and leadership in the global church / edited by Ahida Calderón Pilarski ; foreword by Teresa Maya.

Description: Eugene, OR : Cascade Books, 2023 | Series: Studies in World Catholicism | Includes bibliographical references and index.

Identifiers: ISBN 978-1-7252-9033-4 (paperback) | ISBN 978-1-7252-9018-1 (hardcover) | ISBN 978-1-7252-9032-7 (ebook)

Subjects: LCSH: Christian leadership—Catholic Church. | Women in church work—Catholic Church. | Women in the Catholic Church.

Classification: BV639.W7 D38 2023 (print) | BV639.W7 D38 (ebook)

# Table of Contents

# Contributors

**J. J. Carney** is associate professor of theology at Creighton University (Omaha, Nebraska). He is the author of *For God and My Country: Catholic Leadership in Modern Uganda* (2020) and *Rwanda before the Genocide: Catholic Politics and Ethic Discourse in the Late Colonial Era* (2014). He is also co-author of *Contesting Catholics: Benedicto Kiwanuka and the Birth of Postcolonial Uganda* (2021) and co-editor of *The Surprise of Reconciliation in the Catholic Tradition* (2018). He holds degrees from the University of Arkansas-Fayetteville, Duke University Divinity School, and the Catholic University of America, and he recently served as a US Fulbright Scholar and visiting professor at Uganda Martyrs University.

**Neomi De Anda** is a Tejana scholar/activist and lay Catholic Marianist currently serving as associate professor of religious studies at the University of Dayton (Dayton, Ohio). She holds a PhD in constructive theology, and her research interests include Latinas and Latin American women writers in religion 1600–1900; Christology; Latina theology; theology and breast milk; the intersection of race and migrations; and developing a border theology in partnership with the Hope Border Institute. Currently she serves as president-elect for the Academy of Catholic Hispanic Theologians of the United States. Her honors include the Louisville Institute First Book for Minority Scholars grant and fellowships from the Hispanic Theological Initiative and the Wabash Center for Teaching and Learning in Religion and Theology.

**Wendy M. Louis** has been an active writer and trainer for Basic Ecclesial Communities (BECs) since 1992 and is currently a member of the Federation of Asian Catholic Bishops' Conferences' (FABC) Asian Integral Pastoral Approach Resource (AsIPA) Team, which works to promote a BEC-based participatory church in Asia. She also served eight years as the executive secretary of the FABC's Office of Laity and Family and Women's Desk. Other previous positions include serving as the executive director for the Catholic Schools Commission of the Archdiocese of Singapore and as director of the Singapore Pastoral Institute. She holds a master's degree in pastoral studies from Heythrop College, London University (London).

**Teresa Maya, CCVI,** served from 2016–19 as president of the Leadership Conference of Women Religious (LCWR), an association of leaders of the congregations of Catholic women religious in the United States. Born in Mexico City, she is the second Latina to serve as LCWR president. She holds an MA in systematic theology from the Graduate Theological Union in Berkeley, California, and a PhD in Latin American colonial church history from El Colegio de Mexico in Mexico City.

**MarySylvia Nwachukwu, DDL,** is a sister of the Daughters of Divine Love Congregation. She currently serves as director of academic planning at Godfrey Okoye University (Enugu, Nigeria), where she also teaches biblical languages and courses in Sacred Scripture. In addition, she is a lecturer in theology at Enugu's Bigard Memorial Seminary. She holds a Licentiate in Sacred Scripture (LSS) from the Pontifical Biblical Institute (Rome) and a PhD in biblical theology from the Pontifical Gregorian University (Rome). She is a member of national and international biblical and theological associations, and her research interests include the Pentateuch, St. Paul's letters, and contextual theology. She is author of *Creation–Covenant Scheme and Justification by Faith* (2002) and many journal articles.

**Jeane Caña Peracullo** serves as chair and associate professor of philosophy at De La Salle University (Manila), where she has taught since 2008. A founding member of the Asian Association of Women Philosophers, she has also served as the international coordinator of the Ecclesia of Women in Asia (2016–18) and, in 2016, as a fellow with the Institute for Advanced Study in Asian Cultures and Theologies at The Chinese University of Hong Kong. Her recent publications include the e-book, *Liberating Power: Asian Feminist Theological Perspectives* (2017), and "The Virgin of the Vulnerable Lake: Catholic Engagement with Climate Change in the Philippines" (2020), published in the journal *Religions*.

**Ahida Calderón Pilarski** serves as chair and professor of theology at Saint Anselm College (Manchester, New Hampshire). She holds an MA in Theology with specialization in Old Testament (Catholic Theological Union, Chicago), an MLA (University of Chicago), a ThM in the Old and New Testaments, and a PhD from the Lutheran School of Theology at Chicago. Her research focuses on the intersection of gender and culture/ethnicity/race in the interpretation of the Bible. She is a member of the editorial board of the Wisdom Commentary Series from Liturgical Press, and her recent publications include the co-edited *By Bread Alone: Reading the Bible through the Eyes of the Hungry* (2014) and *Pentateuco: Introducción al Antiguo Testamento/La Biblia Hebrea en Perspectiva Latinoamericana* (2014).

**Barbara E. Reid, OP,** is president of Catholic Theological Union (Chicago), where she has also taught since 1988, and currently serves as the Carroll Stuhlmueller, CP, Distinguished Professor of New Testament Studies. She holds an MA from Aquinas College and a PhD from the Catholic University of America. One of the leading scholars in feminist interpretation of the Scriptures, she is general editor for the Wisdom Commentary Series, a new feminist Bible commentary from Liturgical Press. Her awards include an honorary doctorate from the University of Graz, Austria, in 2019 and induction into the Aquinas College Hall of Fame in 2016. Among her latest publications is *Wisdom's Feast: An Invitation to Feminist Interpretation of the Scriptures* (2016).

**Melinda A. Roper, MM,** has lived and worked in Central America for the majority of her time as a Maryknoll sister. Since 1985, she and a team of sisters have worked with the mestizo and indigenous peoples in the Vicariate of Darien, Panama, instructing Delegates of the Word, catechists, teachers, and young mothers, with the goal of forming Basic Ecclesial Communities. From 1978 to 1984, Sr. Roper served as president of the Maryknoll Congregation; just two years into her term, on December 2, 1980, four US churchwomen were murdered in El Salvador (among them, two Maryknoll sisters). During her time as president, she received numerous honorary degrees, including the Doctor of Humane Letters from Loyola University (Chicago), Fordham University (New York), and Catholic University of America (Washington, DC).

**María del Pilar Silveira** has served since 2018 as a visiting assistant professor in Boston College School of Theology and Ministry's online,

Spanish-language, continuing formation program. Previously, she taught postgraduate and advanced theology at the Institute of Theology for Religious at the Universidad Católica Andrés Bello (UCAB) in Caracas, Venezuela. She holds a PhD in theology from the Pontificia Universidad Javeriana (Bogotá) and an MA in religious studies from Rome's Pontifical Gregorian University. Her research focuses on popular religiosity in the various Marian devotions, especially in Venezuela, and on women's role in their dissemination in both family and society. She is the author of *Mariología Popular Latinoamericana: Fisonomía de la Mariología* (2013), as well as numerous journal articles.

**Niceta M. Vargas, OSA,** is a lecturer and assistant professor of biblical theology, Loyola School of Theology, Quezon City, Philippines. She holds a PhD in religious studies with a specialization in the New Testament, particularly in the Gospel of John, from the Catholic University of Louvain, and her publications on New Testament themes include *Word and Witness: An Introduction to the Gospel of John* (2013). She has served as Superior General of the Augustinian Sisters of Our Lady of Consolation (2013–21); chair of the Asia Pacific Augustinian Conference (2018–21); and twice as director of Tahanan Mapagkalinga ni Madre Rita (TMMR), a home she founded for children in need of special protection in Bulacan, Philippines.

# Foreword

Teresa Maya, CCVI

Invisible no more! Women are the face of the church everywhere, we read in one of the chapters of this book. We know women are the backbone of the church. We also know that many of the younger generations of women are leaving frustrated or, worse, disinterested in a church that fails to listen to and notice them. The women of Latin America have marched in the streets of Chile, Argentina, and Mexico City the last two years—singing to the tune of *La Tesis*, waving green *paliacates* (bandannas), engulfed in purple smoke, and calling themselves the *marea verde* (the green tide)—it's hard to forget that, on one weekend, Mexico saw the greatest number of women marching in the streets of every one of its cities, and then, the following week, COVID sent them all into lockdown, into the silence of their homes, which is often the most unsafe place for them. This volume's authors offer a lens through which to understand this reality emerging in Latin America as well as in Asia and Africa. Each writer provides the insight we need to delve deeper into Pope Francis's teaching that "realities are greater than ideas" (*EG*, 232). The realities women in our global church face every day require a new toolbox of ideas. These authors offer that opportunity.

Women are leaving the church from every generation and culture. Surveys and census data nuance this trend, some more alarmingly than others. Yet the trend remains. Our societies are increasingly more secular. Many of these secularizing societies perceive religion as a construct that underpins the systemic "isms" they are moving away from. For this reason, as Jeane Caña Peracullo explains in her introduction, "feminists around the world steer clear of religion." She asks poignantly, "How can feminism, and feminist principles, which originated from the West, be compatible with religion and its seeming antiwomen nature?" These sorts of questions are why this book inspires a conversation we have yet to have! Nothing is ever that simple, and unless we engage our changing societies with the less visible leadership of women in faith communities, we risk oversimplifying both what is happening and what is possible.

More than fifty years ago, in *Pacem in Terris*, Pope John XXIII wrote that "[w]omen are gaining an increasing awareness of their natural dignity. Far from being content with a purely passive role or allowing themselves to be regarded as a kind of instrument, they are demanding both in domestic and in public life the rights and duties which belong to them as human persons" (*PT*, 41). The role and dignity of women have gradually been recognized in cultures and societies across the globe in differing ways, yet alas, a whole fifty years later, women's dignity remains a work in progress. Why? This book's authors provide insight through the perspectives of women of different cultures.

Women need to find the dignity our gospel offers them. For centuries, however—as Barbara Reid reflects in this volume—biblical texts themselves have justified the suffering and abuse of women. The cross should be a sign of liberation, not subjugation and abuse. Reid explains that the biblical text can "be deadly when it is used to justify the oppression of those who are most disadvantaged; it can also be the liberative force that sets captives free." The text is "never neutral," she reminds us. The global church bears the responsibility of offering the freeing cross of Christ as a symbol "of birthing new life." The seeds of new life are now ours to give to human beings everywhere, panging for transformation.

I have long prayed for the women of our church, the women who have stayed, despite the patriarchy, despite the invisibility. These women have stayed because they learned they are heirs to a long line of women mystics and leaders. These women have stayed because they found an authentic Christian spirituality incarnate in *lo cotidiano*—the everyday life of women at work or in the *mercado*, struggling to make ends meet, finding ways to provide for their families, bringing beauty and hope to their friendships. The essays you will read in this book give us a glimpse into those women; they are a counternarrative that needs to be in dialogue with the lived experience of the hundreds of thousands of women, mothers, and sisters who no longer find meaning in a faith community that fails to speak to their lived experience. The communities of faith the authors refer to are being built everywhere; we can find them in all kinds of places. We get a glimpse in each of the articles. I am still smiling, for example, about reading that a study in the Philippines showed that women professors smile more!

The authors here challenge us to a new understanding of leadership in the Catholic Church. Silveira explains that "female leadership is often invisible." What women have done over the centuries—and continue to do in the Latino/a/x community—builds the church. We have yet to fully recognize this leadership as critical to the transmission of the faith. Perhaps the key is simply to notice the everyday acts of leadership that build a community of faith in the in-between time, from one Sunday to the next. We have a community we call church because of this female leadership. Popular piety—*pastoral popular*—needs to be better integrated into our understanding of the transmission of the faith. However robust our sacramental life is at the parish, it will never be enough to sustain our faith life. What happens at home complements what we celebrate on Sunday. Faith needs to be an everyday love affair with God! The images, smells, and practices of *pastoral popular* are perhaps one of the most beautiful signs of this relationship. We need to recover their meaning for the twenty-first century. We are people of the incarnation, and *pastoral popular* teaches us to embody our faith practice, to make it visible beyond the official liturgies of our tradition. Silveira uses the beautiful expression of "the living tissue in popular religiosity" to describe the gestures and prayers. A living faith needs practice!

Several authors begin with an analysis of family culture. They challenge us to appreciate the complexity of male and female roles in the family to start to see how they can contribute to the organization of our church into the future. MarySylvia Nwachukwu, DDL, shows that, even in the most patriarchal structures, "women are appreciated for their contemporary roles and resourcefulness." Throughout the book, we find that culture represents a critical hermeneutical lens through which to discover the complexity of women's roles in church and society. In each of the chapters, we are warned not to oversimplify culture. We find different nuances and transitions that are taking place, and we are challenged to demystify and de-Westernize our thinking. As Jeane Caña Peracullo explains, we need to "unpack" Asia—"two-thirds of the earth's total landmass"—which was "sequestered by Western epistemological trajectories." Generalizations around a culture or place distort the ever-transforming kaleidoscope of the Christian community.

The debate over access to the ministerial priesthood continues. I wonder where the outrage has gone. What happened to the questions around women's ordination that fueled intense opinion? What happened to the challenge that Theresa Kane, RSM, offered John Paul II on his first pastoral visit to the United States? Could it be that the next generations of women are simply less engaged with the church? Are they tired of the exclusion? Several of the authors here address this concern, but they also move us beyond this debate. Recognizing the place and leadership in our faith communities goes beyond belonging in the "presbytery"—it needs to understand what weaves and sustains the community.

The insights collected here present an alternative path for our Christian churches. I hope that they also reach the men of our church, the ones in leadership, the ones in the pews—our fathers, brothers, and partners. We can only move forward if we forge a culture of inclusion, where all are welcome. This volume reminds us that we need to forge the church of the twenty-first century. I will pray with the words of Celine Ugwu, one of the women interviewed in Nigeria by Nwachukwu: "The Church is our own; so we carry the Church just as we carry our families. It is our Church!"

## Bibliography

Francis, Pope. *Evangelii Gaudium: The Joy of the Gospel.* New York: Image, 2014.
John XXIII, Pope. *Pacem in Terris: On Establishing Universal Peace in Truth, Justice, Charity, and Liberty.* Washington, DC: National Catholic Welfare Council, 1963.

# Introduction

## Ahida Calderón Pilarski

On October 9, 2021, Pope Francis spoke at the opening of the XVI Ordinary General Assembly of the Synod of Bishops which took place in Vatican City.[1] The central theme for the General Assembly revolved around the call "For a Synodal Church: Communion, Participation, and Mission." As Pope Francis reflected upon the three distinctive keywords stated in this theme, he reminded people that baptism is an essential component in the understanding of the mission of the church, especially when responding to its call to be a synodal church. Synodality means "walking together" (composed of the Greek preposition συν [meaning "with"] and noun ὁδός [meaning "path"]).[2] This sense of togetherness as a community or assembly finds its biblical roots in the Hebrew term *qahal* and in the Greek term *ekklesia*.[3]

In this walking together of the people of God as a church, Pope Francis explains that participation—one of the keywords in the theme—"is a requirement of the faith received in baptism," and in responding to this requirement or call, "[b]aptism, the source of our life, gives rise to the equal dignity of the children of God, albeit in the diversity of ministries and charisms."[4] It is in this same light, one of equal dignity as the children of God, that an adequate conversation on women's leadership in the church can be fruitful. Catholicism in the Third Millennium is called

1. The Synod of Bishops was established by Pope Paul VI in 1965 (see his Apostolic Letter, *Apostolica Sollicitudo*, issued *motu proprio* with the aim of keeping among the bishops the spirit of collegiality and dialogue started at the Second Vatican Council).

2. International Theological Commission, "Synodality," 3.

3. International Theological Commission, "Synodality," 12–23.

4. Francis, "Address for the Opening of the Synod," para. 5.

to bring to the fore the abounding wisdom that has been always present in the centuries-long ministries and charisms exercised by women in a diversity of leadership roles.

Yet, in this conversation on women's leadership in a synodal church, this introduction also wants to address briefly the existent (almost tectonic) rift that has created an uneven "path" (ὁδός) for women to exercise their leadership. The unevenness of this path has at least two distinctive levels. On the one side are the (actual and potential) leadership positions that women (were and) are occupying within the hierarchical structures of the (early and contemporary) institutional church. And on the other side are the many and diverse actual and hidden (or ignored) leadership roles that women have been exercising and continue to exercise in ecclesial settings throughout history, as well as in other spaces in society at the local and global levels. Despite the fact that a challenging asymmetry in equality and equity remains in the unevenness of the path toward synodality, women have found the way to participate in responding to their call as baptized children of God to advance the larger mission of the church. Paradoxically, this heuristic distinction of uneven levels on a path provides a wider framework to analyze and value the critical roles and models of leadership that women have been exercising throughout history. While the contributions to this volume focus especially on the latter setting or level, this introduction wants to acknowledge that, during the papacy of Francis, there have been significant signs of hope and progress in the pursuit of equity in the former setting or level.

In the last decade, there has been an increase of female employees (about 22 percent)[5] in a variety of positions at the Vatican and Holy See. Gradually and consistently, Pope Francis has been appointing women to key senior leadership positions. In January of 2020, he appointed Francesca Di Giovanni as undersecretary for multilateral affairs in the Secretariat of State, and in August of the same year, six women[6] became members of the Vatican's Council for the Economy (an entity established in 2014). In February of 2021, Pope Francis appointed Nathalie Becquart as one of the undersecretaries of the Synod of Bishops, and most recently,

5. O'Kane, "Pope Francis Appoints Six Women," para. 8.

6. "Pope Chooses Six Women as Lay Experts." The appointees are Charlotte Kreuter-Kirchhof of Germany; Eva Castillo Sanz of Spain; Leslie Jane Ferrar of Great Britain; Marija Kolak of Germany; María Concepción Osákar Garaicoechea of Spain; and Ruth Maria Kelly of Great Britain.

on November 4, 2021, he appointed Raffaela Petrini as the new Secretary General of Vatican City.

Equally important to notice are Pope Francis's efforts to advance timely conversations about women's leadership roles. He has appointed two commissions to study women deacons. The first commission was formed in 2016, and their final report was inconclusive. Then in 2020, after listening to the proceedings of the Special Assembly of the Synod of Bishops for the Pan-Amazon region, Pope Francis appointed a new commission to continue this study on women deacons. Two paragraphs from Pope Francis's postsynodal apostolic exhortation *Querida Amazonia*,[7] which are relevant to the larger conversation on women's leadership in the global church, deserve to be included here in their totality:

> 99. In the Amazon region, there are communities that have long preserved and handed on the faith even though no priest has come their way, even for decades. This could happen because of the presence of strong and generous women who, undoubtedly called and prompted by the Holy Spirit, baptized, catechized, prayed and acted as missionaries. For centuries, women have kept the Church alive in those places through their remarkable devotion and deep faith. Some of them, speaking at the Synod, moved us profoundly by their testimony. . . .
>
> 103. In a synodal Church, those women who in fact have a central part to play in Amazonian communities should have access to positions, including ecclesial services, that do not entail Holy Orders and that can better signify the role that is theirs. Here it should be noted that these services entail stability, public recognition, and a commission from the bishop. This would also allow women to have a real and effective impact on the organization, the most important decisions and the direction of communities, while continuing to do so in a way that reflects their womanhood.

Pope Francis's call to reflect on a synodal church reveals his deep commitment to assume his responsibility as the highest leader of the Catholic Church to be attentive to the *sensus fidei*. The International Theological Commission's document "Synodality in the Life and Mission of the Church," issued in May of 2018, explains this dimension, the *sensus fidei*, as follows:

7. Francis, *Querida Amazonia*, 99, 103.

> All the faithful are called by virtue of their baptism to witness to and proclaim the Word of truth and life, in that they are members of the prophetic, priestly and royal People of God [cf. *Catechism of the Catholic Church*, 783–86]. . . . The anointing of the Holy Spirit is manifested in the *sensus fidei* of the faithful [Vatican II, *Lumen Gentium*, 12a]. "In all the baptized, from first to last, the sanctifying power of the Spirit is at work, impelling us to evangelization. The People of God is holy thanks to this anointing, which makes it infallible *in credendo*. This means that it does not err in faith, even when it cannot find words to explain that faith. The Spirit guides it in truth and leads it to salvation. As part of His mysterious love for humanity, God furnishes the totality of the faithful with an instinct of faith—*sensus fidei*—which helps them to discern what is truly of God. The presence of the Spirit gives Christians a certain connaturality with divine realities, and a wisdom which enables them to grasp those realities intuitively" [Francis, *Evangelii Gaudium*, 119]. This connaturality shows itself in a "*sentire cum Ecclesia*: to feel, sense and perceive in harmony with the Church. This is required not just of theologians, but of all the faithful; it unites all the members of the People of God as they make their pilgrim journey. It is the key to their 'walking together'" [International Theological Commission, *Sensus Fidei*, 90].[8]

Reflecting on three foundational elements—baptism, synodality, and *sensus fidei*—to speak about women's leadership in the church, the preamble in this introduction sets the stage to present now the title of this book, *Daughters of Wisdom: Women and Leadership in the Global Church*. This title was the theme for the international conference organized by the Center for World Catholicism and Intercultural Theology (CWCIT) at DePaul University in April 2018.[9] Many of the participants were asked to further develop their essays for this volume. Their contributions offer a window into current realities regarding women's leadership in the global church and explore strategic recommendations to nurture this leadership in the twenty-first century.

The authors are lay and religious people from Mexico, Venezuela, Peru, the US, Uganda, Nigeria, Ghana, Indonesia, and the Philippines. They address particularly different aspects of women's leadership in the

8. International Theological Commission, "Synodality," para. 56.

9. For more information about this conference, see https://las.depaul.edu/centers-and-institutes/center-for-world-catholicism-cultural-theology/World-Catholicism-Week/past-world-cath/Pages/2018.aspx.

Catholic Church, with a special emphasis on the Global South. The topics explored include women's use of Scripture, the ecclesiological basis for women in church leadership, and the leadership roles that women are already exercising in grassroots church communities, faith-based social movements, and theological education.

The essays in this book have been divided according to the authors' respective three continental contexts (America, Africa, and Asia), and their contributions in the corresponding continent are presented alphabetically. The conclusion draws on some significant correlations across the continents and gathers a few strategic recommendations raised by the participants themselves. The first five chapters are dedicated to America, chapters 6 and 7 to Africa, and the last three to Asia. Here is a brief summary of each of the chapters.

## America

In chapter 1, Roper (a keynote speaker during the conference) offers a profound analysis of the expression "Living Questions," taking the readers on a journey to reflect on the living questions emerging out of her experience as a woman of faith in mission in the tropical rainforest of Darién, Panama. One key question she asks is: "How did the way that Jesus related to women—that is, with deep trust and respect—come to be set aside and forgotten by the official church?" (see page 5). Her response to this question dwells on a passage from the Gospel of John: "the wind blows wherever it wishes; you hear the sound it makes, but you do not know where it comes from or where it is going" (3:8). Looking at four experiential points, Roper calls for a careful listening of how the Spirit (*ruah*—the divine wind) is blowing in our times. If the Church, "as a living sacrament of God present," were to listen attentively to the *ruah*, it "should be in the forefront of discovering new organizational models for and with the human community" (see page 11). In other words, it would be a model that embraces the laity, especially women.

In chapter 2, Calderón Pilarski provides an overview of the challenging, yet hopeful, journey of Latin American women in the field of theology, particularly biblical studies, in the past fifty years. Although it has been a difficult undertaking, their increased presence as subject(s) in theology has contributed to the changing landscape of academia. The emerging horizon of the twenty-first century requires, however, deep thinking and to be more strategic in order to advance women's integral dignity and leadership. In Catholic arenas of critical thinking and reflection, concepts like a "theology of the people" (*teología del pueblo*) and synodality (*sinodalidad*)—which are central to Francis's papacy—might contribute to this task.

In chapter 3, DeAnda offers an overview of the life and work of Sor María Anna Águeda de San Ignacio (1695–1750), the first woman foundress of a Dominican convent in Puebla, Mexico, and a theologian. Author of a four-volume theological treatise, *Las Marabillas del Divino Amor Selladas con el Sello de la Verdad*, Sor María Anna develops a theology of breast milk using the image of Mary. DeAnda observes that, in Sor María Anna's four books, "she explains connections between Mary and each person of the Trinity, with particular attention to Mary's relationship with Jesus" (see page 79). Sor María Anna's leadership (as a woman, nun, and theologian) in the context of the late seventeenth century in Latin America was exceptional. Despite the fact that her work was marginalized by mainstream theologies, DeAnda argues that the impact of Sor María Anna's life and work makes her a leading figure not only for the theologies developed in seventeenth-century Latin America but also for LatinoXa theology in the United States of America today.

In chapter 4, Silveira speaks about women's leadership exemplified through the Marian devotion at three sanctuaries in Venezuela: La Virgen de Coromoto, La Divina Pastora, and Nuestra Señora del Rosario de Chiquinquirá. In 2013, Silveira conducted a survey interviewing women participants at festivities in these three locations. In her essay, she shares some of their words and insights, showing not only their leadership but also the theological richness in their expressions of popular faith. Central to Silveira's reflection about the women's religious practices is the interconnection she notices between the motherhood of Mary and women devotees. This connection has inspired women to pass on the Marian devotion as a tradition in their families for many generations. While the popular Marian devotion presents some challenges, women's faith and leadership have remained as a hidden treasure for centuries.

In chapter 5, through the reading of passages from the gospels, Reid shows the dynamics, relevance, and timeliness of reading the Scriptures with the mind, eyes, and heart of a woman. Reid begins by clarifying the concepts of feminism and feminist biblical interpretation. Next, she focuses on biblical references to the phrase, "taking up the cross" (also the title of one of her books), which is generally connected to the suffering that led to death. Then, Reid demonstrates that, from a feminist perspective, its meaning can also be that of birthing hope. Reid shares some conversations she had with Latin American women to present how their stories unveil a variety of hidden realities of oppression. At the basis of this oppression and violence are biblical misinterpretations and indoctrinations that perpetuate false notions of deserved suffering (including, for example, cases of domestic violence). In sharp contrast, Reid analyzes several passages from the Gospel of John to show that the image of birthing new life challenges Christians today "to replicate in our own lives the actions and attitudes of the Christ who came to engender new, full life for all" (see page 32).

## Africa

In chapter 6, Carney introduces three women leaders in the Catholic Church of Uganda (two natives and one foreigner). These women exemplify what he calls an "ecclesiology of solidarity in the streets": Sr. Rose Mystica Muyinza (the mother of "the people without people"), Mrs. Rosalba Oywa (the "social analyst and peace activist"), and Ms. Sherry Meyer (a "postcolonial missionary"). This ecclesiology offers a pastoral vision of leadership based on three key dimensions: it entails relocating to the streets, speaking from the streets, and it is aimed at transforming the streets. Carney labels these three dimensions as relocation, advocacy, and transformation. These dimensions embody not only the call to solidarity in Catholic social teaching, but they also offer "powerful and creative examples of Catholic women's grassroots leadership" (see page 105) in the challenging postcolonial context of Uganda.

In chapter 7, Nwachukwu describes the importance of knowing that the image of church in Africa is strongly connected to the concept of "family," and therefore, to understand women's leadership in the church, one needs to have a sense of women's status and role in the family according to the African worldview and culture. In her essay, Nwachukwu shares the results of a questionnaire-survey she conducted with Nigerian Igbos and the matrilineal Akan people of Ghana regarding the status of women in modern African families. Among her findings is the significant improvement in women's access to education, health care, and the labor market. Nwachukwu argues that these changes have also impacted women's current roles in the African church, and this phenomenon brings hope for the future of women's leadership in the church in Africa. At the end of her essay, Nwachukwu compares some of the women's roles in the African church to those of a few biblical female characters, especially Rebecca in Genesis 25–27.

## Asia

In chapter 8, Peracullo argues for the need to explore the role of faith in the public sphere in order to understand more adequately women's religious practices in twenty-first-century non-Western societies, especially in Asia. Her essay examines two important Catholic women's movements/organizations in Asia: Ecclesia of Women in Asia (EWA) and Wanita Katolik Republik Indonesia (WKRI). Peracullo calls for a deeper analysis of the small (or silenced) stories of Catholics worldwide, especially those of women, and she offers two recommendations: (1) "We need to appreciate female-centered praxis," and (2) "we must not lose sight of the quest for justice" (see page 147).

In chapter 9, Louis offers a description of Basic Ecclesial Communities (BECs) in Asia. BECs began in the 1970s, and in 1990, a renewal of this ecclesial model was encouraged by the Federation of Asian Bishops' Conferences (FABC). Louis argues that BECs were and are essential to advancing the mission of the church as community and that these also have created a platform for the development of women's leadership opportunities given the nature of some key characteristics and roles within these organizations. Louis highlights some areas of community life in the BECs where women have taken initiatives and developed their talents. However, the hope for evangelization and communion in mission through the BECs in Asia requires an appreciation of diverse work and skills and a reexamination of how to enable "their leaders, who are mostly women, to become confident and compassionate missionary disciples working in the front lines" (see page 166).

In chapter 10, Vargas provides an overview of the landscape of theological education for women (profiling students and faculty) in the Philippines, eventually focusing her analysis on four schools based on the International Theological Commission's (ITC) twofold criteria: (1) a solid theological curriculum and (2) being in dialogue with the world. The four selected schools for her analysis are the Institute of Formation of Religious Studies, the Loyola School of Theology, the St. Vincent School of Theology, and the Institute of Consecrated Life in Asia. Vargas argues that, despite the advancements in diversity and inclusiveness achieved by these schools and the demonstrated positive academic impact of women theologians in the field, the presence of Filipino women theologians (especially religious sisters) is still insufficient.

The aim of the conference, and of this book, is to offer a contribution to the larger conversation about women's leadership in the church. Our hope is to restore the evenness of the path toward a synodal church where every baptized person, with equal dignity as a child of God, can continue to participate in a more integral way in advancing the mission of the church.

## Bibliography

Catechism of the Catholic Church. Vatican.va, 1993. https://www.vatican.va/archive/ENG0015/_INDEX.HTM.

Francis, Pope. "Address for the Opening of the Synod." Address given in New Synod Hall, Vatican City, October 9, 2021. https://www.vatican.va/content/francesco/en/speeches/2021/october/documents/20211009-apertura-camminosinodale.html.

———. Evangelii Gaudium. Vatican.va, November 24, 2013. https://www.vatican.va/content/francesco/en/apost_exhortations/documents/papa-francesco_esortazione-ap_20131124_evangelii-gaudium.html.

———. "Querida Amazonia." Vatican.va, February 2, 2020. https://www.vatican.va/content/francesco/en/apost_exhortations/documents/papa-francesco_esortazione-ap_20200202_querida-amazonia.html.

International Theological Commission (ITC). "Sensus Fidei: In the Life of the Church." Vatican.va, 2014. https://www.vatican.va/roman_curia/congregations/cfaith/cti_documents/rc_cti_20140610_sensus-fidei_en.html.

———. "Synodality in the Life and Mission of the Church." Vatican.va, 2018. https://www.vatican.va/roman_curia/congregations/cfaith/cti_documents/rc_cti_20180302_sinodalita_en.html.

O'Kane, Caitlin. "Pope Francis Appoints Six Women to Senior Vatican Positions—A Historic First." CBS News, August 6, 2020. https://www.cbsnews.com/news/pope-francis-appoints-six-women-to-senior-vatican-positions-a-historic-first/.

Paul VI, Pope. Apostolica Sollicitudo. Vatican.va, September 15, 1965. https://www.vatican.va/content/paul-vi/en/motu_proprio/documents/hf_p-vi_motu-proprio_19650915_apostolica-sollicitudo.html.

"Pope Chooses Six Women as Lay Experts for Council for the Economy." Vatican News, August 6, 2020. https://www.vaticannews.va/en/pope/news/2020-08/pope-francis-new-members-for-economy-council.html.

Vatican II. Lumen Gentium. Vatican.va, November 21, 1964. https://www.vatican.va/archive/hist_councils/ii_vatican_council/documents/vat-ii_const_19641121_lumen-gentium_en.html.

# PART ONE:

*Women's Leadership in the Americas*

# I

## The Wind Blows Where It Wishes

Melinda A. Roper, MM

In forests, trees fall when their time comes. Where I live, we have just cut down four big trees, because they were close to our buildings and had grown too tall. With the summer winds, the danger of their falling had increased significantly. From our perspective, they had become dangerous and had to be eliminated.

My greetings to each of you as we continue to explore the illusions, contradictions, challenges, and wonders of living today, as women, with planet Earth. For more than thirty years, we have been attempting to live in harmony with the tropical rainforest of Darién, Panama. When the trees were taken down, I wondered if we had learned anything. I am not referring simply to a gap in our learning process or our lack of knowledge. I am referring to evolving consciousness that is a fascinating, creative, and demanding dynamic that springs from the transformation of relationships as well as of ideas.

Thus, I begin this essay with questions and contradictions which intend to be helpful and stimulating for the adventure of living into the future. Most of you are familiar with Rainer Maria Rilke's quote taken from *Letters to a Young Poet*: "And the point is, to live everything. Live the questions now. Perhaps you will then, gradually without noticing it, live along some distant day into the answers."[1] Living questions is an impor-

1. Rilke and Kappus, *Letters to a Young Poet*, 35.

3

tant life experience for me, because it keeps me open and alert to mystery, to wonder, and to adventure. The illusion of security in having the right answers can keep us frozen, limiting our ability to forgive those whom we perceive to be wrong and, in the end, curtailing the opportunity to be forgiven ourselves, limiting every possibility for growth.

One of the marvels of being alive today is that we can be very certain that what we don't know is so much greater than what we think we know. For example, I grew up thinking that the world was about 6,000 years old; 13.8 billion is quite different, and not just numerically. The experience of finding one's self within an evolutionary process billions of years old, floating on a "pale blue dot"[2] through an ever-expanding universe, has been, for me, an adventure in faith. An adventure where all relationships are continually challenged and renewed.

From this experience, I share the following questions which come to me as a woman of faith in mission:

- When and how did parable and story give way to doctrine and catechism?

- When and how did gospel give way to dogma, certainty, and creed?

- When and how did prayer give way to reciting prayers?

- When and how did Eucharist give way to saying Mass?

- When did the seed, the leaven, the nesting birds of the kingdom of God, give way to a kingdom, temples, and altars of human design and construction?

- When did church as community give way to church as institution?

- When did the widow's mite give way to tax-free fundraising and weekly envelopes?

- When did authority as service give way to apostolic succession, canon law, and the curia?

- When did the justice of forgiveness give way to the right to judge and exclude according to the law?

- When did Jesus of Nazareth, prophet, give way to Christ the King and High Priest?

- When did Mary of Nazareth, wife of Joseph and mother of Jesus, become the Queen of heaven, adorned with jewels and costly robes?

2. A nod to Carl Sagan's book, *A Pale Blue Dot*.

While these questions are the kind that come forth from living and are ultimately answered by how we live, I believe that academic exploration, as part of the human experience, is vital to our evolving awareness and commitment to life and to the future.

In this context, there is one more question which must be asked considering the theme of this conference, and I would phrase it in the following manner: How did the way that Jesus related to women—that is, with deep trust and respect—come to be set aside and forgotten by the official church?

I am not necessarily referring to the personal attitudes and behavior of individuals, but I do mean the operating structures, policies, and laws by which the church functions and is governed and which in turn dictate the modes of relationship within it. For some clerics, to live the gospel within this context must be deeply painful as it certainly is for many of us women. The pain to which I refer is not that we are excluded from the hierarchical structures of the institutionalized church, but rather that those particular structures exist at all. In the human community, structure reflects and reinforces values, attitudes, beliefs, and relationships, while at the same time these strengthen and maintain the structures.

Now, we may ask: What are the structures that can facilitate the spirit and style of Jesus to flow freely today? It seems to me that this conference is providing a forum to challenge and explore the logic, philosophies, and theologies essential to a new practice of living and celebrating our faith.

I think that most of us look for ideas or experiences that help us understand life, ourselves, and alternatives for the future. The following four ideas and quotes reflect major experiences and learnings in my life as a woman in the church and have led me to know deeply in my heart that "the wind blows wherever it wishes; you hear the sound it makes, but you do not know where it comes from or where it is going" (John 3:8 GNT).[3] I find the following helpful when deciding how to live as a woman of faith today in Darién:

1. A few years ago, a Scripture scholar shared with us some of the implications of the destruction of Jerusalem in AD 70. He left us with the following observation: when Jerusalem was destroyed, the temple, the altar, and the priesthood ceased to exist. This was an experience of the early Christian community in Jerusalem as well as the Jewish community. Can we imagine the church of tomorrow without temple, altar, and priest? If not, can we perhaps imagine an alternative organization

3. All Scripture quotations are taken from the Good News Translation (GNT).

where administrative, economic, and political functions are separated from what is presently the liturgical ministry?

2. In the gospel story, the women are given the mission to share the news of the resurrection with the disciples. According to Matthew and Mark, the women were to tell the disciples that Jesus would meet them in Galilee, not in the capital city of Jerusalem. According to Mark, the disciples did not believe Mary Magdalene, and Luke says, "But the apostles thought that what the women said was nonsense and did not believe them" (24:11). Why is there so much fear and resistance in the contemporary church concerning our mission to bring the good news of resurrection and of life to all of creation? Given the outrageous destruction of the whole community of life today, we women cannot speak in the temple, but we do go and are present in Galilee.

3. In Luke 10:21, we read, "At that time, Jesus was filled with joy by the Holy Spirit and said, 'Father, lord of heaven and earth! I thank you because you have shown to the unlearned what you have hidden from the wise and learned. Yes, Father, this was how you were pleased to have it happen.'" Most of my adult life I have lived among people who have had little formal schooling. I have participated in celebrations of the word where the delegate of the word's reflection is filled with the wisdom of life according to Jesus. I have also heard abstract ideas in homilies laced with anecdotes and reminiscences that frequently don't even mention the gospel. One day, when my frustration level was very high and I was spouting off about environmental destruction caused by big teak tree plantations, Adelia (a member of the community) said to me, "but Melinda, we know all that. We just don't believe." What is hidden from those of us who study and are learned? Adelia would ask us not what we know, but "what do you believe?"

4. Also, in chapter 10 of Luke, Jesus tells the parable of the good Samaritan to a teacher of the law who tries to trap him. The theme or issue of religious practice is extremely difficult and sensitive to talk about and deal with. I truly hesitate to bring it up, because as a public religious figure I am, in a certain sense, in the role of teacher of the law. On the other hand, I think I understand what Jesus is saying in this parable. What I am so profoundly challenged by is the respect that Jesus shows the teacher, even though the teacher was trying to trap him. This is the lesson for me today: by encouraging the teacher to respond to his own question in light of the parable, Jesus defuses the debate (which will always have the same winner—that is, the one most proficient in the law). Jesus changes the question from one of religious practice to

one of living faith. "And Jesus concluded, 'In your opinion, which one of these three acted like a neighbor toward the man attacked by the robbers?' The teacher of the law answered, 'The one who was kind to him.' Jesus replied, 'You go then, and do the same'" (Luke 10:36–37). Jesus changed the situation from a debate about religious law to one of living faith.

The living awareness of these four points—that is, questioning the centrality of temple, altar, and priest to our religious practice; the mission of the women to announce the resurrection and new life to the disciples; the wisdom of the unlearned; and the priority of kindness over the fulfillment of the law—has led me to feel the wind. At the end of chapter 2 of John's Gospel, Jesus has a violent encounter with the authorities of the temple. Conversation with them was impossible because, according to the author, "he himself [Jesus] knew what was in their hearts" (v. 25).

After this incident, we are introduced to Nicodemus, a Jewish leader, member of the party of the Pharisees, and a great teacher in Israel (John 3). He represented a dimension of the religious establishment quite different from the temple authorities. Before reflecting on this encounter between Jesus and Nicodemus, I would like to recall another moment when Nicodemus appears in John's Gospel. In chapter 7, there is a discussion among religious authorities about Jesus' identity and mission. I think it best to refer to the text:

> When the guards went back, the chief priests and Pharisees asked them, "Why did you not bring him?" The guards answered, "Nobody has ever talked the way this man does!" "Did he fool you too?" the Pharisees asked them. "Have you ever known one of the authorities or one Pharisee to believe in him? This crowd does not know the Law of Moses, so they are under God's curse!" One of the Pharisees there was Nicodemus, the man who had gone to see Jesus before. He said to the others, "According to the Law we cannot condemn people before hearing them and finding out what they have done." "Well," they answered, "are you also from Galilee? Study the Scriptures and you will learn that no prophet ever comes from Galilee" (vv. 45–52).

With this additional information about Nicodemus, let's return to his nocturnal meeting with Jesus. Jesus expresses surprise that Nicodemus doesn't understand the freedom of God's Spirit. Perhaps because he, Nicodemus, had only experienced God's presence through the Scripture, the temple, and his own attempt to live according to the Law. He also knew that prophets were vital to Israel's history and to their living faith. I think that he sensed that Jesus was a prophet.

Jesus does not quote Scripture to Nicodemus but uses the images of wind, water, and being born to convey the experience of new life and energy as God's presence. I understand these images to signal God as being present beyond our imagining and, above all, beyond our control.

From what I have been able to gather, wind as well as water are universal symbols present in most cultures. Wind symbolizes the unknown, the unpredictable, and the uncontrollable. It represents the mystery which is perceived and felt but not seen. For me, the wind symbolizes the creativity and freedom of God and all that gives life. The biblical imagery is exciting—*ruah*,[4] the breath of God present, creative, moving, evolving. In the poetry of the Psalms, God rides on the wings of the wind and uses the winds as messengers (Ps 104:3–4). Speaking with God, the psalmist says, "But when you give them breath, they are created, you give new life to the earth" (Ps 104:30).

There are numerous spiritualities both within and beyond the Judeo-Christian traditions that describe the activity and presence of wind/air/breath as the creative energy of the cosmos. The following is not traditional Christian vocabulary, but the underlying experience seems similar: "The energy of the dance of creation arises out of pure awareness or existence, the unlimited energy of the universe; this energy is love."[5]

Perhaps the political and religious institutions following the destruction of Jerusalem were in survival mode, and the law had become their security. But be that as it may, I suggest that one of the greatest obstacles to experiencing the wind that blows wherever it wishes is the illusion that we can control God's presence through knowledge, ritual, and law.

I perceive that Nicodemus was a good religious person who couldn't let the Spirit of God flow freely in his life. He was faithful to his religious tradition at a confusing and troubling time. He probably experienced anxiety and fear at the unpredictability of the wind, and this limited his understanding of what Jesus was sharing and wanted him to grasp.

It is an anxiety that many of us can identify with. Yet, at the same time, we are fortunate to be alive during this moment in history when

---

4. The Hebrew term *ruah* refers to the "divine wind" present already from the very beginning of creation (see Gen 1:2).

5. Morrison, *Book of Ayurveda*, 19. This description is of Sankhya's philosophy of creation, the foundation of *Ayurveda*, India's traditional system of medicine.

science is revealing so many aspects of the mystery of life and the universe—a moment when open discussion and dialogue among science, spirituality, and religion are more and more inclusive, and when our awareness and consciousness continue to evolve. It seems that the wind, as usual, is unpredictable, both wild and gentle.

How will the church of the future be a living sign of the coming of the kingdom of God? How can its organization and structures feel and hear the wind as it blows so freely? How can our worship be in spirit and in truth? How do we move into the answers of these living questions?

My personal experience and how I understand the gospel tell me that to be excluded from the hierarchical aspect of church offers us, as women, the space and freedom to serve and worship without fear. At times, we do experience hurt, anger, and even fear as members of this church. We live in a particularly shameful time when violence against women is increasingly blatant in societies around the world. This violence is not absent from the church. Can we name it spiritual violence?

The theme of the Latin American *Calendar* for the year 2018, a Claretian publication, was gender equality. The bishops of Guatemala have forbidden its sale in the country. In the publication, there is an article by David Molineaux of Chile where we read, "Machismo continues causing incalculable suffering and tragedy: it is enough, for example, to be aware of the drama of femicide in the different countries of our region. But machismo is not patriarchy: it is its pathetic bastard son."[6]

The role of religions in the Western patriarchal societies is well-documented, and the documentation of femicide in the West is currently being carefully analyzed. The following quote from the Latin American writer Eduardo Galeano bears scrutiny:

> There are criminals that blatantly proclaim, "I killed her because she was mine," just as though it were common sense, the height of all justice, as is the right to private property, that makes the man the owner of the woman. But not one, not one—even the most macho of the supermachos—has the courage to confess, "I killed her from fear," because after all, women's fear of the

6. Molineaux, "*Patriarcado y Machismo*," 41. Translation mine. The original Spanish reads: *El machismo sigue causando incalculable sufrimiento y tragedia: basta tomar conciencia, por ejemplo, del drama del feminicidio en los diferentes países de nuestra región. Pero el machismo no es patriarcado: es su patético hijo bastardo.*

violence of men *is the mirror of the fear that a man has of a woman who is fearless.*"[7]

But let's move beyond fear. How does the wind blow in our world today? Quite similarly to the days of Jesus, I should think. Outside of officialdom, how does Jesus inspire us to live? I'll share my list with you:

- To live so that the quality of our relationships be based on profound respect for the dignity of the other with preference for the excluded, children, women, the elderly, and those who are not like us.

- To live so that unlimited kindness and compassion in the use of our time, energy, and resources be the style of how we live.

- To live so that unlimited forgiveness calls forth the beauty and goodness of each other.

- To live so that healing the pain and wounds of the lonely, the injured, the sick, and the hungry be the living sacrament of God present.

- To live so that our words, teaching, and reflections reveal the loving kindness of our God and encourage those who listen to live with the Spirit of Jesus.

- To live so that our wisdom flows from the totality of our commitment to the common good.

- To live so that we contemplate, pray, and celebrate our faith in community.

If we are learning to live with the idea that the Spirit blows where it wishes, we need not be overly concerned with the hierarchical church.

I suggest that new organizational models of church will be created by those who experience the wind that blows where it wishes. And I venture to say that most of these folks will be those most free of the present operational structure—that is, the laity, and especially women. What could happen if church structures and organization began to take form from planet Earth, where the wind blows where it wishes?

---

7. "Eduardo Galeano y la Mujer sin Miedo," para. 1. Translation mine; emphasis added. The original quote in Spanish reads: *Hay criminales que proclaman tan campantes 'la maté porque era mía', así no más, como si fuera cosa de sentido común y justo de toda justicia y derecho de propiedad privada, que hace al hombre dueño de la mujer. Pero ninguno, ninguno, ni el más macho de los supermachos tiene la valentía de confesar 'la maté por miedo', porque al fin y al cabo el miedo de la mujer a la violencia del hombre es el espejo del miedo del hombre a la mujer sin miedo.*

The earth flag, with the photo of our planet in space, is beautiful in and of itself. It offers us many opportunities to contemplate the wonders of the wind. One observation that becomes clear to the observer is that superimposed political boundaries do not appear. They simply are not there. The photo invites us to dream dreams and have visions beyond the nation-state and beyond the current operative, competitive economic systems. I do not believe that the nation-state is an adequate model of an operating structure for the church and much less for the dream of the kingdom.

Science is offering us inspiring organizational principles such as differentiation, interiority, and communion, not to mention quantum entanglement. From microbiology to astrophysics, dynamic structures of life and the universe are being discovered. Are these the new parables of the coming of the kingdom? It seems to me that the church, as a living sacrament of God present, should be in the forefront of discovering new organizational models for and with the human community. It is under-standable that the human community throughout its history has created social, economic, political, and religious structures as part of its own development. But we are at a new moment. We have new tools and new information that allow us to understand and analyze more carefully the superimposed structures which we have placed on both the planet Earth and on the gospel. The beauty, energy, and wonders of both the gospel and planet Earth are revealing themselves to us today. We are being in-vited to a new moment of creativity and integrity as our living structures reflect more faithfully those of planet Earth and those of the gospel. Both Earth and gospel are alive. Changing structures is risky but so exciting and so necessary.

We can't wait 500 years as did the official church to admit the truth of planet Earth's relationship with the sun. Science tells us that the universe is ever expanding. What a wonderful image for God: an ever-expanding, evolving energy beyond our calculations and imagining. Do we of the human community reduce God to our short history and limited experience? Rather, let us feel and hear the wind as we venture forth in consciousness ever more aware, through the gratuitousness of faith, that we are little living signs of a God whose love is ever expanding.

The following gospel experiences shed light on our present mo-ment. The first is from our courageous but cautious friend Nicodemus: "After this, Joseph, who was from the town of Arimathea, asked Pilate if he could take Jesus's body. (Joseph was a follower of Jesus, but in secret, because he was afraid of the Jewish authorities.) Pilate told him he could have the body, so Joseph went and took it away. Nicodemus, who at first had gone to see Jesus at night, went with Joseph, taking with him about one hundred pounds of spices, a mixture of myrrh and aloes. The two men took Jesus's body and wrapped it in linen cloths with the spices according to the Jewish custom of preparing a body for burial" (John 19:38–40).

The second is an extravagant sacramental gesture beyond custom, tradition, and law. Let us listen and be inspired: "Now when Jesus was at Bethany in the house of Simon the Leper, a woman came up to him with an alabaster flask of very expensive ointment, and she poured it on his head as he sat at the table. But when the disciples saw it, they were indignant, saying, 'Why this waste? For this ointment might have been sold for a large sum and given to the poor.' But Jesus, aware of this, said to them, 'Why do you trouble the woman? For she has done a beautiful thing to me. For you always have the poor with you, but you will not always have me. In pouring this ointment on my body, she has done it to prepare me for burial. Truly, I say to you, wherever this gospel is preached in the whole world, what she has done will be told in memory of her" (Matt 26:6–13).

Nicodemus and the woman who anoints Jesus are present among us here today. How will we move into the future together, both cautiously and extravagantly? The wind will continue to blow where it wishes. Now I must return to the forest, to my home where we cut down the trees. Yet before I do, I will leave you with two more questions: What once grew where you now live? How will we grow into the future?

## Bibliography

"Eduardo Galeano y la Mujer sin Miedo." *Cosecha Roja,* April 13, 2015. http:// cosecharoja.org/eduardo-galeano-y-la-mujer-sin-miedo.

Molineaux, David. *"Patriarcardo y Machismo: Patologías Emparentadas."* In *Agenda Latinoamericana Mundial 2018,* edited by José María Vigil and Pedro Casaldáliga, 40–41. Panama: José María Vigil and Pedro Casaldáliga, 2018. https:// latinoamericana.org/digital/2018AgendaLatinoamericana.pdf.

Morrison, Judith H. *The Book of* Ayurveda: *A Holistic Approach to Health and Longevity.* New York: Simon and Schuster, 1995.

Rilke, Rainer M., and Franz X. Kappus. *Letters to a Young Poet.* New York: Norton, 1954.

Sagan, Carl. *A Pale Blue Dot: A Vision of the Human Future in Space.* New York: Random House, 1994.

# 2

# A Challenging Hope: A Journey of Latin American Women in Theology and Biblical Studies

Ahida Calderón Pilarski

## Introduction

THE LAST FIFTY YEARS have been a challenging, yet hopeful, journey for Latin American women in the field of theology (particularly in biblical studies). This essay offers a snapshot of this journey and some elements for reflection. Despite a path filled with obstacles, the increased presence of women as subjects "in" (the doing of) theology[1] has contributed to the changing landscape of academia in Latin America. Still, the emerging horizons of the twenty-first century world require that more strategic and deep thinking be in place to advance women's integral dignity, presence, and leadership, and this is not limited to academia. In Catholic arenas of critical[2] thinking and reflection, concepts like the "theology of the peo-

---

1. In contrast to being just a subject "of" theological studies. See Azcuy, "El Lugar Teológico de las Mujeres," 11–34.

2. I am using the term "critical" in the way Elisabeth Schüssler Fiorenza connects it to its original sense. She says, "this expression is derived from the Greek word, *krinein/ krisis*, which means judging and judgment, evaluation and assessment. A critical approach is interested in weighing, evaluating, and judging texts and their contexts, in exploring *crisis* situations and seeking for their adjudications" (Schüssler Fiorenza, *Power of the Word*, 14).

ple" (*teología del pueblo*) and synodality (*sinodalidad*)—which are central to Francis's papacy—might contribute to this endeavor.

To address some of the points mentioned above, this essay is divided into three main parts. The first section offers a brief overview of the journey of Latin American women in theology, especially in the areas where a gradual integration of their experiences and voices has been significant; this overview is based on two important studies (Elsa Tamez's and Nancy Viviana Raimondo's) that heuristically identify stages (or moments) in this journey. The second section of this essay shows a sample snapshot of this journey in numbers, revealing discouraging and challenging realities for the present and the future of women in theology. As a way of conclusion, the last section elaborates on three concepts—"emergence" in complexity theory, the "theology of the people," and "synodality"—which provide an extension to the platform to speak about leadership and hope for a better future, not only for women, but also for the church and for humanity.

## A Fifty Years' Journey (1970s–2010s)

Looking back at the landscape to sketch a fifty years' overview of the work and presence of Latin American women in theology, particularly in biblical studies, is a challenging task. On the one hand, there is limited access to information about and from women (and their publications) in this academic field, and on the other hand, most importantly, women's presence in academia (particularly in theology) still shows the impact of a much larger issue—that is, their limited "access" to higher education. The subrepresentation of women in academic fields in the Americas, as María Pilar Aquino observes, "is not due to our [women's] lack of will or vocation, but to the impact on our lives of the interlocking systemic forces of colonization, of racist and sexist exclusion, and of socioeconomic injustice."[3] Exposing these realities in Latin America is a necessary step to have a sober conversation about women's leadership in academia as well as in the church.

The overview presented here is based on two important studies (Tamez's and Raimondo's) that incorporate two key aspects in the journey of Latin American women in theology: the chronological and the epistemological. Tamez's 1998 essay entitled "Latin American Feminist

---

3. Aquino, "Latina Feminist Theology," 146; addition mine.

Hermeneutics: A Retrospective"[4] lays out three phases in women's development of feminist consciousness which reflect changes in their approach
to the biblical texts and in their subsequent theological discourse(s).
These three phases are structured chronologically (by decades: the 1970s,
1980s, and 1990s), using some key ecumenical congresses of Latin American women theologians and biblical scholars as points of reference or
landmarks of development (Mexico 1979, Buenos Aires 1985, and Rio
1993, correspondingly). Tamez clarifies that these phases are not meant
to show a chronological development per se, but they show characteristics that she noticed in her participation at these three events. Tamez
further observes that the "hermeneutical experiences of one decade do
not cancel out those of the other. Very often, different and even conflict-
ing experiences coexist, sometimes within the same person, because of
the different levels of feminist awareness."[5]

Returning to the three phases, the first (in the 1970s) "corresponds
to women's discovery of themselves as autonomous subjects: oppressed
but capable of liberation and actively producing theology."[6] In the second phase (1980s), women attempt "to rework the biblical-theological
discourse in the light of women's aspirations, suffering, and spirituality,
seeking to complete it with women's experience."[7] In the third phase
(1990s), women strive toward "a new biblical-theological discourse with
the help of gender theories."[8] As she continues her analysis, Tamez breaks
down each chronological phase into four areas:

1. She describes the historical context and the biblical and theological
   themes that were emphasized in each particular decade;

2. She identifies some aspects in the feminist consciousness that were
   developed during each specific decade;

3. She elucidates major characteristics of Latin American women's feminist hermeneutics; and

---

4. Tamez, "Latin American Feminist Hermeneutics," 1–14. This same year, two
other significant essays were published: Tepedino, "La Mujer y la Teología en América
Latina," 13–40, and Aquino's original "Latina Feminist Theology," in *Journal of Feminist Studies in Religion* 14 (1998) 89–107. A more recent article is that of Vélez, "Teología Feminista Latinoamericana de la Liberación," 1801–12.

5. Tamez, "Latin American Feminist Hermeneutics," 2.

6. Tamez, "Latin American Feminist Hermeneutics," 13.

7. Tamez, "Latin American Feminist Hermeneutics," 13.

8. Tamez, "Latin American Feminist Hermeneutics," 13.

4. She notices that inclusive language can serve as a relevant indicator of the advancement in the reception of the feminist perspective in Latin America.

The first area listed above is of particular interest to my essay, because it addresses the use of the Bible. The following are key insights (under the first area) from each of the three phases shown chronologically in Tamez's study. In the 1970s, she describes women's reading of the Bible as "popular and militant, intended to be liberating and transforming. The starting point was God as liberator, in solidarity with women and men who were oppressed."[9] Moreover, she continues, "only texts which spoke of liberation were chosen and applied to the double oppressed situation of women," and the hermeneutical approach focused on "the Exodus and the Christology of the historical Jesus because of their practice of justice."[10] In the 1980s, Tamez points out that there are three ways that women are working with the Bible: (a) women search for greater freedom in their way of speaking about God; (b) women affirm the value of "virtues such as motherliness, unselfishness, and tenderness, which society has assigned to women and which had not been considered important in the prevailing theories of knowledge"[11]; and (c) there is a hermeneutical advance in the treatment of the Bible shown in the fact that "when the text did not allow re-interpretation, it was classed as non-normative."[12] For the third phase, the 1990s, Tamez's remarks are rather brief, yet important. She says that, in this decade, women begin to raise "questions on concrete biblical work,"[13] meaning that women not only have questions about the biblical texts, but also, about how these biblical texts have been interpreted.

Tamez's framework of analysis provides an important insight into her work. She contextualizes (chronologically and historically) each of the phases in the process of building women's critical feminist consciousness. In other words, her analysis of "feminist hermeneutics"[14] is not done in the abstract (through theoretical discourses only), but on the contrary, she emphasizes the importance of the context in each of these phases.

9. Tamez, "Latin American Feminist Hermeneutics," 4.

10. Tamez, "Latin American Feminist Hermeneutics," 4.

11. Tamez, "Latin American Feminist Hermeneutics," 7.

12. Tamez, "Latin American Feminist Hermeneutics," 7.

13. Tamez, "Latin American Feminist Hermeneutics," 11.

14. This is how Tamez labels (through the headings) each of the phases in her analysis.

Tamez returns to this insight in her conclusion when she observes that, "given the serious economic and political situation in the continent . . . there is also a certain difficulty in working with radically feminist concepts in theological discourse without a clear, practical method to link economic, political, racial, and feminist concerns."[15]

Making reference also to the work of Tamez (and the three phases), Nancy Raimondo extends the chronology to the next decade and millennium (until 2005), adding other significant works and insights. Raimondo observes that, similar to the analysis of Tamez, Ivone Gebara (in 1993) also alluded to similar phases; one significant difference in Gebara's work is that she identifies these phases as "moments." This category looks at women's individual level of consciousness about their identity as an existential process. Regarding the category of "moments," Raimondo explains that these allow "for spatial and temporal flexibility regarding the different moments of emergence . . . [in this way] it is possible for it [the initial moment] to coexist with diverse developments or theological understandings without excluding each other or becoming unilateral."[16] Raimondo refers to these three moments as *irruption, growth,* and *consolidation*. She points out that for many Latin American women entering the moment of growth has required them to emigrate from their countries of origin (e.g., this has been actually my [diasporic] journey to the US as a native Peruvian). Looking at the three moments of *irruption, growth,* and *consolidation,* Raimondo also explains that the continual process of always having someone entering the moment of irruption creates a referential framework for women theologians, and this framework encompasses the value given to life in the everyday (or *lo cotidiano*). This referential framework points to the preferential option for women, the primacy of praxis, and the affirmation of the body in theology as well as in spirituality.[17]

As Raimondo expands the historical-chronological analysis of Latin American women's presence in theology until 2005, she includes three prominent projects: the first one done at the Universidad Javeriana in Colombia, and the other two in Argentina. In Colombia, a reflection group gathered in 2003 to address students' concerns about gender in theology, and these reflections turned into a research report entitled

15. Tamez, "Latin American Feminist Hermeneutics," 13.

16. Raimondo, "Recuperación del Caminar de las Mujeres," 77; translation mine.

17. Raimondo, "Recuperación del Caminar de las Mujeres," 84.

"Reflections around Feminism and Gender" (published in 2004).[18] In Argentina, a forum entitled "Theology and Gender" took place at the Instituto Superior Evangélico de Estudios Teológicos (ISEDET) in 2003; this evolved into a series of research seminars that was eventually coined Teologanda. This created a larger platform for advancing the theological discourse from the perspective of women; this platform also served as a springboard for the emergence of new leaders in academia. Moreover, Teologanda has been functioning as a network of support for the challenging yet hopeful journey of Latin American women doing theology in all its traditional subdisciplines (biblical studies, systematics, etc.). I believe that this particular research project, Teologanda, has been so far one of the most influential projects and models of leadership in advancing the presence of Latin American women in theology.[19] Teologanda has produced three important research studies: a dictionary (2007), an anthology (2008), and essays on the trajectory of relevant women figures in theology and biblical studies (2009).[20]

The studies included in Raimondo's essay incorporate gender theory, which is one of the aspects/details noticed by Tamez in the third phase (or moment). Connected to this practice, Consuelo Vélez (a prominent Latin American theologian) also notices that feminist theology has advanced the most in the area of Latin American biblical hermeneutics, and one significant factor has been the use of the gender perspective in its approach. Vélez explains that the approach to the Bible from this perspective has been

> characterized by the liberation from the androcentric and patriarchal ways of referring to God, by the re-valuation of the feminine traces present in God and therefore also in hu-mankind—male and female—([like] maternity, selflessness, tenderness), by the welcoming of hermeneutical categories for the body and the quotidian, [and] the work to integrate in the theological discourse [themes like] the "fiesta," happiness, [and] the joy of corporality and sexuality.[21]

18. Raimondo, "Recuperación del Caminar de las Mujeres," 74.

19. See Azcuy, "Andares Teológicos de Teologanda," 113–37.

20. Azcuy et al., *Diccionario de Obras de Autoras en Latino América, el Caribe y Estados Unidos*; Azcuy and García Bachmann et al., *Antología de Textos de Autoras en América Latina, el Caribe y los Estados Unidos*; and Azcuy and García Bachmann et al., *Estudios de Autoras en Américan Latina, el Caribe y Estados Unidos*.

21. Vélez, "Teología Feminista Latinoamericana de la Liberación," 1807; translation mine. Worth noticing in this citation is that, in the incorporation of the gender

Vélez further argues for the need to incorporate the gender perspective in the theological discourse, because it is consistent with a Christian vision of the kingdom of God. She elaborates on this point by saying that "what is at play [referring to gender] is not a particular reality, a contextual theology or a social movement, rather it is the human race [*el género humano*] that is called to be in the image and likeness of God Triune."[22] This insight provides an important theological mediation to further appreciate the significance of Tamez's and Raimondo's analyses of the chronological and epistemological journey of Latin American women in theology.

## A Fifty Years' Journey (in Numbers)

This section is shorter compared to the prior and subsequent one, and its length speaks of the limitations mentioned above regarding the gathering of data and information. Nonetheless, this snapshot moderately illustrates a latent reality of inequality and inequity in the representation of women in the academic context of theology. For this section, I refer to the work done by Carolina Bacher Martínez. She surveyed three academic institutions in Latin America to find out the number of women (students and faculty) attending school or teaching at the selected locations. The institutions included in her study were the Universidad Javeriana (in Bogotá, Colombia), the Pontificia Universidad Católica in Rio de Janeiro, Brazil (PUC-Rio), and the Instituto Superior Evangélico de Estudios Teológicos (ISEDET) in Buenos Aires, Argentina.[23]

Through a series of interviews, Bacher collected information and data from available time periods at each of these institutions, and based on this information, she was able to determine approximate percentages of women's presence at the selected locations (see table).

perspective, Vélez still refers to the biological "binary" male-female.

22. Vélez, "Teología Feminista Latinoamericana de la Liberación," 1812; translation and addition mine.

23. Bacher Martínez, "¡Hay Mujeres en las Facultades de Teología!," 29–46.

| Universidad Javeriana (Bogotá, Colombia) [1999–2002] | Pontificia Universidad Católica [PUC-Rio] (Rio de Janeiro, Brazil) [2004–2010] | ISEDET (Buenos Aires, Argentina) [2004–2008] |
|---|---|---|
| 25 percent of student body (women) | 40 percent of student body (women) | 40 percent of student body (women) |
| 18 percent faculty (women) | 30 percent faculty (women) | 40 percent faculty (women) |

Compared to the twentieth century, the increased percentage of women in academic institutions is remarkable. Bacher sees in this presence a new "sign of the times"[24]; the emergence of women as historical subjects in society and in academia has contributed to the development of a presence that is "active and protagonistic" and growing in communal leadership.[25] Through these signs, one must recognize, Bacher says, "a presence of God that opens processes of humanization that are offered to the world and to the church as *a gift from God*."[26] Moreover, Bacher recommends that for the church these signs should be accompanied by an institutional commitment to change, especially at the structural level. She actually claims that, if one pays attention to the way these changes are already influencing transformations at the institutional level in academic settings, one can see that these changes are offering "institutional options which are at the same time concrete pastoral [ministry] options"[27] for the future.

Bacher notices that the changes in the selected academic institutions correspond to known aspects in processes of institutional change. So, using a framework for organizational change (one specifically focused on gender),[28] Bacher outlines four stages of development—quantitative, compensatory, institutional adaptation, and structural transformation[29]— to illustrate the significance of the changes that have already happened at

24. Paul VI, *Gaudium et Spes,* 4; Bacher, "¡Hay Mujeres en las Facultades de Teología!," 39–41. See also Eckholt, "La Cuestión de las Mujeres como Signo Permanente de los Tiempos," 11–28.

25. Bacher, "¡Hay Mujeres en las Facultades de Teología!," 40.

26. Bacher, "¡Hay Mujeres en las Facultades de Teología!," 40; emphasis original.

27. Bacher, "¡Hay Mujeres en las Facultades de Teología!," 44; addition mine.

28. See Kolb et al., "Making Change," 1–4.

29. Bacher, "¡Hay Mujeres en las Facultades de Teología!," 42–43.

the three selected institutions, and also to show that these changes point towards future steps to continue advancing institutional transformations. For instance, in the third stage (institutional adaptation), Bacher refers to the new faculty spaces that these institutions opened for women by creating endowed chairs, or by creating and supporting research groups formed by women theologians.[30] These changes have allowed women to engage actively in their academic lives. So, Bacher argues that an analysis through this lens can assist as a platform of reflection to foster institutional transformations that can adequately support and respond to the increased emergence of women studying or teaching theology in academic institutions in Latin America, or everywhere else.

In 2018, in preparation for the presentation that eventually became this essay, I did a quick Google search on these same three institutions to see if the percentages presented by Bacher in 2013 remained stable. Although this was an informal search (which included information only on faculty) gathering details through these institutions' websites, I noticed some stability in the percentages and one significant change; additionally, I looked at the number of female faculty teaching in biblical studies. In the Universidad Javeriana, out of a total of forty-seven faculty, ten were women (that is, about 19 percent [so there was a 1 percent increase]), and out of those ten women, only two were in the area of Bible. At PUC-Rio, out of a total of eighteen faculty, four were women (that is, about 20 percent [so there was a 10 percent decrease]), and of those four women, only one teaches Bible. The third institution, the ISEDET in Buenos Aires, closed its doors in 2016 (due to financial issues). Since I am a native Peruvian, I decided to look also at one institution in Peru—the Pontificia Universidad Católica (PUC) in Lima where, out of a total of thirteen faculty, two were women (that is, about 18 percent); interestingly, both have masters degrees only, and neither teaches Bible. Overall, a quick glance at this journey in numbers remains challenging, yet hopeful—a challenging hope.

## A Fifty Years' Journey (in Hope)

As a way of conclusion, this final section is aimed at doing some "deep thinking," and this will be done through three concepts: "emergence" in complexity theory, the theology of the people, and synodality. Deep

---

30. Bacher, "¡Hay Mujeres en las Facultades de Teología!," 43.

thinking is actually a technical term to refer to the kind of thinking that "results in significant learning. Deep thinking is a different . . . way of using the mind. It results in the discontinuous 'aha!' experience, which is the essence of creativity. It is at the heart of every paradigm shift or reframing of a problematic situation."[31] Deep thinking may allow readers to see the seeds of hope embedded in the challenging journey of Latin American women in the past fifty years and in the path ahead.

Emergence of Hope

In 2015, Mercedes Navarro Puerto wrote an essay entitled "La Teología y la Exégesis Bíblica Feministas en la Emergencia Creativa del Futuro Inmediato" (Theology and Feminist Biblical Exegesis in the Creative Emergence of an Immediate Future).[32] Looking at the specific geographical contexts of northern and central Europe and northern America, Navarro Puerto uses terminology from complexity theory to explain the importance of being attentive to the signs of the times because—despite the shocking numbers given in the second section of this paper—these signs still point to a horizon of hope.

*Emergence*, in complexity theory, "refers to the evolution from a simple system to a more complex one. Therefore, emergence is a process."[33] As a process, it revolves around two dynamic movements. The first movement implies an agent, someone who can constantly observe and identify patterns; the second movement focuses on what is being observed and perceives the slow appearances of new patterns. So, when looking at the past fifty years' journey of Latin American women in theology, one is observing two things happening at once—women as agents and processes in motion. Although the numbers are discouraging (i.e., quantifying women's presence in academic settings in theology and biblical studies in Latin America), through a much larger framework of thinking and understanding, these same numbers are better than those from the previous fifty years, because the current numbers reflect new and significant patterns that have been emerging. For instance, if we look through the lens of publications, Navarro Puerto says, "we discover its

31. Byers, "Deep Thinking," back cover.

32. Navarro Puerto, "La Teología y la Exégesis Bíblica Feministas," 207–38.

33. Navarro Puerto, "La Teología y la Exégesis Bíblica Feministas," 207–8. Translation mine.

directions, its traces, its evolution, its addressees, the means used for its communication, the rank it occupies and the public niches that are still unattended . . . [all these are pointing to] a promising future line."[34] The concept of emergence facilitates the re-consideration and re-framing of what can be seen as the seemingly minor accomplishments or light presence of Latin American women in theology during the past fifty years. Through this lens, the future of women in theology looks hopeful; their accomplishments are part of a complex system that continues to be in a dynamic emergence.

## The Theology of the People

In the Catholic Church, a return to a more gospel-centered framework of hope has been emphasized during the papacy of Francis—a pope from Latin America—through the theology of the people. Rafael Luciani explains that there is a clear connection between Pope Francis' speeches and "the theological and pastoral guidelines proposed by what is known as the theology of the people, or the theology of culture."[35] This theology may assist people in interpreting the many "new" signs of the times, which, according to Pope Francis, reflect not just the new millennium, but a "change of era"; the very framework of the worldview is changing.[36] This is a fruitful lens through which to observe the signs of the times related to women's presence in academia, especially in theology, because it adds another layer of complexity for deep thinking.

The theology of the people, in its foundation and development, proposes a return to its Christian essence—that is, "the historical praxis of Jesus as a paradigm of humanity."[37] Luciani explains that the "kerygmatic Christology of Francis is faithful to the [Second Vatican] council spirit as it was received in Latin America, granting primacy to following the Jesus of the gospels, the source of humanization and the hermeneutic criterion

34. Navarro Puerto, "La Teología y la Exégesis Bíblica Feministas," 216; translation and addition mine.

35. Luciani, *Pope Francis and the Theology of the People*, xiii. See also Scannone, *Teología del Pueblo*.

36. Bergoglio, "Message of *Aparecida* to Priests." The *Aparecida* document was part of CELAM's V meeting in Brazil, 2007. CELAM refers to the Episcopal Conference of Latin American Bishops. The previous four meetings of CELAM took place in Rio (1955), Medellín (1968), Puebla (1979), and Santo Domingo (1992).

37. Luciani, *Pope Francis and the Theology of the People*, 151.

for our daily life."[38] The Second Vatican Council[39] proposes the figure of Jesus as a model of humanity, "one who works for the humanization of every oppressive relationship through true reconciliation. This model of humanity is revealed concretely in Jesus as originating event and archetype of every authentically human way of being. It is a totally inclusive humanity, one that recognizes in every human being a brother or a sister."[40] This hermeneutic criterion provides a much larger theological and Christocentric framework anchored on the importance of restoring and protecting the dignity of *every* human being. Therefore, this framework furnishes a platform for adequate theological reflections and actions that would also include, engage, and empower women themselves in the restoration of their own dignity. Rooted in this Christocentric paradigm of humanity, women's voices and experiences can no longer be at the margins of the theological discourse; righting this wrong will open new opportunities for the emergence of more women leaders in Latin America and elsewhere—not just in academia, but also in the church and society.

## Synodality

In 2018, the International Theological Commission (ITC) released a document entitled "Synodality in the Life and Mission of the Church."[41] In the very first paragraph, it states that it "is precisely this path of synodality which God expects of the Church of the third millennium." Then, it describes the theological significance of the term "synod"

> as an ancient and venerable word in the Tradition of the Church, whose meaning draws on the deepest themes of Revelation. Composed of a preposition, συν (with), and the noun, ὁδός (path), it indicates the path along which the People of God walk together. Equally, it refers to the Lord Jesus, who presents Himself as "the way, the truth and the life" (Jn 14:6), and to the fact

---

38. Luciani, *Pope Francis and the Theology of the People*, 151; addition mine. In this, Pope Francis follows the Christology of *Gaudium et Spes* 22.

39. See Paul VI, *Gaudium et Spes*, 22.

40. Luciani, *Pope Francis and the Theology of the People*, 152.

41. International Theological Commission, "Synodality in the Life and Mission of the Church."

that Christians, His followers, were originally called "followers of the Way" (cf. Acts 9:2; 19:9–23; 22:4; 24:14–22).[42]

Related to this emphasis on *the walking together of the people of God,* which has profound ramifications when considering the role of women as "active" (walking requires motion) members of the church, the ITC's document elaborates on two other relevant concepts, both also connected to the understanding of synodality: (1) the vocation of all baptized to walking together as a church and (2) Pope Francis's description of the inverted pyramid as the image of a synodal church.

Regarding the first point, the document states that "[a]ll the faithful are called by virtue of their baptism to witness to and proclaim the Word of truth and life, in that they are members of the prophetic, priestly, and royal People of God."[43] Sandra Arenas explains that these three functions, known as the *tria munera,* constitute the general framework for the Second Vatican Council's documents, particularly *Lumen Gentium,* and they are the subjacent principle in the ecclesiology of the 1983 Canon Law.[44] However, she observes that while the *tria munera* applies to all of the baptized, the reality is that ordained ministers and laity have been individualized when it comes to juridical and pastoral matters. In her study, Arenas addresses the issue of "why, if there is common participation [in witnessing to and proclaiming the word of truth and life], there is no movement toward a major gender homogeneity regarding leadership and administration of ecclesial power."[45] She acknowledges that "to interpret and/or discern the spirit and the conciliar letter—and its norms—is a complex matter. On the one hand, one has to detangle the excesses of centralization which generate the ties between ordination-ministry-leadership-ecclesial governance, and on the other hand is the excess of masculinization."[46] Sadly, despite the fact that there have been some exceptions during the postconciliar period to include more lay people in some ecclesial spaces, these have favored men and segregated

42. International Theological Commission, "Synodality in the Life and Mission of the Church," 2; emphasis mine.

43. International Theological Commission, "Synodality in the Life and Mission of the Church," 56.

44. Arenas, "Sin Exclusiones," 541.

45. Arenas, "Sin Exclusiones," 542; addition and translation mine.

46. Arenas, "Sin Exclusiones," 542; translation mine.

women, even in academia and in the teaching of theology.[47] In her study, Arenas proposes a shared governance model as a heuristic tool to rethink leadership in the church, and I believe that her insight requires further research in the future.

The second concept, a synodal church, is based on the ecclesiological perspective of Vatican II. Pope Francis has taken up this perspective and sketched this image of a synodal church as an inverted pyramid, "which comprises the People of God and the College of Bishops, one of whose members, the Successor of Peter, has a specific ministry of unity. Here, the summit is below the base."[48] The renewal of the church's synodal life in this inverted pyramid "demands that we initiate processes for consulting the entire People of God."[49] In attending to these processes, women's voices and roles as members of the people of God must be equally considered and represented in conversations. Worth pointing out is that, in his 2013 apostolic exhortation, *Evangelii Gaudium*, Pope Francis was already calling for "the legitimate rights of women to be respected . . . [and] for pastors and theologians . . . to recognize more fully what this entails with regard to the possible role of women in decision-making in different areas of the Church's life."[50] In a recent study of Pope Francis's magisterium regarding the role of women in the church, Miren Junkal Guevara identifies two main points in Pope Francis's agenda: (1) the clues for a "theology of women" and (2) women's presence in decision-making places.[51] In looking at the challenges for the future, among other things, Guevara recommends an explicit support for the professionalization of women who want to study theology so that they can serve the church with a "stronger presence."[52]

This "stronger presence" refers back to the words of Pope Francis during an interview (on his return trip from Rio de Janeiro) regarding the role of women in the life of the church. Interestingly, the previous topic addressed in the interview was synodality. Pope Francis was asked how he envisions the future unity of the church. His response was "[w]e

---

47. Arenas, "Sin Exclusiones," 550.

48. International Theological Commission, "Synodality in the Life and Mission of the Church," 57.

49. International Theological Commission, "Synodality in the Life and Mission of the Church," 65.

50. Francis, *Evangelii Gaudium*, 104.

51. Guevara, "El Magisterio de Francisco sobre la Mujer," 475.

52. Guevara, "El Magisterio de Francisco sobre la Mujer," 495.

must walk united with our differences: there is no other way to become one. This is the way of Jesus."[53]

I end this essay with Pope Francis's response to the specific question of "what about the role of women in the church?," which I believe applies to the role of women in academia and theology:

> It is necessary to broaden the opportunities for a *stronger presence* of women in the church. . . . Women are asking deep questions that must be addressed. The church cannot be herself without the woman and her role. The woman is essential for the church. . . . We must therefore investigate further the role of women in the church. We have to work harder to develop a profound theology of the woman. Only by making this step will it be possible to better reflect on their function within the church. The feminine genius is needed wherever we make important decisions. The challenge today is this: to think about the specific place of women also in those places where the authority of the church is exercised for various areas of the church.[54]

## Bibliography

Aquino, María Pilar. "Latina Feminist Theology: Central Features." In *A Reader in Latina Feminist Theology: Religion and Justice,* edited by María Pilar Aquino et al., 134–60. Austin: University of Texas Press, 2002.

Arenas, Sandra. "Sin Exclusiones: Catolicismo, Mujeres y Liderazgo Distribuido." *Teología y Vida* 61 (2020) 537–53.

Azcuy, Virginia R. "Andares Teológicos de Teologanda (2003–2013): Una Lectura desde las Prácticas." *Proyecto* 63–64 (2013) 113–37.

———. "El Lugar Teológico de las Mujeres." *Proyecto* 39 (2001) 11–34.

Azcuy, Virginia R., et al. *Diccionario de Obras de Autoras en Latino América, el Caribe y Estados Unidos.* Buenos Aires: San Pablo, 2007.

Azcuy, Virginia R., and Mercedes García Bachmann, et al. *Antología de Textos de Autoras en América Latina, el Caribe y los Estados Unidos.* Buenos Aires: San Pablo, 2008.

———. *Estudios de Autoras en Américan Latina, el Caribe y Estados Unidos.* Buenos Aires: San Pablo, 2009.

Bacher Martínez, Carolina. "¡Hay Mujeres en las Facultades de Teología! Reflexión Teológica-Pastoral a Partir de Tres Experiencias en América Latina." *Proyecto* 63–64 (2013) 29–46.

Bergoglio, Jorge Mario. "The Message of *Aparecida* to Priests." Homily given at Villa Cura Brochero, Argentina, September 11, 2008.

---

53. Spadaro, "Interview with Pope Francis."
54. Spadaro, "Interview with Pope Francis"; italics mine.

Byers, William. *Deep Thinking: What Mathematics Can Teach Us about the Mind.* Montreal: World Scientific, 2014.

Eckholt, Margit. "La Cuestión de las Mujeres como Signo Permanente de los Tiempos: Legado y Misión del Concilio Vaticano II." *Proyecto* 25 (2013) 11–28.

Francis, Pope. *Evangelii Gaudium: The Joy of the Gospel.* New York: Image, 2014.

Guevara, Miren Junkal. "El Magisterio de Francisco sobre la Mujer: Continuidad, Novedad y Desafío." *Teología y Vida* 61 (2020) 473–96.

International Theological Commission. "Synodality in the Life and Mission of the Church." *Vatican.va,* March 2, 2018. http://www.vatican.va/roman_curia/congregations/cfaith/cti_documents/rc_cti_20180302_sinodalita_en.html#.

Kolb, Deborah, et al. "Making Change: A Framework for Promoting Gender Equity in Organizations." *CGO Insights* (October 1998) 1–4. https://www.simmons.edu/sites/default/files/2019–03/Insights%2001.pdf.

Luciani, Rafael. *Pope Francis and the Theology of the People.* Maryknoll, NY: Orbis, 2017.

Navarro Puerto, Mercedes. "La Teología y la Exégesis Bíblica Feministas en la Emergencia Creativa del Futuro Inmediato." In *Resistencia y Creatividad: Ayer, Hoy y Mañana de las Teologías Feministas,* edited by Carmen Picó, 207–38. Estella (Navarra), Spain: Verbo Divino, 2015.

Paul VI, Pope. *Gaudium et Spes: Pastoral Constitution on the Church in the Modern World.* Boston: St. Paul's, 1990.

Raimondo, Nancy Viviana. "Recuperación del Caminar de las Mujeres en América Latina y el Caribe: Una Mirada Histórico-Teológica (1975-2005)." *Proyecto* 63–64 (2013) 65–84.

Scannone, Juan Carlos. *La Teología del Pueblo: Raíces Teológicas del Papa Francisco.* Maliaño, Spain: Sal Terrae, 2017.

Schüssler Fiorenza, Elisabeth. *The Power of the Word: Scripture and the Rhetoric of Empire.* Minneapolis: Fortress, 2007.

Spadaro, Antonio. "Interview with Pope Francis." *Vatican.va,* August 19, 2013. http://www.vatican.va/content/francesco/en/speeches/2013/september/documents/papa-francesco_20130921_intervista-spadaro.html.

Tamez, Elsa. "Latin American Feminist Hermeneutics: A Retrospective." In *To Be Fully Human: EATWOT Women's Theologies,* edited by EATWOT Executive Committee, 1–14. Manila: Ecumenical Association of Third World Theologians (EATWOT), 1998.

Tepedino, Ana María. "La Mujer y la Teología en América Latina: Antecedentes Históricos." In *Entre la Indignación y la Esperanza: Teología Feminista Latinoamericana,* edited by Ana María Tepedino and María Pilar Aquino, 13–40. Santa Fé de Bogotá, Colombia: Indo-American Service Ltd., 1998.

Vélez, Olga Consuelo. "Teología Feminista Latinoamericana de la Liberación: Balance y Futuro." *Horizonte* 11 (2013) 1801–12.

# 3

# A Woman's Leadership in Seventeenth-Century Mexico: A Model for Latina Leadership Today

Neomi De Anda

Sor María Anna Águeda de San Ignacio's (1695–1756) *Marabillas del Divino Amor Selladas con el Sello de la Verdad,* published posthumously in Puebla, Mexico in 1758, offers an eighteenth-century theology based on *El Camino de la Leche,* or the Milky Way. Her writings exist today because her bishop, Sr. Dr. D. Domingo Pantaleón Álvarez de Abreu paid for the publication of her texts soon after her death.

The lack of historical voices from Latin America found in theological scholarship in the United States of America raises concern for the Catholic Church with a large LatinoXa[1] population. However, we should not consider such a lacuna only a contemporary pastoral problem. As

---

1. As stated in Cruz et al., "Respondiendo a las Demandas Históricas," 5, "We have chosen to use this format to signify the naming of our complex realities for the following reasons. The inclusive 'a' and 'o' point to the need to omit an often created gender binary and allow for more fluidity as the 'X' can also be seen as bridging the 'o' and 'a' together. . . . The thin horizontal line symbolizes that no matter which descriptor is used for identifying our communities, none fully engages/reveals the complexity of realities. We understand the aforementioned list to be descriptive and limited, not prescriptive and all encompassing." Furthermore, this term allowed for multiple colors, which signify "the diversity of our communities with particular attention to race, ethnicity, and sexuality." I now add that the "X" can also be seen as annihilating the need for a gender binary or gendering all together.

Michelle Gonzalez states, "Very few women's voices emerge in the history books and theological texts of the late seventeenth century in Latin America. In fact, many would argue that there are few substantial figures in this region, male or female, whose impact is significant beyond their local context."[22] Overall, historical figures from Latin America have been considered marginal and insignificant to wider theological discourse, as some consider these figures to be spiritual writers rather than theologians. One reason most of these figures have not been brought forward into the United States of America may not be because of their lack of theological insight or possible contribution for our time, but because they are seen as outside of the mainstream. Some consider these historical figures as part of USA LatinoXa theologies and in the mainstream. For instance, Gary Macy argues that

> whatever can be said of Latino/a theology, it cannot be said that it is out of the mainstream of Western European theological tradition. On the contrary, it is the heir of an ancient tradition that was greatly responsible not only for the preservation of the Western European traditions and learning, but also was one of the most influential creators of that tradition and of that learning. From this historical vantage point, then, Latino/a theology is as much, or more so, a part of mainstream theology than any other theological grouping.[3]

In light of this recognition, two historical facts must be remembered. One, the Catholic Church was first brought to the Americas[4] by the Spanish and was translated into a complex matrix of faith and religious experiences. As Macy states, "[the] colonial background was shaped by sixteenth-century Iberian theology, which in turn was influenced by the *Convivencia* that continued into that century of encounter and mutual discovery."[5] Two, some of the oldest Catholic settlements in the United States of America are found in St. Augustine, Florida, and in the American Southwest in what is now Texas. This Catholic history needs to be remembered as we continue Catholic theological scholarship in the United

---

2. Gonzalez, *Sor Juana*, xi.

3. Macy, "Iberian Heritage of US Latino/a Theology," 44.

4. I use the term "Americas" as the name known today. I recognize that, when Columbus and other Spanish settlers landed on the continents we now call North and South America, these names did not exist and the names themselves comply with a complex matrix of colonization.

5. Macy, "Iberian Heritage of US Latino/a Theology," 51–52.

States of America. While Catholic histories of the southwestern United States must be remembered as histories rooted in Spain and Mexico, these histories and historical figures should not be considered as belonging only to Latin America but also need to be understood as belonging to the United States of America. Part of my purpose for the theology I do is to uncover historical roots for deepening our theological reflections.

The retrieval of historical voices, especially those of women, remains an important and necessary function for theologies constructed in the twenty-first century. It is important to have a diversity of historical voices for women in leadership in the Catholic Church. It is also important to exemplify women as leaders throughout the history of the church. Sor María Anna Águeda de San Ignacio renders a voice from seventeenth- and eighteenth-century Mexico which should not be lost in the folds and depths of Christian histories and traditions. María Anna adds another original voice to those we know from New Spain and early Mexico. Furthermore, she was both a leader in the establishment of her convent and a theologian as first prioress of the community of Santa Rosa. As a leader in the conversion of her *beaterio* to a convent, she helped realize a goal of a project that began in 1609 which was to establish an ecclesial institution which belonged only to the Mexican Catholic Church and not the Spanish Catholic Church.[6]

María Anna Águeda de San Ignacio's work exists because she remained in positive relationships with her local ordinary (bishop), Sr. Dr. D. Domingo Pantaleón Álvarez de Abreu, and her confessor, Joseph Bellido, who documented her *vida,* or life story. Not only did the local ordinary place his seal on her work, but he also paid for the professional printing of numerous copies. Five copies still exist in public venues with the possibility of other copies being held in private collections.

Sor María Anna employs the image of Mary's breast milk to appropriate simultaneous authority for herself as leader and foundress of her Dominican convent in Puebla and her theological treatise, *Las Marabillas,* within the context of Christian traditions.[7] Through the four books of *Las Marabillas,* María Anna adopts *el Camino de la Leche*[8] as the spiritual path to develop her theological treatise. Through the image of Mary's

6. Archivo General de Indias, "Expediente sobre beaterio de Santa Rosa de Puebla."

7. Águeda de San Ignacio, *Marabillas del Divino Amor,* 3–7.

8. The Path of Milk, The Way of Milk (my translations); Milky Way (translation by Néstor Medina).

breast milk, she explains connections between Mary and each person of the Trinity, with particular attention to Mary's relationship with Jesus. In this relationship, the fullness of what is human and divine comes to be known to humanity. Through this spiritual milk, humanity may also come to know and be in union with God.

María Anna develops her theology of breast milk within each of the four books of *Las Marabillas*; each contains a specific focus and purpose. In Book One, she focuses on Mary and Mary's relationship to the Trinity by situating her work within deep Catholic traditions. She makes a direct link between her writings on Mary's breast milk and Saints Augustine and Bernard of Clairvaux. María Anna also gives numerous persuasive reasons why the reader should follow the *Camino de la Leche*.

In Book Two, María Anna uses the fifteen mysteries of the rosary to develop a theology of gift, with each decade of the rosary based on a particular gift. Examples include Mary's children coming to know the fruits of the Eternal Incarnate Word and matters of justice, one of María Anna's main themes throughout *Las Marabillas*. The fifth mystery is dedicated to Mary's children coming to know necessary doctrine to find Jesus. Themes of suffering, nudity, and the Holy Spirit are treated in mysteries seven through fifteen.

Book Three focuses on the soul's relationship to Christ. In this book, María Anna articulates how humanity should measure union with Christ. By explaining these measurements, such as wisdom,[9] María Anna develops a Christology based on a Jesus:Mary:Humanity model, where the union with Christ results in both relationship and community.[10] Finally, Book Four names rules for life in the Convento de Santa Rosa. María Anna explains the rules of divine love, which a faithful nun in the convent of Santa Rosa should follow.

Overall, within *Las Marabillas*, María Anna situates her own theology within extended Christian traditions. In particular, her employment of the image of breast milk places her firmly in a tradition created by both male and female leaders of religious communities through the history of Christianity, such as Augustine and Bernard of Clairvaux.

María Anna Águeda de San Ignacio stands as one more mystical voice who should be studied in light of theological inquiry and Christian traditioning from a Roman Catholic perspective. While she wrote *Las*

9. Águeda de San Ignacio, *Marabillas del Divino Amor*, 228.

10. I use the term "community" to include more than two persons gathered in relationship.

*Marabillas* primarily for her convent community, she not only shared her understandings of Christian traditions but included new understandings, particularly of the richness of the *Camino de la Leche*, which reached a broader audience through the multiple copies printed upon publication.

María Anna Águeda de San Ignacio lived during a period in which the Catholic Church strongly influenced Mexican society, particularly women's roles in that society. Although the church was understood as primarily a religious force, it also wielded much power over and within the socioeconomic-racial[11] structures of Mexican society.

Little is known about Sor María Anna's formal education. We do know, however, that she was born to lower-middle-class/lower-class Mexicans in Mexico, rather than to members of the elite. It is more than likely she was raised in a Catholic church, which lived with a fluid, complex, and even synchronistic understanding of some Christian doctrines, such as that of God and God's relationship to humanity. The historical context of the seventeenth- and eighteenth-century Mexican Catholic churches strongly influenced María Anna's life. Born on Friday, March 3, 1695[12] to two Mexican parents, her lineage is more complex than the label of *criolla* may describe. Her father, Pedro de la Cruz y Aguilar, was born in Puerto de Santa María, a city close to the empire of Gaditano, while her mother, Doña Micaela Velarde, was from Puebla. Her genealogical lines prior to her parents are not definitively known, but a strong probability exists that María Anna was at least of partial indigenous heritage and not only of full Spanish descent as would be the proper description for one labeled a *criolla*, as Jennifer Eich[13] and others' building upon Eich's work have labeled her. Through using context as a foundational contributor to the creation of theological thought, a concept central to LatinoXa theologies and religious discourses, this distinction becomes noteworthy, because María Anna's theological constructs found in *Las Marabillas* should be read as thoughts from a woman of mixed heritages and backgrounds, not only Spanish.[14]

---

11. I see these factors as all working together in the context of Mexico in the early eighteenth century. The histories of the sixteenth century, which set the stage for the modern history of Mexico, show that these factors were structurally systematized all in the name of God. For further explanation, see Espín, *Faith of the People*, 37.

12. Bellido, *Vida*, 10.

13. Eich, *Other Mexican Muse*.

14. I wish to dispel a misconception that the Spanish Catholic Church acted only as religious (sometimes social and cultural) colonizers of the Americas during the

Although *vidas,* religious biographies and autobiographies of that era, were written for the specific purpose of showing how holy certain members of religious life were in the stories of New Spain, one can learn much from these religious biographies. Her parents were joined through the Catholic sacrament of marriage and were blessed with many children—understood as the reward for those pure souls whose procreation was not determined by lust or passion, as we see from Bellido, Maria Anna's biographer:

> *Felicitò el Cielo su Matrimonio, dandoles multiplicado fruto de bendicion, que es el primario fin de la institucion de este Sacramento; sin duda, que por averlo recibido, como tan Cristianos, aviendo purificado antes sus almas con las saludables aguas de la penitencia, no arrastrados de la pasión, ciegos del interès, ni con otro bastardo motivo, de los muchos que se suelen mezclar, y de que resultan tantas, y tan lastimosas monstruosidades en el Mundo.*[15]

María Anna was one of eight children, four girls and four boys.[16] We know that she outlived three sisters and one brother,[17] and that the brother who died before she did was a priest.[18] Bellido furthermore notes that María Anna's parents gave her preferential treatment over her siblings: *"María Anna, que se le siguiò, todo alivio, amparo y Consuelo."*[19] While this piece of information may not be factual, but more hagiographical and idealized, Bellido's inclusion of it sets María Anna apart as one

---

periods of the fifteenth to eighteenth centuries. Once members of the Spanish Church arrived on the continent of the Americas, something new began to transpire. Of course, this history is not a peaceful one, nor should it be remembered as such, but María Anna's mixed background shows that people of mixed backgrounds and contexts (many different levels of these distinctions existed in Mexico, and I do not know into which category María Anna fit) contributed to the development of the theological discourse of the Mexican Catholic Church of the seventeenth and eighteenth centuries.

15. Bellido, *Vida,* 2. In English (my translation), this reads, "The heavens celebrated their marriage by giving them multiple fruitful blessings, which is the primary end of this Sacrament, without a doubt, having received it in such a Christian way, having purified their souls with the healthy waters of penance, not led by passion, blind of interest, nor with any other bastard motive, of the many which can be mixed together which result in so many pitiful monstrosities in the world."

16. Bellido, *Vida,* 2.

17. Bellido, *Vida,* 3.

18. Bellido, *Vida,* 3

19. Bellido, *Vida,* 2. In English (my translation), this reads, "María Anna, who received all care, protection, and comfort."

destined for a particularly holy life. He also describes María Anna's virtue as exemplary: "*Estaban tan unidas en la virtud, que iban â competencia, de quien amaba mas á su querido Jesus, repitiendo María Anna con innata humildad, que en todo, y siempre le ganaba a Teresa.*"[20]

*Vidas,* of course, had a particular cultural purpose. Certain people's lives were recorded, because they demonstrated a certain holiness of people to the society of New Spain—in María Anna's particular case, Mexico. Coupled with a baroque Spanish characterized by hyperbole, these pieces presented examples of human beings who lived stellar religious vocations from a very young age and whose family background permitted and enabled them to live these saintly lives.[21]

From our twenty-first-century perspective, these family backgrounds are described in heterosexist, racist, and classist ways so typical of the times. But these *vidas* also give us a lens to understand lives—in this case, María Anna's—within a particular social construct and situation. They help us grasp how society understood and even deliberately constructed her; however, through her writing, we can also see how she framed or set up her own social world beyond the normative societal expectations.

That Bellido writes about her family life is very important, because it reinforces that she came from an appropriate background for a saintly woman, one who should be lauded for her leadership. The following is a prime example of his many similar descriptions:

> *Cuidaban con el mayor espero los Padres de nuestra Maria Anna de la crianza de sus hijos, doctrinandolos, insundiendoles el santo temor de Dios, y teniendolos recogidos; pero mas que todo dandoles siempre en las acciones vivos exemplos, de lo que avian de hacer, y caminando delante como guias, que los encaminaban por los senderos seguros de las virtudes; porque unidos con el yugo matrimonial de comun acuerdo las practicaban.*[22]

20. Bellido, *Vida*, 2. In English (my translation) this reads, "They were so united in virtue, that they even had competitions about who loved Jesus more, and over and over, María Anna with innate humility as in everything, would always beat Teresa."

21. Lavrin, *Brides of Christ*, 34.

22. Bellido, *Vida*, 3. In English (my translation), this reads, "María Anna's parents cared with the greatest of hope in the beliefs of their children, through always keeping them together, they indoctrinated them and instilled in them the holy fear of God, but more than anything, were always giving them living examples in action of what they should do, and walking ahead of them like guides who walked them through secure footpaths of virtues, because [they were] united in the yoke of marriage and agreed

Of course, her siblings were raised in the same religious and pious home. But María Anna was given special attention, as mentioned above: "*Desde edad tierna acostumbrò su Padre rezar tres Salves todos los dias à Maria Santissima, rogandole, le deisfe à conocer la cercanía de su muerte.*"[23] María Anna's father told her that if God could do such great things with him who was a great sinner, then how much more could he do with one who served God with as great care as she did.[24] We know also that both her father[25] and mother[26] were strongly devoted to Mary, and we can thus begin to see that María Anna's dedication and devotion to Mary and Marian images in her writings find their roots in her childhood family life.

María Anna's familial socioeconomic context plays a pivotal role in my understanding of her context and place in eighteenth-century Mexican society. Bellido informs us that she was born poor. He quickly moves beyond this less-than-culturally-acceptable fact for a saintly life by stating how she was, in fact, chosen to be a bride of Jesus, because she was born into the same poor conditions as Jesus.[27] Her father, who was unemployed for an extended length of time during her childhood,[28] died when María Anna was still a girl,[29] leaving the family of nine quite poor.[30] At one point, Maria Anna's mother was asked for María Anna's hand in marriage in exchange for medical care for the rest of the family.[31] Her mother believed that María Anna's religious call was so strong that she rejected the offer,[32] telling María Anna to follow that divine calling.[33] While one may not be certain of the historical accuracy of this account, Bellido intends for the reader to conclude that María Anna was destined to be

---

practices."

23. Bellido, *Vida*, 3. In English (my translation), this reads, "From a young age, they were accustomed by their father to pray three Holy Marys every day to the Most Blessed Mary, begging, they understand the proximity of their death."

24. Bellido, *Vida*, 4.

25. Bellido, *Vida*, 5.

26. Bellido, *Vida*, 6.

27. Bellido, *Vida*, 10.

28. Bellido, *Vida*, 4.

29. Bellido, *Vida*, 5.

30. Bellido, *Vida*, 6.

31. Bellido, *Vida*, 7.

32. Bellido, *Vida*, 32.

33. Bellido, *Vida*, 7.

a remarkable nun despite her socioeconomic circumstances. Of course, this story may also be Bellido justifying how a poor girl could become such a respected leader, which would have been strongly contrary to the cultural norms and expectations of the time.

## Entering Religious Life

María Anna chose to enter the *beaterio* at the age of nineteen.[34] As Eich states, "Sor María Anna was admitted without the necessary 'economic contribution' although her biographer never explains the 'miraculous' event that enabled this startling exception,"[35] as dowries were expected for all women to enter *beaterios*. It may be that this *beaterio*, because of its foundational endowment, did not require dowries as others in Puebla did at that time. Some think Fr. Juan de Torres, her spiritual director who also served as the *beaterio's*[36] chaplain, saw to her admittance in the *beaterio*.[37] Here, one should note that important differences existed between nuns and *beatas*. Further research explains that this "miraculous event" was part of the desired social change on behalf of the Mexican Catholic Church as it moved away from the control held by the Spanish Catholic Church.[38] As Eich states, "Beatas were pious laywomen who adopted the rules and living habits of a religious order, sometimes professing as a tertiary or lay sister of an established religious order."[39] Whether or not to wear the religious order's habit was their choice.

María Anna's lack of dowry did not go unnoticed. Bellido makes a point of discussing the questions other women posed to and about María Anna because of her lack of dowry:

> *Què palabras le decian? Què estylos, y modos tenian en tratarla? Què pesares no le daban? No era lo de menos decirle; para què entraria esta aqui? Quièn hizo tal disparate? Quitate de delante,*

---

34. Bellido, *Vida*, 48.

35. Eich, *Other Mexican Muse*, 11.

36. A *beaterio* is a place where lay women lived together in prayer. These women made temporary but never permanent vows.

37. Eich, *Other Mexican Muse*, 12; Muriel, *Cultura Feminina Novohispana*, 263.

38. Archivo General de Indias, "Expediente sobre beaterio de Santa Rosa de Puebla."

39. Eich, *Other Mexican Muse*, 12; Muriel, *Cultura Feminina Novohispana*, 263.

*que ni vèrte, ni oìrte queremos? Nos estás comiendo, y gastando*
*las rentas del Beaterio.*[40]

So, like many other young women who entered *conventos* and *beaterios*
without a dowry, María Anna was more than likely treated as a lower-
class citizen within the social structure of the *beaterio*.

Although María Anna's role and station at the *beaterio* were initially
questioned and at times scorned, she made considerable contributions as
a *beata* and later as a nun, both to her own *beaterio*, to at least one other
*convento*, and to theological discourse.

## Becoming a Nun in Eighteenth-Century Mexico

As in all cultures, particular constructs of and for women existed in and
shaped New Spanish society. Lavrin states, "Historians and literary historians agree that sacred biography and even autobiography intend to
'represent' or create models of behavior that fit well-established canons
of sacred writing."[41] By the sixteenth century, "the fact still stands that
the official 'construct' of women as weak and threatened, and the beaterios and convents as sites of shelter, was part of the mind-set of those
who were shaping New Spain's society."[42] In the world of María Anna,
socioeconomic and racial matters strongly influenced women's choices in
life. For example, poorer but nonetheless pure-blooded women entered
convents to maintain racial class and purity of blood rather than lower
their family's racial status by marrying down.[43] Asunción Lavrin names
four standards for becoming a nun: purity of blood as a racial category;
legitimacy of birth as a result of conception within the boundaries of
marriage; virginity; and a dowry. According to Bellido, María Anna met
some of these categories, with the possible exception of purity of blood
and the exception of a dowry as I have previously stated. Yet, she met two
other categories delineated by Bellido: call and high intelligence.

40. Bellido, *Vida*, 63. In English (my translation), this reads: "What words did they
tell her? In which ways did they treat her? What grief did they give? It was not beneath
them to say, 'Why did this one enter here?' Who did such a silly thing? Move away
from here, because we neither want to see nor hear you. You are eating and wasting the
rents collected from the Beaterio."

41. Lavrin, *Brides of Christ*, 26.

42. Lavrin, *Brides of Christ*, 19.

43. Lavrin, *Brides of Christ*, 18.

He begins by establishing her parents' ancestry: "*Ambos Confortes fueron de conocida limpieza en la sangre, de honrados procederes en el trato, de muy cristianos costumbres, y de muy competentes bienes de fortuna, para una mas que mediana decencia.*"[44] This notion was so important that a direct statement needed to be made in her *Vida* so that no question would ever exist as to whether María Anna was of the right lineage, not only to be a bride of Christ but also to have such a significant place as a mystic, foundress, and leader in her convent community, as well as the broader church of Puebla.

Bellido demonstrates legitimacy of birth as a result of conception within the boundaries of marriage through her parents having conceived all of their children thanks to their own pure souls rather than as a result of some untoward passion.[45] They entered into a "*contraxo legitimo Matrimonio*"[46] which was not only a legal agreement but, more importantly, a religious, sacramental union.

Bellido highlights María Anna's virginity by focusing on one significant event. When she believed it time to enter the convent, she prayed diligently before making the final decision.

During one of these acts of prayer, she had a mystical vision in which a large serpent tempted her to sin in a manner that would mean the loss of her virginity. In her vision, she resisted the serpent and remained a virgin.[47]

So, María Anna was accepted to the *beaterio*, because she met extra requirements for entry. Yet, her lack of dowry was not without consequence. Lavrin mentions that many of the nuns of sixteenth- through eighteenth-century New Spain were described as being precocious and highly intelligent but does not include those attributes as being ones sought after in candidates entering a *beaterio* or *convento*. But Bellido describes María Anna as highly intelligent to the point of exaggeration, saying, for example, that she learned to read with just one lesson and could read anything given to her.[48] Nevertheless, María Anna's theologi-

44. Bellido, *Vida*, 2. In English (my translation), this reads: "Both caregivers were known to be pure of blood, honorably partnered (married), upholding very Christian customs, and very competent backgrounds, which meant she was above average descendance."

45. Bellido, *Vida*, 2.

46. Bellido, *Vida*, 2.

47. Bellido, *Vida*, 31–32.

48. Bellido, *Vida*, 18.

cal abilities are revealed in her writings, moving beyond the questionable examples provided by Bellido. Finally, although the notion of a call to a religious vocation is not mentioned as one of Lavrin's themes, it was proposed as critical in María Anna's *Vida*. We see the critical nature of this call in the above examples of her mother foregoing health care for the family because she considered María Anna's call to be so strong. We also see it in the story of proof of her virginity, and in her final choice to enter the *beaterio* at the age of nineteen, after completing the spiritual exercises of Ignacio de Loyola.[49]

## Converting the *Beaterio* to a *Convento*

Fr. Bernardo Andía was the provincial who oversaw the spiritual lives of the Province of Santo Domingo. According to Bellido, he cared zealously and tirelessly for the women in María Anna's *beaterio*. He took those whom he considered to have a stronger vocation than that of a *beata* and placed them in one house. These women professed to be *Beatas del Tercer Orden de Santo Domingo* and consecrated themselves to God in the *beaterio, Virgen Limana Santa Rosa de Santa Maria*.[50] After seventy years, Fr. Andía knew he could not continue the work of growing the convent from a *beaterio* and appointed María Anna as his successor.[51] Fr. Juan Ignacio de Uribe, a Jesuit priest, became one of the *procuradores*[52] sent by the Mexican province to the courts of Madrid and Rome. On one of his trips to Veracruz, he stopped in Puebla to visit María Anna.[53] María Anna, who had been working—to no avail—for a number of years at this point to convert the *beaterio* to a convent, had petitioned multiple bishops to grant this conversion. In a moment of desperation during Fr. Uribe's visit, "*le propuso la pretension, le rogó se hiciesse cargo de ella, y que la tomasse con empeño.*"[54] Fr. Uribe could not excuse himself from

---

49. Bellido, *Vida*, 48.

50. Bellido, *Vida*, 93.

51. Bellido, *Vida*, 94.

52. In English (my translation), this means an "ecclesial representative."

53. Bellido, *Vida*, 94.

54. Bellido, *Vida*, 94. In English, (my translation), this reads, "She affectionately proposed to him; she begged him to put himself in charge of her cause and to try to achieve this goal."

this request and promised María Anna that he would see this wish to its completion.[55]

> ... *aviendo llegado à Madrid* [Fr. Uribe at 26 years of age], *puso por obra algunas diligencias, que le parecieron necessarias, y suficientes para obtener un feliz despacho en Roma. En esta Curia se valio nada menos, que del Poderoso brazo del Eminentissimo Señor Cardenal Alvaro Cienfuegos, Jesuita de tan Superior herarquia por sus letras; Religiosidad, bizarrias, y valimiento, por ser Ministro del Imperio, que para no dar el lleno que merece à sus elogios, mas vale passarlos en silencio. Tomò el encargo aquel Eminentissimo, con el ardoroso empeño, que expressa su Apellido, y que mostrò bien en quantos negocios se pusieron à su cuidado.*[56]

> *Interessose de modo en este, que se apersonò como Ponente, ò Postulador de esta causa. Presentò à su Santidad un Memorial, en que le proponia su pedimento, apoyado de razones, y urgentes poderosos motivos, Luego que el Papa lo leyò, lo remitiò à la Congregacion de Obispos, y Regulares; para que lo examinanssen, y diessen su parecer. Lo hicieron con tanta exaccion, y rectitude, que juzgaron no se debia conceder, lo que se pedia. Con esta repulse se acalorò mas en el assumpto el Cardenal Ponente. Hizo segunda instancio con Nuevo refuerzo de razones, consentimiento expresso del Rey de España D. Phelipe V. positivos derechos, y muy justificados motivos. Registrados esto nuevamente por la Congregacion, mudò de parcer, y lo diò, para que se concediesse la gracia, que se pedia, si benignamente se inclinasse la Suprema Cabeza de la Iglesia.*[57]

---

55. Bellido, *Vida*, 94.

56. Bellido, *Vida*, 95. In English (my translation), this reads, "... having arrived in Madrid [Fr. Uribe at 26 years of age] began to work diligently on that which seemed necessary and sufficient to a successful trip in Rome. In this curia was none other than the powerful arm of the most eminent Cardinal Alvaro Cienfuegos, a Jesuit of such a superior hierarchy because of his letters, religiosity, gallantries, and valor for being a minister of the empire that, for as not to give the fullness of all of the praises he deserves, it is better to remain silent. He took charge of the most eminent with an arduous persistence, which his last name expressed, and which worked well in all of the businesses which were put in his care."

57. Bellido, *Vida*, 95. In English (my translation), this reads, "He interested himself in the following way: he made himself the personal reporter and postulator of this cause (to convert the beaterio to a convent). He presented to his Sanctity a memorandum in which he gave his proposal, filled with reasons and urgent powerful motives; then the Pope read it, submitted it to the Congregation of Bishops and Ordinaries for their examination and decision on the matter. The report had been written with such

On May 22, 1739, Pope Clement XII issued a papal bull in which he supported the conversion of the Beaterio de Santa Rosa into the convent of Religiosas Recoletas de Santo Domingo, furthermore stating that the *beatas* who were considered the foundresses were to take solemn vows with those who enter after this date, taking solemn vows one year after entering the novitiate.[58] As soon as Fr. Uribe learned of this, he returned from Madrid to Puebla to deliver the news in person to María Anna.[59] Consequently, on July 12, 1740, all of the *beatas* reconsecrated themselves to God by taking solemn vows.[60]

Beyond playing the pivotal role in converting her *beaterio* to a *convento*, María Anna made a notable contribution to the convent's constitution, possibly because of her own treatment when a novice. She included a clause abolishing the need for women wishing to enter the Convent of Santa Rosa to provide a dowry. *Constituciones* reads that women will be

> recibidas sin dote; pero se advierte, que si lo tuvieren pueden dexarlo voluntariamente al Convento, ê instituírlo por heredero; pues aunque se admitan en lugar, y por esso sin dote, no ha de ser este motivo para que se les prive hazer bien al Monasterio, concurriendo â obra tan piadosa, como es fomentar sus Rentas, conque se evitarà el inconveniente, de que la que tuviere dote se retaìga de pretender, juzgando que es obice para ser admitida. Pero si alguna traxere algo al Convento, nunca diga lo que traxo, ô traxeron otras, porque no resulte de esto algun desambimiento en la Communidad.[61]

precision and rectitude that they decided against conceding what was asked. With this rejection, the reporting Cardinal became extremely angered. He made a second attempt with a new list of rationale. Consciously, he expressed to the King of Spain D. Philip V's positive rights and justified motives. He registered this new document with the Congregation so they may concede their grace which was blessedly asked if the Supreme Head of the Church was so inclined."

58. Bellido, *Vida*, 96.
59. Bellido, *Vida*, 96.
60. Bellido, *Vida*, 96.
61. Águeda de San Ignacio, *Regla y Constituciones de las Religiosas*, 72. In English (my translation), this reads, "received without a dowry, but with notice that those who have one can leave it voluntarily to the convent and name the convent as an heir; even for those who admittedly have no dowry, this should not be the motive not to allow them to enter the monastery, concurrent with such a pious labor, even if this provokes an inconvenience in the rents of those who do enter with a dowry; it is required that they pretend otherwise and not judge [the dowry] as an obstacle of admittance. But if one leaves something to the convent, she shall never say that she brought it or who brought what so that this does not produce a negative environment in the community."

Beyond this particular example, María Anna made significant contributions both within and beyond her convent. It is difficult to trace the number of María Anna's published works. We know of at least thirteen different works for which original copies still exist today, but many pieces were the same works published under different names, and some short pieces were published in pamphlet form. A few of these pamphlets exist today, at least one of which is a small, bound prayer book that appears to be from the mid-nineteenth century.[62]

## Life in the Eighteenth-Century Mexican Church

María Anna is considered a mystic because of her spiritual writings. Her spiritual devotions and theological writings disclose a strong baroque imagination. At a personal level, Ignacio de Loyola's *Spiritual Exercises* strongly influenced María Anna's initial desire to enter the *beaterio*, as well as her ongoing spiritual direction as her confessors were mainly Jesuits. As Ibsen states, "Loyola's exercises, and those that followed his model of mental prayer, transform meditation into an imaginative act, a powerfully visual force, and this fit perfectly into the baroque notion of art as a means to provoke emotional and spiritual reaction."[63]

Influenced by the 1562 Council of Trent's edict regarding the use of "visible signs" and by Spanish cultural influence,

> Baroque spirituality, with its emphasis on the individual experience of God, converted the act of devotion into a work of art. No longer limited to the repetition of ritual formulae, a renewed notion of will and of an active calling to love God formed the nucleus of spiritual treatises throughout the Spanish world. . . . The visual imagery for these mental pilgrimages was reinforced by the pictorial cycles in the churches and by privately commissioned panel paintings. Religious themes predominated, and paintings adorned churches, convents, and private homes.[64]

Yet, Iberian baroque notions of sign, symbol, and mystery were not easily transplanted or readily accepted in New Spain. The church setting of María Anna's life was strongly integrated into many realms of Mexican society and daily life. The process of colonization created a complex

62. Águeda de San Ignacio, *Devoción a la Santísima Vírgen María*.

63. Ibsen, *Women's Spiritual Autobiography in Colonial Spanish America*, 101.

64. Ibsen, *Women's Spiritual Autobiography in Colonial Spanish America*, 102.

milieu in which to understand the Mexican Catholic Church of the sixteenth through eighteenth centuries.

The perspective I have laid out of María Anna's context provides
the foundation for the analysis of her work. Yet, significant questions remain as to the complexity of María Anna's identity. She was not a wealthy
*criolla*, and Bellido overcompensates for her questionable social status
by devoting considerable discussion to her family's commitment to God
and Mary and to the parents' teaching their children the doctrines of
the church. Coupled with her biographer's arduous efforts to ensure her
parents' purity of blood, the fact that she was the child of two parents
who were born in Mexico leads me to believe that she was not necessarily of the normally accepted socioeconomic-racial background of such a
strong theological writer and religious leader.

The use of religious signifiers, particularly of Mary and Marian images, by eighteenth-century religious women of New Spain comes from a
complex history in which one group (in this case, the Spanish) colonized
other groups (in this case, indigenous peoples) in the sixteenth century.
At this point, a pre-Reformation Catholic Church was planted in North
and South America in the regions which today I call América Latina.
Therefore, the labels/names acquired/given/evangelized/theologized are
those of the dominant group, the Spanish, yet the religious practices become religious syncretism and a complex mix of the various cultures.
In this case, María Anna Águeda de San Ignacio's daily lived experience
comes from a Catholic Church which grew out of these perspectives,
which means she more than likely came from mixed backgrounds, and
the lower-middle to lower class, whose popular devotions were typically
a mix of practices from the Spanish Catholic Church of the sixteenth
century and various indigenous beliefs and practices.

## María Anna Águeda de San Ignacio and Authority

María Anna's writings reveal complexities[65] of authority through various
contexts, specifically through the following: (1) official authority as first
prioress of her convent; (2) engagement with and at times resistance to
socio/cultural/religious/political factors; (3) embodied power through
the authority of her mystical experiences; (4) and authority within a

65. For a detailed postcolonial description of scripting complexities of history, see
Said, *Culture and Emperialism*.

Catholic tradition. For a definition of authority, I primarily draw upon David Stagaman's work. The work of Jennifer Eich strongly informs my approach to resistance to the socio/cultural/religious/political factors, while Kristina Eva Routt's analysis of Sor María Anna's writings provides a basis for the embodied authority of a mystic. Finally, an analysis of María Anna's writings on the image of breast milk develops a Catholic tradition of this image.

## An Understanding of/Approach to Authority

A complex approach to authority, like Stagaman's, sheds light on how we view, interpret, and understand both María Anna's writings and those writings about her life. As Stagaman states, "Authority resides in human practices that relate persons to persons or persons and things. These practices give one party in the relationship the initiative and place upon another party an obligation to heed that initiative."[66] Authority is central to how we live in community and society,[67] as well as to what extent humans flourish in life. As a complex concept, authority's meaning consists of at least three dimensions.

First, as Stagaman states, "the meaning of authority is best situated in that process of social construction and the human interaction which constitutes it."[68] So, this processual reality reveals authority as something fluid and nebulous, with different roles, diverse contexts, and plural settings not only shaping and forming authority but also corresponding changes within and among these social constructs. Authority is found in human "social realities and historical creations as well."[69] Second, authority may lead persons to live in communities of friendship where persons not only live free of coercion but also flourish in life.[70] Third, authority presents a bond between and among members of communities. It "gives a particular identity to a community in a manner analogous to the identity an individual gains through free choices."[71]

---

66. Stagaman, *Authority in the Church*, xiv.

67. Stagaman, *Authority in the Church*, 35.

68. Stagaman, *Authority in the Church*, 25.

69. Stagaman, *Authority in the Church*, 37.

70. Stagaman, *Authority in the Church*, 36.

71. Stagaman, *Authority in the Church*, xiv.

From this perspective on authority, human sinfulness presents many challenges for the full flourishing of life.[72] Because human sinfulness limits the full flourishing of life, authority must be constantly negotiated by members of a community. At some levels, authority may never be questioned. For example, in a family, the authority to pay the electric bill may be designated to one member of the family and never questioned again. Yet, children not having clean clothes to wear to school will lead to the questioning and renegotiating of the authority of who is and is not responsible for the laundry. Free will, friendship, and flourishing of life are key factors that should both guide and be positive societal outcomes of authority. Because human sinfulness, like authority, exists as a social creation,[73] it can limit the possibilities of friendship, free will, and full flourishing of life. Furthermore, because authority and sin are social creations, the guidelines for judgment come from communities. While some forms of sin are universal—for example, murder—interpretations of such sins must be placed in the context of a community.

## Perspectives on Authority in María Anna's Writings

María Anna worked far outside the limits of her office and role as a woman to ensure that the *beaterio* became a convent. She developed alliances and relationships with both women and men to secure her goal. Authority in this context functioned as both a human practice and a competence. According to Stagaman, "Human practices are interactions that link individuals together and establish the relationship that constitutes human sociability. . . . Not only are human practices not isolating actions, but they are social realities and historical creations as well."[74] María Anna's preestablished relationship with Fr. Juan Ignacio de Uribe, a relationship of human practice, made possible the competence[75] of authority fulfilled between María Anna and Fr. Uribe when she begged him for assistance in converting the *beaterio*, after he had become one of the *procuradores*.

72. Stagaman, *Authority in the Church*, 38.

73. For a further discussion of sinfulness as a complex topic, see chapter 4 of De Anda, "Images of God, *Imago Dei*, and God's Relationship with Humanity."

74. Stagaman, *Authority in the Church*, 37.

75. "We consider people competent for one of two reasons: either they are endowed with certain personal qualities that are held in high esteem, or they have received their ability to act through a particular delegation or a pattern of doing so in the society" (Stagaman, *Authority in the Church*, 38).

Fr. Uribe promised María Anna that he would ensure the conversion of the *beaterio* to a convent, and through this promise, María Anna's goal was fulfilled. Because of this promise, Pope Clement XII converted the Beaterio de Santa Rosa to a Convento de Religiosas Recoletas de Santo Domingo.

While a large corpus of María Anna's work is extant, she was not the only woman who wrote during this time and in this context. I do not wish to create a declension narrative[76] that this woman was the only one of the few in her situation who wrote at the time. She may be one of the few whose writings exist with us today, but most foundresses and first prioresses were asked to write for their convent communities. Lavrin provides the following description, which proves accurate for María Anna's historical and theological place as compared to religious men and women of this her time:

> Ironically, their own immobility and sheltered condition as cloistered women were to create a different culture of female archetypes in the colonial setting. They introduced devotional practices specifically promoted to cater to female affectivity, with Christ and Mary at their center.[77]

I further claim that María Anna was one among a number of women who wrote in New Spain. Routt situates María Anna's "work in the context of the plethora of religious literature that appeared in her time as well as an exploration of her unique place in the particularly female tradition of using the body to access the divine."[78]

Furthermore, women religious were not banned from writing, but women's writings were expected to shy away from prideful philosophical proofs. For example, Sor Philotea's letter to Sor Juana, only one generation earlier than Sor María Anna, insists women are to read more spiritual texts and focus upon heavenly endeavors rather than write.[79] While reprimanding Sor Juana for engaging in theological discourse with Antonio de Vieira's homily, Sor Philotea tells Sor Juana,

---

76. A declension narrative creates a story of over-encompassing characteristics of one person or a particular group of people which is then given/used to label a larger group of people and/or cultural phenomena.

77. Lavrin, *Brides of Christ*, 351.

78. Routt, "Authoring Orthodoxy," 181.

79. Kirk Rappaport, *Sor Juana Inés de la Cruz*, 249–53.

You have spent no little time on these curious studies (philosophy and poetry). Move on, like the great Boethius, to take advantage of them, combining the subtleties of natural science with the usefulness of moral philosophy. . . . It is a pity that your great mind should become confused by the despicable things of the earth and not desire to penetrate the things of heaven.[80]

In the particular instance of Sor Philotea and Sor Juana, the practice of writing for one's community is used as a way to silence Sor Juana by Sor Philotea, a pen name believed to be used by the local ordinary, Manuel Fernández de Santa Cruz, bishop of Puebla, Mexico. However, through this act of silencing, we learn that writing for one's convent community was an accepted act by most first prioresses and many of the educated nuns of a community.

## Conclusion

This overview of Sor María Anna Águeda de San Ignacio points to some significant directions of her as a female ecclesial leader. First, unlike Sor Juana, Sor María Anna was able to maintain a relationship with her bishop. This difference in relationship shows the difference in fate for women during this time. Second, the rhetoric integrated in her writings allowed her to maintain a position as a spiritual leader while not seeming too theological. And this becomes fascinating because she presents concepts which could seem very questionable theologically, such as the kenotic act of God needing to happen for Jesus to be filled with Mary's human milk. Another theological theme of Mary as first teacher to Jesus may also be raised as theologically questionable by some but can also be found in the writings of other eighteenth-century thinkers such as William Joseph Chaminade, one of the founders of the Marianist Family. Third, and maybe most importantly, Sor María Anna was one of various women religious from this time period in the Americas who left behind spiritual writings, such as entire rosaries—all fifteen decades—and books of prayers. These women were making strong contributions in their times to their religious communities and some far beyond their communities as well. Furthermore, because we have these writings today, they inform both our scholarship and ministry. In her writings, I am finding answers to some of our own theological questions in the twenty-first century.

80. Kirk Rappaport, "Letter of 'Sor Philotea,'" 252.

These writings allow for some braiding of cultures, which systems of domination have otherwise tried to strip away from many of us, especially those of us who are Latinas.

## Bibliography

Águeda de San Ignacio, María Anna. *Devoción a la Santísima Vírgen María en Honra de su Purisíma Leche.* Guadalajara, Mexico: Impressa por Manuel Brambila, 1840.

———. *Marabillas del Divino Amor, Selladas con el Sello de la Verdad.* Puebla, Mexico: Imprenta de la Bibliotheca Mexicana, 1758.

———. *Regla y Constituciones de las Religiosas de la Gloriosa Virgin Sta. Rosa [de] Maria de Lima, Nuevamente Fundada en la Ciudad de la Puebla de los Angeles, en Virtud de la Bula Expedida por N. S. P. Clemente XII. De Feliz Memoria, en Roma en Sta. María la Mayor, â las que Entran, y Professan, Fin el Modo de Dàr el Habito, y Profession, â las que Entran, y Professan Conforme â la Observancia de sus Estatutos.* Mexico City: Imprenta Real del Superior Gobierno, y del Nuevo Rezado, de Doña Maria de Rivera, 1746.

Archivo General de Indias. "Expediente sobre beaterio de Santa Rosa de Puebla." http://pares.mcu.es/ParesBusquedas20/catalogo/description/370410.

Bellido, José. *Vida de la V. M. R. M. María Anna Agueda de S. Ignacio Primera Priora del Religiosissimo Convento de Dominicas Recoletas de Santa Rosa de la Puebla de los Angeles.* Mexico City: La Imprenta de la Bibliotheca Mexicana, 1758.

Cruz, Jeremy, et al. "Respondiendo a las Demandas Históricas: Analysis of the Transformative Legacy of Samuel Ruiz García of Chiapas, México." *Journal of Hispanic/Latino Theology* 19:1 (November 2013) 2–8.

De Anda, Neomi. "Images of God, *Imago Dei,* and God's Relationship with Humanity through the Image of Mary's Breast Milk: A Focus upon Sor María Anna Águeda de San Ignacio (1695–1756)." PhD diss., Loyola University Chicago, 2011.

Espín, Orlando. *The Faith of the People: Theological Reflections on Popular Catholicism.* Maryknoll, NY: Orbis, 1997.

Eich, Jennifer. *The Other Mexican Muse: Sor María Anna Águeda de San Ignacio (1695–1756).* New Orleans: University Press of the South, 2004.

Gonzalez, Michelle. *Sor Juana: Beauty and Justice in the Americas.* Maryknoll, NY: Orbis, 2003.

Ibsen, Kristine. *Women's Spiritual Autobiography in Colonial Spanish America.* Miami: University of Florida Press, 1999.

Kirk Rappaport, Pamela. "Letter of 'Sor Philotea.'" In *The Classics of Western Spirituality: Sor Juana Inés de la Cruz,* edited and translated by Pamela Kirk Rappaport, 249–52. New York: Paulist, 2005.

———. *Sor Juana Inés de la Cruz: Selected Writings.* New York: Paulist, 2005.

Lavrin, Asunción. *Brides of Christ.* Stanford, CA: Stanford University Press, 2008.

Macy, Gary. "The Iberian Heritage of US Latino/a Theology." In *Futuring Our Past,* edited by Orlando Espín and Gary Macy, 43–82. Maryknoll, NY: Orbis, 2006.

Muriel, Josefina. *Cultura Feminina Novohispana.* Mexico City: Universidad Nacional Autónoma de Mexico, 1982.

Routt, Kristina Eva. "Authoring Orthodoxy: The Body and the *Camino de Perfección* in Spanish American Colonial Convent Writings." PhD diss., Indiana University, 1998.

Said, Edward. *Culture and Emperialism.* New York: Vintage, 1994.

Stagaman, David J. *Authority in the Church.* Collegeville, MN: Liturgical, 1999.

# 4

## The Marian Devotion
## Led by Latin American Women

María del Pilar Silveira

THE LATIN AMERICAN CATHOLIC Church has the face of a woman because most of its members are women.[1] Women have been the communicators of the faith through various evangelizing expressions; unfortunately, their leadership is often invisible because their collaboration in the transmission of faith has been done through simple acts in the everyday. This essay focuses on the Marian devotion in Latin America as an example of this kind of invisible leadership. In approaching women (and this may apply to other "invisible" people of faith) to gather their testimony at diverse religious events, one can discover the presence of God. This essay offers an insight into this kind of women's leadership through a research survey, which I conducted between 2008–09, about Marian devotion in Venezuela. The survey delves into women's experiences—expressed in their own words—as they participated in festivities at three shrines: La Virgen de Coromoto, La Divina Pastora, and Nuestra Señora del Rosario de Chiquinquirá.[2] The survey included 279 participants, and their responses detail the popular Marian faith lived by women with the aim of elaborating a "border" theology. As Pope Francis tells theologians,

1. CELAM, *Documento de Aparecida*.

2. The survey information provided in this essay comes from my 2013 book. See Silveira, *Mariología Popular Latinoamericana*.

"Do not settle for a desktop theology. Your place for reflection is the frontier. Do not fall into the temptation to embellish, to add fragrance, to adjust them to some degree and domesticate them. Even good theologians, like good shepherds, have the odor of the people and of the street and, by their reflection, pour oil and wine onto the wounds of mankind."[3] My hope is that, through the women's voices I share here, the readers will sense and connect with the smell of the people and of the streets that is embedded in their words such that their own faith and love for the "other" as a brother or sister will grow.

In addition to the introduction and conclusion, this essay includes four sections. The first speaks about the expressions of popular faith; the second focuses on the leadership role of women and mothers as evangelizers; the third focuses on healing and miracles in the Marian devotion; and the last section considers hopes and challenges regarding popular Marian devotion in the future.

## Expressions of Popular Faith

Different devotions were brought to Latin America by European missionaries from diverse congregations: Dominicans, Franciscans, and Jesuits, among others. These missionaries founded towns and, in the central plazas, built a chapel with an image of either the Virgin, Jesus, or a saint; the saints, such as San Isidro Labrador or San Pancracio, were generally associated with agricultural tasks. The Dominican missionaries played a very important role in catechization through the recitation of the rosary, and this may explain the centrality of the Marian devotion in the early centuries of the conquest. Juan Carlos Villa-Larroudet explains how Pope Pius V's bulla, *Consueverunt Romani Pontifices* (December 17, 1569), officially established the devotion to the holy rosary, and he attributes the institution of the holy rosary to Saint Dominic of Osma, founder of the Dominican Order.[4] Furthermore, Pope John Paul II, in October of 1992, affirmed that

> The arrival of the Gospel of Christ in the Americas bears the seal of the Virgin Mary. Her name and her image stood out in Christopher Columbus' caravel, the "Santa Maria," which five centuries ago landed in the New World. She was the "Star of the

3. Francis, "Letter of His Holiness Pope Francis," para. 3.
4. See Villa-Larroudet, "Prehistoria del Rosario," 216–18.

Sea" in the risky and providential crossing of the ocean, which opened unsuspected horizons for humanity.[5]

While the hierarchy of the church, constituted mostly of celibate men, has always been one that "officially" proposed diverse ways of expressing the faith through different devotions, women have also played an important role from the very beginning. They have contributed significantly to the growth and diffusion of the faith and devotions. Why is this the case? In a later section I describe the various reasons for this that women generously offered in their survey answers.

Faith is based on and generally shaped by the tradition handed down to a person; as affirmed by John the Evangelist, "[w]hat we have seen and heard, we proclaim also to you" (John 1:1–4). Home, on the other hand, is also a privileged space for the transmission of values and faith through word and symbols, from the ancestors to the present time. Thus, the love for the Virgin Mary and its various expressions have been also transmitted through the environment of the family, generating a powerful and silent evangelization. Referring to this kind of evangelization in 2013 on the Day of Confraternities and of Popular Piety, Pope Francis says,

> When you visit shrines, when you bring your family, your children, you are engaged in a real work of evangelization. This needs to continue. May you also be true evangelizers! May your initiatives be "bridges," means of bringing others to Christ, so as to journey together with him. And in this spirit may you always be attentive to charity. Each individual Christian and every community is missionary to the extent that they bring to others and live the Gospel, and testify to God's love for all, especially those experiencing difficulties. Be missionaries of God's love and tenderness![6]

Pope Francis mentions an action that generally goes unnoticed because of its simplicity, and that is taking the family and children to visit the shrine. This action contains several elements that are part of the rich treasure of popular religiosity[7] where the Marian devotion occupies a prominent place. It implies a relationship of friendship, of love, of faith

---

5. John Paul II, "Ángelus," 2; translation mine.

6. Francis, "On the Occasion," para. 3.

7. See CELAM, *Documento de Aparecida*.

with the image of the Virgin that rests in the shrine, one that makes visible an invisible reality, symbolizing "the tenderness and closeness of God."[8]

As an expression of popular faith, the Marian devotion at shrines has developed a few relevant characteristics over time. For instance, the image (in this case, of the Virgin Mary) associated with the devotion has a long history of linking the Marian devotion at a particular place to the "miraculous" actions that have taken place at those locations, and then these experiences are passed from generation to generation through verbal or written means. Another characteristic is the act of going to the shrine itself. It brings with it an experience of encounter with the Virgin that develops a history with the devotee; this comes to motivate a person to visit her shrine regularly. The visit itself requires action, movement, going out of a person's own house, in search of someone who is important. Because this visit is so meaningful to the devotees, they must generously offer their time "to be with" the Virgin Mary, and by doing so, they leave behind other activities. Finally, going to the shrine is also an occasion to invite others, to take the loved ones, especially children, who will then become familiarized with the patronal festival, and imitate the expressions of faith that they observe around them. This is, in a sense, an evangelizing experience. A survey participant, in her own words, explains this practice: "We come every year. We have come as long as I can remember. My mom has brought us to the procession, and this year we came to ask her [the Virgin] for the health of my grandfather, who is very sick, my mom's dad. All the family is here."[9]

Other elements of popular faith are expressed through various symbolic manifestations. Using images and gestures in particular ways, people display and share their devotion in public demonstrations. For example, in patronal festivals, the contributions of women can be observed in the way the images are dressed (in local costumes) in preparation for the procession. The confraternities that continue to exist today keep alive the memory of this preparation, done with creativity and care, passing this aspect of the devotion down to the next generation.

Corporal gestures are also significant. Walking, entering the shrine, praying, offering flowers, lighting candles, etc., are ways to give testimony of favors the Virgin has granted in a person's life. The Aparecida

8. See CELAM, *Documento de Aparecida,* para. 259; translation mine.

9. Silveira, "Nueva Búsqueda," 136; translation mine.

Document[10] acknowledges the relevance of these gestures. They represent a process that devotees go through, and they contain a vivid spiritual experience because they are, as Pope Francis affirms, "the manifestation of a theological life nourished by the working of the Holy Spirit who has been poured into our hearts (cf. Rom 5:5)."[11] The simplicity of these gestures, as expressions of faith, must not be diminished. In fact, Pope Francis writes that "[e]xpressions of popular piety have much to teach us; for those who are capable of reading them, they are a *locus theologicus* which demands our attention, especially at a time when we are looking to the new evangelization" (*EG*, 126).

Pope Francis also recommends to pastoral agents that, especially when approaching popular religiosity, they imitate the gaze of the Good Shepherd who "seeks not to judge but to love" (*EG*, 125). Indifference  and feelings of superiority towards others can lead to erroneous interpretations of faith expressions, which cause ruptures and wounds among people and weakens the bonds of solidarity. In certain cases, these attitudes cause the faithful to walk away from the Catholic Church to other religious denominations. Interestingly, in spite of this, the love towards the Virgin Mary operates as an "umbilical cord" that continues to unite devotees to the mother church and brings them back, because they are not able to find spaces in other faith traditions to express their faith and love towards the mother of God. The words of one survey participant illustrates this experience: "I show it [love] to her in many ways, telling my children: 'God bless you and my little Virgin be with you'; and the middle names of my two daughters are Chiquinquirá [the name of the location of one of the shrines]."[12] We can say that love and faith for the Virgin Mary, cultivated in the family through popular expressions of faith, work as a sort of remedy to keep devotees within the church and help them to move away from groups that do not sympathize with Marian devotion. Another survey participant expresses her devotion to Mary in this way: "I believe that the love and appreciation we have for the Most Holy Virgin Mary, this day, during which we celebrate this feast, through pilgrimage and love, is the manifestation of us Catholics, towards our Mother."[13]

10. CELAM, *Documento de Aparecida*, 259.

11. Francis, *Evangelii Gaudium*, 125; hereafter cited within the text as *EG*.

12. Silveira, "Nueva Búsqueda," 128; translation mine.

13. Silveira, "Nueva Búsqueda," 124; translation mine.

When is it OTT?

## Mothers and Women as Evangelizers

The survey revealed three particular aspects of the Marian devotion. First, women—especially mothers—identified themselves with the motherhood of Mary who dedicated her life to accompany her son Jesus in his sufferings; these women have taken the responsibility to share these beliefs with their own children. Second, women—especially mothers—found in the Virgin Mary a model of faith and love which they try to imitate in their own daily lives. Finally, women's way of living and expressing their faith reflects something particular about their anthropological capacity. Because these practices have been lived within the everyday family environment, they have not received much attention. However, these faith practices and leadership reflect a way of evangelizing that should no longer be invisible or silent.

Regarding the first aspect that emphasizes the role of the mothers as teachers of the faith, a devotee described her experience in this way:

> Since I was a small child, my mom taught me this love that I now have. I pray everything my mom taught me when I was a small kid, starting with the Lord's prayer, until . . . well . . . she taught me all prayers. I have great faith in everything, first in God, but we as Christians believe in the Virgin because she was the Mother of the Son and also, I (at least me) have a lot of things to be thankful for, because I ask the Virgin for something and in many occasions that thing has been granted. . . . I transmit that faith to everyone: grandchildren and great-grandchildren.[14]

This survey response shows that this evangelizing practice has a multigenerational component. The interviewee appreciates and values the faith received through her mother, and spontaneously imitates her mother in communicating such faith to her children. One can see this same dynamic happening, of course, with sons as well and not only daughters.

The following two survey responses also highlight the importance of the mother's teaching and the multigenerational component:

- "[E]very year I come to welcome the patroness of this place, Barquisimeto—every year. My mom died, and now I come in her place, because she [the mother] came every year."

- "I have had many very beautiful experiences, I owe many favors to Our Lady, our vocation and our faith. My mother taught that to us,

14. Silveira, "Nueva Búsqueda," 119; translation mine.

since very early in life. She brought us here, to the Divina Pastora . . . we waited for her here, in Barquisimeto. When we returned after she [the Virgin] fulfilled the promise, we prayed the rosary. For two years, I didn't come, because of a disease. But this year, I'm here."[15]

These expressions of faith reveal a diverse way of evangelizing through words and actions. For instance, while praying the rosary, the devotees focus not so much on the biblical and theological content of the rosary itself, but rather, praying the rosary is a means to communicate their love and faith for Mary. At the same time, it is also a way to demonstrate their motherly love and care for their families. Similarly, also in connection to the rosary, Pope Francis describes maternal love in this way:

> I think of the steadfast faith of those mothers tending their sick children who, though perhaps barely familiar with the articles of the creed, cling to a rosary; or of all the hope poured into a candle lighted in a humble home with a prayer help from Mary, or in the gaze of tender love directed to Christ crucified. (*EG*, 125)

The second aspect of women's Marian devotion sees in the motherhood of the Virgin Mary a model of faith and love. One particular connection exists in the identification between mothers and the motherhood of Mary, or between women and the womanhood of Mary. The Virgin Mary is a woman and a mother, and this fact facilitates for women the possibility of imitating Mary's examples in their everyday lives. Mary's way, as narrated in the Scriptures, of celebrating life and of responding with faith against injustice, pain, sickness, and death offers a testimony of a life full of faith and love. One of my research survey questions asked about the way of praying to Mary, and one of the respondents emphasized the connection to Mary's motherhood:

> How can I express that? Trying to imitate the way she was with her son, trying to half-imitate her, because it is very difficult, I swear it, because now I have a son and know what it is like. She suffered all those things, from the birth of Jesus until his death, thinking that one day what actually happened would indeed happen. Imagine the moment he was hanging on the cross. I imagine that, with every whip he received, she was being killed, too, and then came to live again. Because it is horrible, isn't it?

15. Silveira, "Nueva Búsqueda," 120; translation mine.

I had an experience in which I felt I could lose my son, and I felt that I was dying; imagine everything that she suffered. I mean, for that reason she has to be given all the devotion in the world; she is a worthy example for humanity—I mean, she is truly incredible.[16]

This description, emphasizing the link to the motherhood of Mary, shows that a very deep bond of union was created between the Virgin and the devotee, especially through the shared experience in a time of difficulty. In this case, this mother's experience of having a very ill child prompted her to pray to Mary and to ask for God's intervention. This same interviewee tells the story about what happened to her son as follows:

My son was born with a small problem, and he had to go through surgery, and it was delicate because it was on the spine, but there he is—look at him—he is grown. I know she protects him; I asked her to do that very often, and I know that she intervened a lot because my son came out of surgery safe and sound. That's why I try to teach him, so that he knows that she exists and that he has to respect her, love her, and revere her.[17]

The cry of a mother for her child's health is something that shakes a person to their core. Jesus himself had compassion for the widow's only son who had died, giving him back to his mother, alive (Luke 7:11–17). When looking at the experiences of healing in the context of the Marian devotion, one finds another aspect, which I will discuss next.

The third aspect of women's Marian devotion is connected to their faith. Women of faith "see" the action of God through Mary in their daily lives and events, and they communicate that by giving testimony of what they have seen and heard. One interviewee speaks about this faith in her daily life:

As a mother, I express this faith to her; I always make petitions to her, you know, when I have many conflicts with my sons, you know: "well, Mother help me, because you are also a mother." . . . And it must be because of the faith that we see that, yes, she manifests herself . . . and in one way or another, she always manifests herself.[18]

16. Silveira, "Nueva Búsqueda," 129; translation mine. See Cuadro (chart) 107.

17. Silveira, "Nueva Búsqueda," 129; translation mine. See Cuadro 107.

18. Silveira, "Nueva Búsqueda," 121; translation mine.

Another devotee speaks about her experience of faith, and how vital it is to attract and invite other people: "First you have to live it internally—I mean, to internally celebrate her, in order to manifest the celebration."[19]

St. Paul helps us understand the dimension of leadership in the dynamics of faith: "Faith is the realization of what is hoped for and evidence of things not seen. Because of it, the ancients were well attested. By faith we understand that the universe was ordered by the word of God, so that what is visible came into being through the invisible" (Heb 11:1–3). In other words, women's leadership and wisdom are evidence of the way they internally embrace (make visible the invisible) their faith throughout their lives. This anthropological capacity to embrace life in this way makes them more sensitive to the action of God (e.g., the Magnificat, Luke 1:46–56), which also illustrates another aspect of motherhood. María Teresa Porcile speaks about a woman's capacity to embrace life in this way: "[her] body is conditioned to receive life and welcome it in her interiority. She collaborates [with this life] during pregnancy, nurturing it through her blood and distinguishing her alterity . . . the body of the woman is an 'open space' that can be habitable, and where she guards, protects, and nurtures"[20] the new life.[21]

## Healing and Miracles in the Marian Devotion

Experiences of healing uncover two dimensions in women's Marian devotion. On the one hand is the mediation of the Virgin Mary in so-called miracles and, on the other hand is the way women emphasize the importance of faith. In Marian devotion, the image of the Virgin Mary serves to mediate in the experiences of healing, especially in cases when a devotee's petition is granted. In popular belief, these healing experiences are called "miracles" (milagros, in Spanish).[22] At the individual level, the women interviewed expressed the change that these miracles caused in their lives. According to them, these miracles contain the presence of the Spirit of God that is capable of giving back health through healing.

19. Silveira, "Nueva Búsqueda," 124; translation mine.

20. Porcile, La Mujer, Espacio de Salvación, 188.

21. This anthropological capacity has been analyzed by several Latin American theologians. See Gebara and Bingemer, María, Mujer Profética, and Azcuy, "Teología ante el Reto del Género," 9–37.

22. Silveira, Mariología Popular Latinoamericana, 315.

Furthermore, when women devotees who were granted a miracle repeat the stories about it, they are sharing their particular faith in the Virgin, and although it may not be their intention they are also inspiring others to become Marian devotees in particular shrines and developing a certain kind of Marian spirituality. One could say that in sharing their experiences, the women are participating, at some level, in a process of evangelization.

In the sharing of stories and events, these women are also contributing to the development of a Marian theology, because, through their stories, the devotees assign important theological titles to identify the Virgin—for example, "miraculous," "mother," "protector," "advocate," "saint," etc. The following survey response also emphasizes the importance of the "remembrance" of the events that took place in the devotees' lives:

> I have a lot of faith in the Divina Pastora, in her miracles. I asked her for a lot of things, and I am very devoted to her. . . . I mean . . . because of the miracles she has granted me, I always keep her present, and I come . . . every year, I walk with her after she leaves [the church, in the procession]; I walk behind her or ahead of her. Now, I'm waiting for her.[23]

While in this case the "miracles" are not detailed, the woman takes for granted that the Virgin Mary will listen to and grant her petitions. It is common to encounter these expressions of faith, because women see in their devotion a sort of friendship with Mary. According to Cardinal Bergoglio:

> The miraculous action of Mary is the main sign of individualized protection of a place and from a place. The supplication and request for favors are a manifestation of the maternal-filial alliance, of interpersonal relationships, of mutual commitment. Although they are people of little sacramental practice, they react to illness or suffering by making a promise. It may consist of walking to the shrine, making the way in silence, walking around the shrine on their knees, with their arms forming a cross, carrying candles or donations, but most of the promises remain anonymous, and their motivation remains private to the person or the family.[24]

23. Silveira, *Mariología Popular Latinoamericana*, 169; translation mine. See the "milagros" category in Cuadro 141 of the Encuesta Divina Pastora.

24. Bergoglio, "Religiosidad Popular," 5th paragraph from the end; translation

To illustrate this description of popular religiosity, I have chosen the following story about the experience of a mother in a critical situation that marked her life:

> I am fulfilling a vow because of my daughter, Maria Auxiliadora, I entrusted her to the Virgin; that is why she is named Maria Auxiliadora—we baptized her here in the Divina Pastora. The Virgin did a miracle—it was a very beautiful experience; they were twins. The other, a boy, died in the womb, and she [the baby girl] had to be taken out, six and a half months into my pregnancy. When I received the news that the boy was dead, I entrusted her [the baby girl] to the Virgin Maria Auxiliadora, because she was where I was hospitalized [I felt her presence with me at the hospital]. There she was, that Virgin, that got my attention, and she got my attention, because I am very devoted to the Virgin but didn't know Maria Auxiliadora. At the time she [my daughter] was born, her weight was one kilogram and five hundred grams [about 3.3 pounds]. She also suffered respiratory arrest, but she overcame all of that.[25]

Every year when the mother comes to the feast of the Divina Pastora, celebrated in her city, she is grateful that Maria Auxiliadora is the only Virgin who interceded to God for her daughter, and in remembrance, she tells her story about the event that took place.

## Hopes and Challenges of Popular Marian Devotion

Marian devotion provides signs of hope for the future of the church and for evangelization, and women's leadership roles are definitely essential to the growth of each. As illustrated by the survey responses provided in this chapter, Marian devotion was born spontaneously from the faith and filial love of the people of God. According to Pope Paul VI, "[t]he Blessed Virgin's role as Mother leads the People of God to turn with filial confidence to her who is ever ready to listen with a mother's affection and efficacious assistance."[26]

In shaping the devotee's capability to trust, mothers (or grandmothers) play an important role, because they are essential agents in the transmission of faith in everyday life. Within a population that respects

mine.

25. Silveira, "Nueva Búsqueda," 143; translation mine.
26. Paul VI, *Marialis Cultus*, 57.

the figures of mothers and grandmothers, women's leadership is characterized by their influence through examples, and not by imposition or authority. This practice reflects a kind of leadership method that involves the repetition of Christian prayers and imitation of popular/traditional gestures; this leadership has been successful in creating a dynamic and vibrant popular religiosity. Through these practices, people identify themselves with a particular Marian devotion; Cardinal Bergoglio describes this phenomenon as follows:

> Marian devotion, strongly rooted in the faith of our people, constitutes one of the main signs of identity, as did the alliance with Yahweh for Israel. . . . People identify with the image of Mary because their parents came to her, and they come today to her with their problems. Admiring the personal virtues of Mary, popular piety uses her attributes to reach God.[27]

Yet, the strengths of women's leadership in Marian devotion raise a couple of key questions: Does this leadership really transform the lives of Latin American women? Does it liberate them from (patriarchal) cultural patterns?

Based on the research responses that I have included in this chapter, I would like to address these questions by elaborating on two particular challenges. The first is machismo and its various related situations of violence that continue to affect women's lives. The second challenge is that of the individualistic devotional practices that create other difficulties in the current transfer of faith within the family and society.

Regarding the first challenge, in *Evangelii Gaudium*, Pope Francis refers (especially in paragraphs 69 and 70) to some of the issues mentioned above when speaking about relationship models found in popular culture that dehumanize people:

> In the case of the popular cultures of Catholic peoples, we can see deficiencies which need to be healed by the Gospel: machismo, alcoholism, domestic violence, low Mass attendance, fatalistic or superstitious notions which lead to sorcery, and the like. Popular piety itself can be the starting point for healing and liberation from these deficiencies. (*EG*, 69)

Very often, the victims of these dehumanizing deficiencies are women. At the same time, Pope Francis indicates that it is necessary to

---

27. Bergoglio, "Religiosidad Popular," 6th paragraph from the end; translation mine.

continue evangelizing through the spiritual force of Marian faith, using it as a starting point to heal wounds and to liberate people from these situations of oppression. Furthermore, it is important to understand that for the devotees to succeed in evangelizing they must have consciences formed such that their relationships respect the dignity of every human being, including women.

Regarding the second challenge of individualistic devotional practices, we must pay attention to the fact that devotional practices by nature require of the devotee an individual and emotive experience of faith that should lead the person to serve others; an authentic popular piety is other-centered. However, when the devotional practice is more self-centered and revolves around personal interests, or economic benefits, or power over others, then this "piety" is enslaving the person rather than liberating him or her. Related to these challenges of individualism, we must also take into account the rupture in the generational transmission of the Christian faith that is happening in the Catholic Church. With so many parents abandoning sacramental practices and the habit of prayer, the faith often is simply not being transmitted via the family. Moreover, we are living in a world influenced by the media, which distracts and confuses people. Messages are socialized with elements of relativistic subjectivism, inciting the unbridled consumerism that primarily strengthens the market economy. These and other situations are threatening the spontaneous transmission of popular faith, which in spite of all these challenges continues on its way. It is necessary to read its signs to accompany the silent presence of the Spirit that beats in the hearts of the faithful, especially in the hearts of women who have exhibited such strong leadership in Marian devotion.

## Conclusion

This brief review of women's leadership in Marian devotion in Venezuela focused on expressions that contain the faith lived by devotees. Approaching people's living faith with open minds and hearts—and in solidarity with their challenging realities—allows for the possibility of sensing the "smell of the sheep" (*EG*, 24) that Pope Francis speaks about often. It is with the humble attitude of the shepherd who listens, observes, imagines, and sees alongside and with the people that one should approach women's experiences with the Virgin. These experiences increase the faith of both the person who recounts and the one who listens to the presence of the living God. Human life is dynamic, always changing, like water in a rushing river. Thus, the attitude of the Good Shepherd is necessary, especially when approaching popular religiosity, in order to see the signs of the times. In people's faith experiences, there will continue to be situations to be thankful for, to praise God for, and to ask for God's help. And in the human heart, there will be always a space for friendship with the divine. Moreover, it seems that women will continue to play an important role in Marian devotion as illustrated in this chapter's description of their current leadership in Venezuela.

The stories collected here show the richness of the popular Marian faith; however, women's leadership remains anonymous in these practices. It is necessary to approach these realities seeking appropriate and authentic interpretations with adequate tools. For example, the research survey I conducted in 2008–09, and on which this chapter is based, allowed me to gather the experiences and voices of the women devotees themselves. The institutional church must value and provide resources to interpret and come to understand these Marian faith experiences so that this treasure will no longer remain hidden.

I end this chapter with a prayer written by a woman devotee at the shrine of the Divina Pastora:

> Blessed Virgin. I have looked for you,
>
> and I always find you.
>
> I pray to you, I cry out to you.
>
> With faith and tears, I come to you with prayers from my sinful heart. I have followed you throughout my life.
>
> Thank you Mother, for loving me so much; thank you for being with me always. In my old age, I appreciate what I have, my home, and my family. Your mantle protects me and guides me. Hail Mary, Mother of God.

## Bibliography

Azcuy, Virginia. "Teología ante el Reto del Género: La Cuestión y el Debate Antropológico." *Proyecto* 45 (2004) 9–37.

Bergoglio, Jorge Mario. "Religiosidad Popular como Inculturación de la Fe en el Espíritu de Aparecida." Homily given in Buenos Aires, January 19, 2008. http://www.arzbaires.org.ar/inicio/homilias/homilias2008.htm#cultura_y_Religiosidad_popular__.

Conferencia General del Episcopado Latinoamericano (CELAM). *Documento de Aparecida, 13–31 de Mayo de 2007*. Bogotá: San Pablo, 2007. https:// asambleaeclesial.lat/wp-content/uploads/2021/01/documento-de-aparecida.pdf.

Francis, Pope. *Evangelii Gaudium. Vatican.va*, November 24, 2013. http://www.vatican .va/content/francesco/en/apost_exhortations/documents/papa-francesco _esortazione-ap_20131124_evangelii-gaudium.html.

———. "Letter of His Holiness Pope Francis to the Grand Chancellor of the 'Pontificia Universidad Católica Argentina' for the 100th Anniversary of the Founding of the Faculty of Theology." *Vatican.va*, March 3, 2015. https://www.vatican.va/content/ francesco/en/letters/2015/documents/papa-francesco_20150303_lettera-universita-cattolica-argentina.html.

———. "On the Occasion of the Day of Confraternities and of Popular Piety." *Vatican. va*, May 5, 2013. http://w2.vatican.va/content/francesco/en/homilies/2013/ documents/papa-francesco_20130505_omelia-confraternite.html.

Gebara, Ivone, and Maria Clara Bingemer. *María, Mujer Profética: Ensayo Teológico a Partir de la Mujer y de América Latina*. Madrid: Paulinas, 1988.

John Paul II, Pope. "Ángelus: Viaje Apostólico a la República Dominicana." *Vatican.va*, October 11, 1992. http://www.vatican.va/content/john-paul-ii/es/angelus/1992/ documents/hf_jp-ii_ang_19921011.html.

Paul VI, Pope. *Marialis Cultus. Vatican.va*, February 2, 1974. http://www.vatican.va/ content/paul-vi/es/apost_exhortations/documents/hf_p-vi_exh_19740202_ marialis-cultus.html.

Porcile, María Teresa. *La Mujer, Espacio de Salvación: Misión de la Mujer en la Iglesia, una Perspectiva Antropológica*. Montevideo: Trilce, 1991.

Silveira, María del Pilar. *Mariología Popular Latinoamericana: Fisonomía de la Mariología Popular Venezolana*. Caracas: Archdiocese of Mérida, 2013.

———. "Nueva Búsqueda de la Mariología Popular Latinoamericana: Aportes de la Fisonomía de la Mariología Popular Venezolana al Conocimiento Teológico." PhD diss., Pontificia Universidad Javeriana, 2011. https://repository. javeriana.edu.co/bitstream/handle/10554/1528/SilveiraMariadelPilar2011. pdf?sequence=1&isAllowed=y.

Villa-Larroudet, Juan Carlos. "Prehistoria del Rosario." *Scripta de Maria* 2:12 (2015) 211–48. https://www.torreciudad.org/wp-content/uploads/2018/10/ scripta_2015_villa_larroudet.pdf.

# 5

## Reading the Scriptures
## with the Mind, Eyes, and Heart of a Woman

BARBARA E. REID, OP

IT IS A GREAT privilege to be among such an august group of women leaders of the global church to reflect together on how women have provided
leadership in the past and how our leadership is sorely needed for the
future. As a biblical scholar, I want to focus on the ways in which women
have led the way in developing feminist critical methods of interpreting
the Scriptures, work that is vitally important for shaping the stories we
tell and by which we live. Reading the Scriptures with the mind, eyes, and
heart of a woman is not only the esoteric work of professional exegetes
(even though that is of utmost importance), but is a life-enhancing endeavor for all the faithful, profoundly rooted in *lo cotidiano*, our everyday
lives.[1]

To enter into our topic, I want to begin with a story of one of the
moments in which my eyes were opened to the importance of being
aware of the lenses one brings to scriptural texts. It happened about
twenty years ago. I was teaching a course on the Gospel of Mark and we
got to the climactic midpoint in chapter 8 where Jesus asks the disciples,
"Who do you say that I am?" (v. 28),[2] to which Peter responds, "You are

1. See Isasi-Díaz, *"Lo Cotidiano,"* 5–17.
2. All scripture quotations are from the New Revised Standard Version (NRSV).

the Messiah" (v. 30). Jesus then says that he will undergo great suffering and be rejected by the elders, the chief priests, and the scribes, and will be killed and then rise again. As Peter struggles with this, Jesus says to the crowd accompanying his disciples, "If any want to become my followers, let them deny themselves and take up their cross and follow me" (v. 34).

I was waxing eloquent on what taking up the cross might mean in a context in which most of us are not likely to face actual crucifixion. A student suddenly raised her hand, and even though I was slightly peeved at the interruption, I called on her. She declared, "I hate this text! It is the single most deadly passage in the whole Bible, and if it were up to me, I would rip it out and never proclaim it again!" I was quite taken aback. I didn't have a clue as to what she was talking about, but I had the good sense to ask her if she could say more about what she found so disturbing in this text. "Gladly," she said.

She proceeded to recount how, in her work in a shelter for women who were abused by their partners, she had seen over and over that the biggest obstacle that kept Christian women from getting the help they needed was the way they interiorized this gospel text. They believed that any abuse or suffering they endured was their way of carrying the cross with Jesus. Worst of all, she said, was that when a woman finally broke her silence about the abuse going on in her home, she would usually confide in her pastor or minister, who, more often than not, would tell her to go home, be subject to her husband (citing Ephesians 5:22), and endure this abuse as her cross. I was aghast. I had never heard such a gross misappropriation of the gospel text, and it set me on a path to investigate the meaning of the cross and where the liberating good news may be found in the New Testament, particularly for women.

Shortly after that I had a sabbatical year, and I began a research project that resulted in my book *Taking Up the Cross: New Testament Interpretations through Latina and Feminist Eyes*. I took advantage of a number of invitations to speak in Mexico, Bolivia, and Peru, and to engage with women in a context very different from my own, trying to learn how they understood the cross. One of the things I did was to ask people everywhere I went, "Why did Jesus die?" Everywhere I got the same simple answer: "To save us from our sins." While this formulation appears a few times in Paul's letters (e.g., 1 Cor 15:3 and Rom 3:25), it is not the only, nor even the primary, explanation for Jesus's death in the New Testament, but it is the explanation accepted by most believers. As Elizabeth Johnson remarked,[3] St. Anselm, who developed atonement theology in the eleventh century, should be considered the most successful theologian of all times—his explanation of the cross stuck!

As I spoke with women in rural Chiapas, I heard how many of them had been indoctrinated with the notion that they were sinful and consequently deserving of all the suffering they experienced. One woman described her understanding of the faith this way:

> Jesus taught us how to sacrifice, how to give our lives for others, how to be humble and not self-centered. We sacrifice especially for our children, for our husbands, for our families. When there is not enough food, we give the best portions to our children and husbands. We sacrifice so our children can go to school, selling whatever we can in the market. We do not follow our own desires, but offer up our lives in service for theirs. . . . I get up at four o'clock every morning to get water and gather wood and start the fire for breakfast. I do all the housework and I work in the fields alongside my husband as well, with my youngest baby strapped to my back. I get no pay for any of my work; we women are completely dependent on what our husbands give us. At the end of the day, I continue to tend the children and fix dinner. Afterward there is more work to prepare for the next day. I don't ever rest or have a day off. Who would carry out my responsibilities? God has made it this way, we have to be humble and sacrifice for others. All the suffering we endure we accept as our way of carrying the cross.[4]

It was hearing stories like these that brought home to me the power of the biblical text. This power can be deadly when it is used to justify the oppression of those who are most disadvantaged, but it can also be a liberative force that sets captives free. It can be used to justify the status quo and maintain inequities and injustices, or it can be the destabilizing word that inspires prophets to speak out and act out with a godly determination to achieve justice. It is never neutral.

---

3. Johnson, "Jesus and Salvation," 5.

4. My translation from personal interviews. Similar observations by women from Chiapas are recorded in CODIMUJ, *Con Mirada, Mente y Corazón de Mujer*.

## Feminism and Feminist Biblical Interpretation

Before I offer an alternative approach to understanding the cross and Jesus' death, I want to explain what I mean by feminism and feminist biblical interpretation. I need to say a few words about what these things are, when they began, how they are done, and why they are important for both women and men.

### Feminism

For some people, the term "feminism" connotes angry, men-hating women. There are many definitions of the term, but as I use it here, feminism is a perspective and a movement that springs from a recognition of inequities facing women; it advocates for changes in structures that prevent full human flourishing. Feminists are both women and men who are committed to the struggle for changes in systems and patterns of relationship that prevent the full flourishing of all creation.

In the US, at least three waves of feminism are commonly recognized. The first, arising in the mid-nineteenth century and lasting into the early twentieth, was sparked by women's efforts to become involved in the public sphere and win the right to vote. The second wave, which peaked in the 1960s and 1970s, focused on civil rights and equality for women. With the third wave, from the 1980s forward, came global feminism and an emphasis on the contextual nature of interpretation. Now a fourth wave may be emerging, with a stronger emphasis on the intersectionality of women's concerns with those of other marginalized groups and the increased use of the internet as a platform for discussion and activism.

Women have benefited from many advances in the last few decades but there are still ongoing concerns about inequities facing women with respect to poverty and wealth, employment and wages, uncompensated labor, and acts of violence, and in the arenas of education, government, business, healthcare, and church ministry. The Bible can be a great asset in addressing these concerns when rightly interpreted.

### Feminist Biblical Interpretation

I want to talk now about feminist biblical interpretation.[5] Women interpreting the Scriptures through the lens of their experience and insight is nothing new. Throughout the ages, women have retold the biblical stories and taught them to their children and others, while interpreting them afresh for their time and circumstances. Written accounts of women's interpretations of the Bible exist from at least the second century AD. One example is Helie, a consecrated virgin who lived in the second century. She was brought before a judge for refusing to marry. When he quoted to her Paul's admonition that "it is better to marry than to be aflame with passion" (1 Cor 7:9), she questioned the notion that the text has only one meaning and responded, "But not for everyone, that is, not for holy virgins."[6] Another is a Jewish woman, Beruriah, who also lived in the second century and who is said to have had "profound knowledge of biblical exegesis and outstanding intelligence." Once when her husband, Rabbi Meir, prayed for the destruction of a sinner, she countered that Psalm 104:35 advocated praying for the destruction of sin, not the sinner.[7]

It was not until medieval times that the first written commentaries on Scripture from a feminist critical point of view emerged with the works of women mystics such as Hildegard of Bingen (1098–1179) and Julian of Norwich (ca. 1342–1416). Hildegard reinterpreted the Genesis narratives in a way that presented women and men as complementary and interdependent, and she frequently wrote about feminine aspects of the divine.[8]

The first person to produce a full-blown feminist commentary on the Bible was Elizabeth Cady Stanton (1815–1902). A leading proponent in the US for women's right to vote, she found that whenever women tried to make inroads into politics, education, or the work world, the Bible was quoted against them. Together with a team of like-minded women, she produced her own commentary on every text of the Bible that concerned

5. Much of the material that follows is taken from my Editor's Introduction (titled "She Is a Breath of the Power of God" (Wis 7:25)), found in each volume of the Wisdom Commentary series published by Liturgical Press. To date, twenty-two of the fifty-eight volumes have been published.

6. Madrid, Escorial MS, a II 9, f. 90 v., as cited in Lerner, *Creation of Feminist Consciousness*, 140.

7. b. Ber. 10a.

8. Hildegard of Bingen, *De Operatione Dei*, I.4.100 PL 197:885bc, cited in Lerner, *Creation of Feminist Consciousness*, 142–43. See also Newman, *Sister of Wisdom*.

women. Her pioneering two-volume project, *The Woman's Bible*, published in 1895 and 1898, urges women to recognize that texts degrading women come from the men who wrote the texts, not from God, and to use their common sense to rethink what has been presented to them as sacred.

Since these early foremothers, there has been a steady stream of works by women whose reflections on the Scriptures question prevailing interpretations. It is only in recent decades, however, that women have had greater access to formal theological education and have taken their place in the world of professional biblical scholars. For centuries, the works of female interpreters of the Bible were largely unknown, both to other women and to their brothers in the synagogue, church, and academy,[9] but now women can build on the work of their foremothers to create global networks in ways not previously possible.

What is feminist biblical interpretation and how does one go about it? First of all, feminist biblical scholars keep uppermost in their minds and use as their starting point a consciousness of women's experiences, both past and present. Feminist biblical scholars follow the three steps of Latin American liberation theology: *ver–juzgar–actuar* (see–judge–act), looking first at reality—women's realities—and foregrounding them as they analyze biblical texts.

In the second step, which involves an analysis of the text, these biblical scholars use all of the critical exegetical tools that have been developed in modern times: historical criticism, literary criticism, rhetorical criticism, and social science criticism, among others, but add questions like: Where were the women? If they aren't mentioned in the text, does  that mean that they were not there? How did women in antiquity receive what was written? For example, when Paul wrote to the Corinthians that "women must keep silent in church" (1 Cor 14:34), how did leaders like deacon Phoebe (Rom 16:1–2) and teachers and heads of house churches like Prisca (Rom 16:3–5) react? Feminist biblical scholars ask whether the single woman apostle identified in the New Testament (Junia in Rom 16:7) might be the tip of the iceberg; that is, whether there were many other such women apostles. They bring to their study questions about who wrote a text, for whom, in what circumstances, and to what purpose. They recognize that for the most part the Bible was written by men, for men, about men, and to serve men's interests. Their intent is not to

*No Kidding*

9. See Lerner, *Creation of Feminist Consciousness*, 138–66.

denigrate men, but simply to call attention to the historical realities lurking behind the construction and interpretation of the text.

Feminist biblical scholars not only try to recover the lost or overlooked history of women in biblical times, but also expose the brutality of the violence against women in "texts of terror" (a phrase coined by Phyllis Trible), such as the story of the rape and dismemberment of the concubine in Judges 19. We do not tear those stories out of the Bible. We tell them to remember and to pledge "that these terrors shall never come to pass again."[10]

Feminist biblical scholars also attend to the importance of sociocultural context. The lenses that a white, well-educated North American woman brings to biblical texts are very different from those of an indigenous woman in rural Chiapas with little experience beyond her male-dominated village. Some feminists have coined terms to highlight the distinctiveness of their own context. Many African American feminists, for example, call themselves "womanists" to draw attention to their experience of oppression resulting from both racism and sexism.[11] Similarly, many Hispanic feminists in the US speak of themselves as *mujeristas* (*mujer* is Spanish for "woman"),[12] while others prefer to be called "Latina feminists."[13] Some feminists prefer to be called ecofeminists, highlighting the fact that the struggle for women's equality and dignity is intimately connected with the struggle for the respect of the earth and the whole of the cosmos.[14]

Finally, feminist biblical interpreters attend carefully to the world in front of the text; that is, how the text is heard and appropriated in contemporary contexts today. They ask: What does the text do to those  who accept it? Does it reinforce domination and oppression? Or does it liberate and lead to the flourishing of life? They often query their work with the question: So what? Feminist biblical interpretation is not a solely intellectual exercise; rather, it provides the impetus for transformative

10. Trible, *Texts of Terror*, 3.

11. Alice Walker coined the term "womanist" in her book, *In Search of Our Mothers' Gardens*. See also Cannon, "Emergence of Black Feminist Consciousness"; Russell, *Feminist Interpretation of the Bible*, 30–40; Junior, *Introduction to Womanist Biblical Interpretation*; Day and Pressler, *Engaging the Bible in a Gendered World*, 37–46.

12. Ada María Isasi Díaz is credited with coining this term in *Mujerista Theology*.

13. For example, see Aquino et al., *Reader in Latina Feminist Theology*, 138–39.

14. See, for example, Gebara, *Longing for Running Water*; see also Ress, *Ecofeminism in Latin America*.

action that changes relationship patterns and dismantles structures that are oppressive of women and other disadvantaged persons. Engaging all the powers of the creative imagination, it dreams of and works toward a world in which there is equality and dignity for all.

## Feminists of All Genders

The work of feminist biblical interpretation is not only by or for women. Men and persons who identify as nonbinary who choose to partner with feminist women in the work of deconstructing systems of domination and building structures of equality are rightly regarded as feminists. Some men and nonbinary persons readily identify with the experiences of women who are discriminated against on the basis of sex/gender, having themselves had comparable experiences; others who may not have faced direct discrimination or stereotyping recognize that inequity and problematic characterizations still occur, and they seek correction.

## Passion and Resurrection:
## From Atoning for Sins to Birthing Hope

Returning to the text of Mark 8:34, "If any want to become my followers, let them deny themselves and take up their cross and follow me," let us continue our discussion of the question of the meaning of "taking up the cross" and of how to understand the death and resurrection of Christ from a feminist perspective. Two important things must be kept in mind. First, in the gospel context, when Jesus speaks to his disciples about taking up the cross, he is talking about a very specific kind of suffering. He is referring to the negative repercussions to which his disciples are willing to expose themselves as a direct consequence of following him. He is not, for example, speaking about the kind of suffering that comes from illness or disease that can befall anyone. There is nothing inherently Christian in bearing that kind of suffering, although Christians certainly derive comfort from relating such suffering to that of Christ. Nor is Jesus talking about accepting suffering that comes from abuse or injustice. He always tried to confront that kind of suffering and do away with it, urging us to do the same.

Understanding "taking up the cross" in this way can have profound consequences. For some of the women I met in Chiapas, it has resulted in a dramatic shift in their lives. Through reflection on the Bible in women's groups, many have come to identify with Mary Magdalene and the other Galilean women disciples. They reason that if these women could find other ways to fulfill their traditional duties while still leaving their homes to preach the gospel, then why not them? The cross, as they understand it now, does not involve submitting to verbal and physical abuse, but instead is the hardship of walking for hours through the rough countryside to reach women's meetings or enduring slander and suspicion when they exercise their newfound ecclesial ministries.

Another element that is extremely important in this discussion is free choice. When Jesus speaks to his disciples about taking up the cross, he is talking to people who have freedom of choice. He is not talking to people who have suffering imposed on them; rather, his disciples have the power to choose whether or not to follow him and to expose themselves to the potential negative consequences of doing so. When women and other abused persons have suffering imposed on them, this is not properly "the cross."

## Johannine Metaphors for Self-Surrender to Love

I want to turn our attention now to the Gospel of John, where we find several metaphors for understanding the cross as something other than sacrifice and atonement. As we explore these, I propose that because of all the pitfalls associated with the language and mentality of sacrifice, we consider the expression used by Elisabeth Moltmann-Wendel of "self-surrender to love." As she explains, in contrast to sacrifice, "self-surrender is an act of one's own free will; it is bound up with responsibility and love, and is interested in the preservation of life."[15] This description of self-surrender emphasizes that an authentic love relationship always includes a costly giving of self, but the emphasis is on the love, not on the cost or the cross to be borne.

### A Friend Who Lays Down His Life for His Friends

An image that concretizes self-surrender to love in the Fourth Gospel is that of a friend who freely lays down his life for his friends out of love (John 15:13). This image builds on what Jesus said earlier, using the

15. Moltmann-Wendel, *Rediscovering Friendship*, 43.

*offering vs taking*

metaphor of a good shepherd, where he asserted that no one takes his life from him; rather, he lays it down of his own accord (John 10:17–18). The theme of a friend who lays down his life for his friends comes to a climactic moment in chapter 11, in which Jesus receives the news that his friend Lazarus is ill. Three times (11:3, 5, 35), Jesus's love for Mary, Martha, and Lazarus is emphasized. When Jesus finally decides to go to them, his disciples protest that his opponents there had just tried to stone him (11:8). Thomas's wry remark, "Let us also go, that we may die with him" (11:16) comes literally true. In this Gospel, it is Jesus' raising of his friend Lazarus that is the last straw for the religious authorities and will lead to his death (11:53).

Adopting such an understanding of the cross can have profound consequences, as illustrated by the following true story from a rural village in Chiapas involving a woman whose husband would frequently beat her after becoming drunk. She had become involved with a women's Bible study group, a movement initiated by Don Samuel Ruiz, the bishop of San Cristóbal de las Casas from 1960 to 2000, in collaboration with the women religious of the diocese. The women had begun to learn how to read the Scriptures *con ojos, mente y corazón de mujer*; that is, with the eyes, mind, and heart of a woman. They were learning how to look at things from their own perspective and were asking questions that challenged the patriarchal underpinnings of their faith and the patterns of their daily lives. One night, the woman attended a Bible study meeting, and when she returned home, her husband was drunk and enraged that she was not there to serve him his coffee when he wanted it. He beat her badly, as he had many times before. The next morning, when her friends saw her bruised face and battered body, they decided to act. Even though realizing that they themselves might suffer repercussions for their actions, they knew it was a moment when they had to lay down their lives for their friend. Some thirty women came together to the house to confront the husband. They informed him that if he ever struck his wife again, it would be he who would have the battered face and bruised body. These women had moved away from emulating the silent suffering Jesus of Mark's Gospel[16] and had become a community of friends who were

---

16. In Mark 15:1–5, Jesus' silence before Pilate is evocative of the servant in Isaiah 53:7 who "was oppressed, and he was afflicted, yet he did not open his mouth; like a lamb that is led to the slaughter, and like a sheep that before its shearers is silent, so he did not open his mouth." Such a portrait of silent endurance of abuse can fuel cycles of violence and victimization rather than counter them.

ready to lay down their lives for their friend. In this particular instance, the result was a happy one, as the husband was so shocked by their intervention that he got the help he needed to stop drinking and beating his wife.[17]

## Death as Birthing New Life

Another Johannine metaphor with great liberative potential is the depiction of Jesus' death as a birthing of new life. We note that one of the unique features of the crucifixion scene in the Fourth Gospel is that immediately after Jesus' death, a soldier pierces his side, from which blood and water flow forth (19:34). Blood and water are highly symbolic. Because these are the liquids that accompany the birthing process, they help interpret Jesus' death as the birthing of new life. This scene brings to a climax a theme that is woven throughout the whole gospel. The presence of Jesus' mother at the foot of the cross (19:25–27), a detail unique to the Fourth Gospel, also helps us to understand this theme: the one who gave him physical birth is a witness to the new life that is birthed in the community of Jesus' beloved disciples. Together with the scene at Cana (2:1–11), the only other place where Jesus' mother appears in this Gospel, an inclusio[18] is formed that helps to draw out the meaning. There are a number of verbal and thematic links between these scenes: Jesus addresses his mother as "woman" (2:4; 19:26), there is reference to "the hour" (2:4; 19:27) and to belief (2:11; 19:35), and water plays an important symbolic role in both.

The theme of birthing is sounded already in the prologue to John's Gospel, where it is said that "all things came into being [*egeneto*] through him [the word, *logos*]" (1:3). The primary meaning of the Greek verb *ginomai* used here is "to come into being through the process of birth or natural production, be born, be produced."[19] Thus, it would be possible to render John 1:3 as "all things *were birthed* through him." Further on, verses 12–13 state, "But to all who received him, who believed in his name, he gave power to become [*genesthai*] children of God, who were

---

17. CODIMUJ, *Con Mirada, Mente y Corazón de Mujer*, 134.

18. Inclusio is a literary device by which an author frames a section by placing similar material at the beginning and end, as a kind of bracket. The Fourth Evangelist uses this device frequently.

19. Bauer et al., *Greek-English Lexicon*, 196–99.

born [*egennēthēsan*], not of blood or of the will of the flesh or of the will of man, but of God." The second verb, *gennaō*, refers more often to female birthing than to male begetting, as is clearly indicated in John 3:4 and 16:21.

In Jesus' conversation with Nicodemus in chapter 3, there are seven instances of the verb *gennaō*, "to be born." Jesus tells Nicodemus that "no one can enter the kingdom of God without being born of water and the Spirit" (3:5). The symbols of water and the spirit link this episode with the crucifixion scene, where the meaning of birth in water and spirit becomes clearer. At Jesus' death, he hands over his spirit (19:30)[20] as water flows from his pierced side (19:34). Just as in Ezekiel 36:25–27, where the prophet proclaims, "I will sprinkle clean water upon you . . . and a new spirit I will put within you," the symbols of water and spirit signal a rebirth accomplished by divine action.[21]

The symbol of water is central to the next chapter, in which Jesus offers the woman from Samaria "living water" (4:10) and elaborates, "Those who drink of the water I give them will never be thirsty. The water that I will give will become in them a spring of water gushing up to eternal life" (4:14). The meaning of "living water" is further developed in the scene during the Feast of Dedication, when Jesus exclaims, "Let anyone who is thirsty come to me, and let the one who believes in me drink. As the scripture has said, 'Out of the believer's heart [*koilia*] shall flow rivers of living water.' Now he said this about the Spirit, which believers in him were to receive; for as yet there was no Spirit, because Jesus was not yet glorified" (7:37–39). In verse 38, the word *koilia*, often translated as "heart,"[22] is actually the word for "womb," or "uterus,"[23] once again evoking a birthing image, and pointing ahead to the water that will flow from

20. See Schneiders, *Written That You May Believe*, 179, and Swetnam, "Bestowal of the Spirit," 556–76, for reasons why the expression "he handed over the Spirit" (19:30) should be understood as the giving of the spirit rather than a euphemism for death.

21. Schneiders, *Written That You May Believe*, 121.

22. See the NRSV and New Jerusalem Bible (NJB). The New American Bible (NAB) renders *koilia* "from within"; the King James Version (KJV) as "out of his belly."

23. This is clearly the meaning in John 3:4, in which Nicodemus puzzles over how a person can "enter a second time into the mother's womb and be born." So also Luke 1:41, 44; 2:21; 11:27; and 23:29. *Koilia* can also mean "belly" or "stomach" as in Matt 15:17; Mark 7:19; Luke 15:16; 1 Cor 6:13; and Rev 10:9. It can also be understood as the seat of inward life, of feelings and desires; thus the rendering of it in English as "heart." See Bauer et al., *Greek-English Lexicon*, 550.

the pierced side of Jesus in 19:34. The referent of the possessive pronoun in 7:38 is ambiguous: it can refer either to the womb of Jesus or to that of the believer. When read in light of 19:34, both referents can be understood to be in view. The life-giving mission birthed by Jesus is carried forward by believers, who are not mere receptacles for living water, but are themselves conduits of it.

The use of the metaphor of birthing is most explicit in the Farewell Discourse, where Jesus speaks to his disciples about his impending passion: "Very truly, I tell you, you will weep and mourn, but the world will rejoice; you will have pain, but your pain will turn into joy. When a woman is in labor, she has pain, because her hour has come. But when her child is born, she no longer remembers the anguish because of the joy of having brought a human being into the world. So you have pain now; but I will see you again, and your hearts will rejoice, and no one can take your joy from you" (16:20–22). This image evokes that of God, who is described by Isaiah as laboring to rebirth Israel after the exile: "For a long time I have held my peace, I have kept still and restrained myself; now I will cry out like a woman in labor, I will gasp and pant" (Isa 42:14).[24] Presenting Jesus' death as birth pangs, the Fourth Evangelist places the focus on the ensuing joy at the new life that will result; the suffering is not an end in itself, nor is it given atoning significance.

Returning to John 19:34, we can envision the women at the foot of the cross, including Jesus' mother, as midwives aiding in the birthing of a renewed community. Jesus' final declaration, "It is finished" (19:30), can be heard as the declaration of a mother who cries out in joy when the birth pangs are over and her child is born. When the body is taken down from the cross, it is wrapped in linen cloths, evocative of the image of swaddling a newborn (as in Luke 2:7). And when the risen Christ appears to his disciples and breathes on them, saying "receive the holy Spirit" (20:22), it is like the moment of the birthing of the first human being, when the Creator breathed into its nostrils the breath of life (Gen 2:7). Finally, the image of the open tomb can symbolize the open womb from which new life has emerged.

24. See Deut 32:18; Isa 42:14; 49:16; 66:9, 12–13; Pss 22:10–11, 131:2; and Job 38:29 for other maternal images of God.

*A Long Tradition*

It is not only modern feminists who see this imagery in the Gospel of John. As early as the turn of the third century, Clement of Alexandria (153–217) wrote about "the body of Christ, which nourishes by the Word the young brood, which the Lord Himself brought forth in throes of flesh, which the Lord Himself swathed in his precious blood," exclaiming, "O amazing birth!"[25] Similarly, Ambrose, Bishop of Milan (d. 397) refers to Christ as the "Virgin who bare us, Who fed us with her own milk."[26] Julian of Norwich (1342–1416) says that Jesus "our savior is our true Mother in whom we are endlessly born and out of whom—we shall come."[27] German Dominican mystic and scholar Meister Eckhart (1260–1328) similarly used birthing language of the First Person of the Trinity, asserting that "God has ever been begetting His only-begotten Son and is giving birth to him now and eternally: and thus He lies in childbed like a woman who has given birth."[28]

## Conclusion

As I hope the real-life stories I have shared today have illustrated, the way we understand the cross of Christ has consequences, either deadly or freeing. The image of birthing new life is far more than a nice way to think about Jesus' death. Rather, it confronts Christians with a challenge to replicate in our own lives the actions and attitudes of the Christ who came to engender new, full life for all. It invites us into relationships in which the gift of self is loving, mutual, and self-replicating, and in which suffering has meaning and value, not as a consequence of sin or the price to be paid to an angry God, but as the labor pangs that must be endured in order to bring forth new life. Furthermore, the image of Christ birthing a renewed community of beloved disciples enhances the ability of female Christians

---

25. Clement of Alexandria, *The Instructor*, 1.6, quoted in Ford, *Redeemer, Friend, and Mother*, 196. For an English translation of the text, see http://www.ccel.org/ccel/schaff/anf02.vi.iii.i.vi.html.

26. Ambrose, *On Virgins*, 1:5, quoted in Ford, *Redeemer, Friend, and Mother*, 196. For the English translation of the text, see http://www.ccel.org/ccel/schaff/npnf210.iv.vii.ii.v.html.

27. Julian of Norwich, *Showings*, 292.

28. Eckhart, Sermon 88, as quoted in Williams, "Feminist Theology and Meister Eckhart's Transgendered Metaphor," 280.

to see ourselves much more clearly as bearing the image of Christ in our world, but it is not an image that excludes males. Finally, appropriating the moral sense of these texts that speak of birthing can lead to actions, both individual and communal, that aim at taking down from the cross the crucified persons in our day, as we act as cocreators with God in a cosmos that is continuously birthing beauty, goodness, and delight.

For many years, feminist biblical scholars have been leading the way in developing these methods of reading the Scriptures with the mind, eyes, and heart of a woman. In these critical times, it is now more important than ever that we learn to read the Scriptures in this way so that all women, men, and children—and all of creation—can flourish.

## Bibliography

Aquino, María Pilar, et al., eds. *A Reader in Latina Feminist Theology*. Austin: University of Texas Press, 2002.

Bauer, Walter, et al. *Greek-English Lexicon of the New Testament and Other Early Christian Literature*. 3rd ed. Chicago: University of Chicago Press, 2000.

Cannon, Katie G. "The Emergence of Black Feminist Consciousness." In *Feminist Interpretation of the Bible*, edited by Letty M. Russell, 30–40. Philadelphia: Westminster, 1985.

CODIMUJ [La Coordinación Diocesana de Mujeres (Diocesan Coordination of Women)]. *Con Mirada, Mente y Corazón de Mujer*. Mexico City: CODIMUJ, 1999.

Day, Linda, and Carolyn Pressler. *Engaging the Bible in a Gendered World: An Introduction to Feminist Biblical Interpretation in Honor of Katharine Doob Sakenfeld*. Louisville: Westminster John Knox, 2006.

Ford, Josephine Massyngbaerde. *Redeemer, Friend, and Mother: Salvation in Antiquity and in the Gospel of John*. Minneapolis: Fortress, 1997.

Gebara, Ivone. *Longing for Running Water: Ecofeminism and Liberation*. Minneapolis: Fortress, 1999.

Isasi-Díaz, Ada María. "*Lo Cotidiano*: A Key Element of Mujerista Theology." *Journal of Hispanic/Latino Theology* 10.1 (2002) 5–17.

———. *Mujerista Theology: A Theology for the Twenty-First Century*. Maryknoll, NY: Orbis, 1996.

Johnson, Elizabeth A. "Jesus and Salvation." In *CTSA Proceedings* 49, edited by Paul Crowley, 1–18. Santa Clara, CA: Catholic Theological Society of America, 1994.

Julian of Norwich. *Showings*. New York: Paulist, 1978.

Junior, Nyasha. *An Introduction to Womanist Biblical Interpretation*. Louisville: Westminster John Knox, 2015.

Lerner, Gerda. *The Creation of Feminist Consciousness: From the Middle Ages to Eighteen-Seventy*. New York: Oxford University Press, 1993.

Moltmann-Wendel, Elisabeth. *Rediscovering Friendship: Awakening to the Promise and Power of Women's Friendships*. Minneapolis: Fortress, 2000.

Newman, Barbara. *Sister of Wisdom: St. Hildegard's Theology of the Feminine*. Berkeley: University of California Press, 1987.

Reid, Barbara E. *Taking Up the Cross: New Testament Interpretations through Latina and Feminist Eyes*. Minneapolis: Fortress, 2007.

Ress, Mary Judith. *Ecofeminism in Latin America: Women from the Margins*. Maryknoll, NY: Orbis, 2006.

Russell, Letty, ed. *Feminist Interpretation of the Bible*. Philadelphia: Westminster, 1985.

Schneiders, Sandra M. *Written That You May Believe: Encountering Jesus in the Fourth Gospel*. Rev. ed. New York: Crossroad, 2003.

Stanton, Elizabeth Cady. *The Woman's Bible*. Charleston, SC: CreateSpace, 2018.

Swetnam, James. "Bestowal of the Spirit in the Fourth Gospel." *Biblica* 74.4 (1993) 556–76.

Trible, Phyllis. *Texts of Terror: Literary-Feminist Readings of Biblical Narratives*. Philadelphia: Fortress, 1984.

Walker, Alice. *In Search of Our Mothers' Gardens: Womanist Prose*. New York: Harcourt Brace Jovanovich, 1983.

Walshe, Maurice, ed. *Meister Eckhart: Sermons and Treatises*. Dorset, UK: Element, 1987.

Williams, Duane. "Feminist Theology and Meister Eckhart's Transgendered Metaphor." *Feminist Theology* 24.3 (2016) 275–90.

# PART TWO

*Women's Leadership in Africa and Asia*

# 6

## Solidarity in the Streets:
## Catholic Women's Leadership in Modern Uganda

J. J. CARNEY

### Introduction: An Ecclesiology of Solidarity in the Streets

IN SPEAKING ABOUT WOMEN's leadership in the Ugandan Catholic
Church, there is an obvious danger of engaging in essentialism. This
danger is even greater for an American male interlocutor such as myself. So rather than try to speak for "all Ugandan female leaders"[1] or "all
Catholic women leaders," I will limit my focus here to three exemplars
of recent grassroots Catholic leadership in Uganda. The first is Sr. Rose
Mystica Muyinza (1938–2009), a Ganda Catholic from southern Uganda
who became renowned in Kampala in the 1980s and '90s for her work
with vulnerable women and orphaned children in the midst of civil war
and Uganda's HIV/AIDS crisis. The second is Mrs. Rosalba Ato Oywa
(b. 1953), an Acholi lay Catholic and social activist who has tirelessly
worked for peace in northern Uganda for over thirty years. The third is
Ms. Sherry Meyer (b. 1951), an American missionary who has spent over
a quarter-century as a lay minister and radio broadcaster in the West Nile
province in northwestern Uganda. Whatever their obvious differences,

1. On the broader themes of women's leadership in Uganda, see Tripp, *Women and
Politics in Uganda*, and Tripp, *Women and Power in Postconflict Africa*, 49–77.

all three of these grassroots Catholic leaders are united by a shared commitment to what I call "solidarity in the streets."

Let me begin by defining terms. When I say "solidarity," I am referring to the concept as expressed in the tradition of Catholic social teaching, namely the call to remember that we are members of one human family, our dignity originating in our creation in the *imago Dei*.[2] Solidarity reflects our fundamentally communal and relational nature; we are not autonomous individuals but rather "social beings" called to find our freedom in self-giving relationships with the other. To quote the *Compendium of the Social Doctrine of the Church*, "solidarity highlights in a particular way the intrinsic social nature of the human person, the equality of all in dignity and rights, and the common path of individuals and peoples towards an ever more committed unity."[3] Solidarity also entails a ministry of presence, walking with people and sharing their lives, even in the most difficult of circumstances. In the words of Pope St. John Paul II, solidarity "is not a feeling of vague compassion or shallow distress at the misfortunes of so many people, both near and far. On the contrary, it is a firm and persevering determination to commit oneself to the common good; that is to say to the good of all and of each individual, because we are all really responsible for all."[4]

When I say "the streets," however, I am veering away from the rarefied discourse of Catholic theology and entering into the tangled world of American English slang. The *Longman Dictionary of Contemporary English* defines "the streets" as "the busy public parts of a city where there is a lot of activity, excitement, and crime, or where people without homes live."[5] Even more revealing are the definitions found in the online *Urban Dictionary*. There, "street" is described as "where the poor urban ghetto people live" and involves "being able to pick up on all things quickly"; "relating to all types of people"; it is "the opposite of *bourgeois*—'street' implies hustle"; and relates to "the cold reality of day-to-day life and achieving."[6] In summary, "the streets" connotes poverty and the social

2. See Gen 1:27–28.

3. Pontifical Council of Justice and Peace, *Compendium of the Social Doctrine of the Church*, 193.

4. John Paul II, *Sollicitudo Rei Socialis*, 38.

5. *Longman Dictionary of Contemporary English*, s.v. "The Streets," lines 1–2. https://www.ldoceonline.com/dictionary/the-streets.

6. *Urban Dictionary*, s.v., "Street," lines 6–8, 13–14. https://www.urbandictionary.com/define.php?term=Street.

margins, but there are also intriguing associations with ingenuity, energy, accessibility, and thinking outside the box. As we will see, all three of the above-mentioned Catholic protagonists have lived in solidarity with the poor on the streets, yet they have also brought creative "street" insight to tackling the root causes of social marginalization.

Combining Catholic social teaching's notion of solidarity with the vernacular understanding of the streets, I propose here a pastoral vision of ecclesial leadership I call "solidarity in the streets." This vision incorporates three key dimensions.

First, "solidarity in the streets" entails *relocating to the streets*. Solidarity involves not just a feeling of "vague sympathy," as Pope St. John Paul II notes; rather, it entails an embodied commitment to those on the margins, even to the point of physical relocation. To quote the African American Christian activist John Perkins, "Relocation is incarnation."[7] As reflected in Perkins's words, this commitment reflects an incarnational vision of God as one who came to live with us in the person of Jesus Christ. This vision also draws on Pope Francis's well-known calls for the church to leave the security of the sacristy in order to encounter the "suffering flesh of others" and "take on the smell of the sheep."[8] In the pope's words, "I prefer a Church which is bruised, hurting, and dirty because it has been out on the streets, rather than a Church which is unhealthy from being confined and from clinging to its own security."[9] In summary, Catholic leaders living out an incarnational ministry do not seek comfort but rather embody compassion.

Second, solidarity in the streets entails *speaking from the streets*. To echo the language of my own Jesuit university, "if relocating embodies the man or woman *with* others, speaking from the streets points to the need for men and women *for* others."[10] Faithful shepherds should live in solidarity with their sheep, but they have typically also benefited from more opportunities for higher education, wider professional networks, and greater financial resources than most of their sheep. In amplifying the "voice of the voiceless," effective Catholic leaders serve as advocates

7. See City Vision University, "CCDA 2006," 44:55. See also Marsh, *Beloved Community*, 174.

8. Francis, *Evangelii Gaudium*, 24.

9. Francis, *Evangelii Gaudium*, 49.

10. This language is taken from a famous speech given by Pedro Arrupe, SJ, superior general of the Society of Jesus, entitled "Men for Others."

who can draw much-needed attention and resources to the long-term social and human challenges in their midst.

Third, solidarity in the streets ultimately aims at *transforming the streets*. In my own city of Omaha, one of the most successful urban apostolates is run by an evangelical Christian organization named Abide Ministries. Abide defines itself as "an inner-city, non-profit organization with a dream that one day, Omaha, Nebraska would have no inner city."[11] Like Abide, the fruitful Christian leader does not leave situations the way she found them but rather helps transform the community in order to better reflect Jesus' already-but-not-yet reign of God. At the same time, such a leader is not a messiah figure who rescues people. Rather, the most effective and long-lasting changes will be carried forward by the people themselves, and the best Christian leaders empower them to do just this. To paraphrase Augustine of Hippo, "God does not save us without us."

In their own unique ways, I argue that all three of these Catholic leaders in Uganda have lived out an ecclesiology of "solidarity in the streets" that entails *relocation, advocacy*, and *transformation*. In so doing, they serve as exemplars of grassroots Catholic leadership for the Pope Francis-inspired church of the twenty-first century.

## Sr. Rose Mystica Muyinza: Mother of the "People without People"

Sr. Rose Mystica Muyinza was born in 1938 into a wealthy, landowning family in the Mukono district of southern Uganda. Baptized an Anglican, she converted to Catholicism at a young age and, as a teenager, chose to pursue a vocation with the Little Sisters of St. Francis of Assisi. Begun by the Irish missionary Mother Kevin in 1923, the Little Sisters were one of the first indigenous women's religious communities in Uganda. They grew to become one of the largest in the region; today they number over 700 sisters in Uganda, with additional religious houses in Rwanda, Burundi, Kenya, Tanzania, and the US. Mother Kevin initially envisioned the Little Sisters as a cloistered, contemplative community, but as time

---

11. See the "About Us" page of Abide Ministries' website (https://www.abideoma-ha.org/), which states that Abide's mission is to "transform the inner city, one neighborhood at a time." Their actual pastoral approach is even more "micro," working on a street-by-street basis with local neighbors to build up families, neighborhood communities, and housing (Dotzler, interview, July 5, 2016). On the vision of Abide and its founder Ron Dotzler, see his appropriately titled *Out of the Seats and into the Streets*.

progressed they embraced an educational apostolate, outreach to the poor, and ministry to the physically and mentally handicapped.[12]

## A. Relocating to the Streets of Kampala

Sr. Rose completed her novitiate and professed her initial vows in the late 1950s. Shortly thereafter, she convinced her reluctant superiors to allow her to become one of the first Ugandan nuns to study social work at Uganda's famous Makerere University in Kampala. As her studies progressed in the early 1960s, Sr. Rose felt an increasing call to live a more radical life of solidarity on the streets of Kampala rather than remaining inside the Little Sisters communities in either Nkokonjeru or Nsambya, a neighborhood in Kampala. Finally, in 1967, Sr. Rose decided to leave the congregation. To support herself financially, she took a job working for the Bank of Uganda, but her creative passion lay with the streets of Uganda's capital city.

In 1971, Sr. Rose founded the Daughters of Charity (DoC) to "help young girls who had social problems" in Kampala.[13] During the 1970s and '80s, young women came to DoC to escape poverty, sex trafficking, family abandonment, and war. Like Sr. Rose, some had also left formal religious life. In their first decade, Sr. Rose's ministries revolved around two houses of charity near Kampala's Nile Hotel. In the late 1980s, she partnered with the Consolata Fathers and an affiliated Italian charity, Insieme Si Puo, to construct three new centers: Kiwanga Charity Home in Mukono, a home for special-needs children; Sabina Home in Masaka, focusing on care for HIV/AIDS patients; and St. Michael Home for street children in Nsambya, Kampala. The next decade saw further growth as Sr. Rose established the twenty-five-acre Namugongo Farm, the Bweyogerere mechanical workshop, and the 100-acre Kirinya Boys Land. By 2000, "Aunt Rose," as she was affectionately called by her children, had

---

12. Sr. Mary Cleophas, interview with author in Nkokonjeru, Uganda, July 13, 2017. At the time of the interview, Sr. Mary Cleophas was the administrator of the Nkokonjeru Mother House of the Little Sisters of St. Francis. For background on the Little Sisters, see Namuddu and D'Arbela, "Congregation of the Little Sisters," 110–20.

13. Archdiocese of Kampala, *2006 Report*, 1. It should be noted that Muyinza's association had no formal links with the Daughters of Charity of St. Vincent de Paul, an international Catholic women's religious community founded in France in the seventeenth century.

provided direct support for over 3,000 youth.[14] Fittingly, the scriptural quotation that marks the entrance to the Kiwanga Home reads "Let the children come unto me" (Mark 10:14). Reflecting her love for its mission to special-needs children, Sr. Rose chose Kiwanga as her burial place. Her grave has become a site of prayer and popular devotion.

While spearheading all of this charitable work, Sr. Rose lived out a radical form of religious life within her DoC community. She maintained a lifelong vow of celibacy and ministered in her Franciscan robes. She also embraced her own vow of poverty, sleeping on a two-by-three mattress on the floor and leading what one friend described as "a life of self-denial and deprivation."[15] She also emphasized prayer. Each of her children's homes had a residential chapel, and Sr. Rose herself spent part of every Thursday in eucharistic adoration. Even during the worst years of the 1980s civil war, she never missed 7:00 a.m. daily Mass at nearby Christ the King Church in downtown Kampala. (In fact, she was known for splashing water on the faces of her girls to wake them for church and for driving them to Mass in her truck as they belted out, "We are the Daughters of Charity!")[16] Sr. Rose and the DoC became fixtures at Christ the King; even today their successors continue to lead a choir at the 7:00 a.m. Sunday Mass.

In relocating to the streets, Sr. Rose was not simply living with the materially poor. Rather, her former associates described her ministry in Uganda as aiding the *okuyamba abanaku*—"the people without people."[17] In other words, she ministered to all of the socially marginalized women of her society, including sex workers, former Catholic sisters, the illegitimate children of priests, and special-needs children. In this sense, this "woman with a golden heart"[18] is better described as a mother of the marginalized than a mother of the poor.

14. Archdiocese of Kampala, *2006 Report*, 1.

15. Leo Kibirango, interview with author in Kampala, July 11, 2017. Leo Kibirango is a former president of the Bank of Uganda and a founding DoC board member. He came to know Sr. Rose during their time studying together at Makerere University in the early 1960s.

16. Annette Nalugo, interview with author at Kiwanga Integrated Skills Training Center, Jinja Road, Uganda, July 8, 2017. Ms. Annette Nalugo is a former Daughter of Charity.

17. Specioza Namazzi, interview with author at Kiwanga Integrated Skills Training Center, Jinja Road, Uganda, July 8, 2017. Ms. Specioza Namazzi works at the Kiwanga Integrated Skills Training Center.

18. Rachel Mirembe, interview with author in Kampala, July 5, 2017.

## B. Speaking from the Streets of Kampala

Sr. Rose drew on her family's connections, her years working in both banking and the civil service, and her own charisma to develop a remarkable network of local and international advocates. This network included a president of the Bank of Uganda, First Lady Janet Museveni, and US president Ronald Reagan's daughter Maureen (who later adopted a DoC member). She cultivated international church partnerships in Italy and the UK and took the DoC choir on several fundraising trips to the US. In 1986, she helped found Luweeso (Uganda Women's Efforts to Save Orphans), and in her final years, DoC partnered with Children of Uganda and the Uganda Children's Charity Foundation. In this sense, Muyinza was a classic networker and advocate, using her elite connections to attract much-needed funds, volunteers, job opportunities, and public attention for her beloved youth.[19] In the words of her former caretaker, Sr. Teresa Basemera, "She could knock anywhere, and they would open."[20] Her reputation as a networker could also get her in trouble. At one point late in the Idi Amin dictatorship she was arrested and tortured at the Nile Hotel on suspicion of collaborating with foreign agents.[21]

These international partnerships were not without ambiguities and tensions, in part due to Muyinza's tendency toward micromanagement. The partnership with Insieme Si Puo ended in 1996 due to a "misunderstanding."[22] A long-standing collaboration with the British group "Help Uganda" collapsed in the 2000s. Muyinza fell sick with Alzheimer's in 2004, a disease most of her colleagues attributed to overwork.[23] Unfortunately, she had so tightly controlled the DoC that the organization became paralyzed after she fell ill. "Before Aunt collapsed

19. Leo Kibirango, interview with author in Kampala, July 11, 2017.

20. Teresa Basemera, interview with author at Kiwanga Integrated Skills Training Center, Jinja Road, Uganda, July 8, 2017. In addition to caring for Sr. Rose in her final years, Sr. Basemera is now the director of the Kiwanga Integrated Skills Training Center.

21. Teresa Basemera, interview with author at Kiwanga Integrated Skills Training Center, Jinja Road, Uganda, July 8, 2017; Frankline Mbamanya Nsubuga, interview with author in Kampala, July 14, 2017. Mrs. Frankline Mbamanya Nsubuga is a former Daughter of Charity who served as a social worker with DoC in the late 1990s.

22. Archdiocese of Kampala, 2006 Report, 2.

23. One former Daughter of Charity described Sr. Rose's work ethic and lack of sleep as so extreme that "she committed suicide in a way" (Justine Babirye, interview with author in Kampala, July 5, 2017).

down, she had been running everything alone. . . . Board members had little room to become involved in the affairs of the home. This explains why when she fell sick, everything at DoC was at a standstill."[24] Taking advantage of her compromised situation, several DoC alumni embezzled money and tried to claim DoC properties.[25] In keeping with Sr. Rose's will, DoC was handed over to the Archdiocese of Kampala after her death in 2009. A decade later, there are signs that the archdiocese is trying to revitalize Sr. Rose's organization with a new investment of resources and leadership.

As evidenced by her will, Sr. Rose maintained positive relations with the Archdiocese of Kampala. She also retained amicable relationships with the Little Sisters of St. Francis, often visiting for feast days. But a recurring theme in her life was her desire for independence and autonomy. In the words of a former associate, Muyinza "didn't want superiors over her. She wanted to be the boss of her own."[26] In part because of her work taking in the illegitimate children of priests and sisters, she also became something of a *persona non grata* in public Catholic circles. Her creativity, charisma, and entrepreneurial spirit enabled Sr. Rose to transform the DoC into one of the most innovative Catholic ministries in Kampala in the 1980s and '90s, but her resistance to systematization and penchant for micromanagement also left the group vulnerable when her health declined.

## C. Transforming the Streets of Kampala

To what degree can one claim that Sr. Rose Muyinza "transformed the streets?" Although she could be justly critiqued for organizational micromanagement, Sr. Rose successfully empowered the young women with whom she worked. DoC women were trained in catering and small business entrepreneurship, and they often spent weekends baking cakes and catering for local weddings. Many went on to higher education and successful careers in these fields; today one of the largest catering services in Kampala is run by a former Daughter of Charity. To be sure, Sr. Rose

24. Archdiocese of Kampala, *2006 Report*, 2.

25. Leo Kibirango, interview with author in Kampala, July 11, 2017; Justine Babirye, interview with author in Kampala, July 5, 2017.

26. Frankline Mbamanya Nsubuga, interview with author in Kampala, July 14, 2017.

was a provider of charitable works rather than a political activist, and she enjoyed close relationships with key players in the post-1986 National Resistance Movement (NRM) government, including with President Yoweri Museveni's wife. However, her charitable mission was not simply to relieve the symptoms of poverty but to help individuals turn their lives around. In the words of the DoC's 1993 mission statement, the organization's purpose was "to engage in and carry on nonprofit making, nonreligious, nonpolitical activities based on love and nonviolence with the object of improving the conditions of health, education, and training of disadvantaged children."[27]

One of the most moving personal testimonies of empowerment came from Mrs. Justine Babirye. Justine's family migrated from Rwanda with many other Tutsi refugees after the Hutu revolution of 1959–62. In the early 1980s, her father was killed during Uganda's civil war, and shortly thereafter, her mother abandoned her and her siblings. Babirye was now one of the thousands of "Luweero Triangle Girls."[28] At thirteen, she found herself in a refugee camp in Toro in western Uganda. Shortly after Museveni's NRM came to power in January 1986, she found her way to Kampala. A friend suggested that she visit the Daughters of Charity home near the Nile Hotel. Here, Sr. Rose welcomed Babirye with joyful tears and a hug: "Justine, now I am going to be your mother! You will have so many sisters and brothers here!"[29] Justine lived at the DoC home for the better part of the next decade. She finished her secondary schooling and went on to study agronomy and health policy at the university. Today, she and her husband run Keith Associates, an agrochemical business in downtown Kampala. Justine attributes all of her professional success and even her survival to Aunt Rose. "I cherish my life and who I am today because of her. I would have died of HIV/AIDS without her."[30] Sr. Rose Mystica Muyinza's ultimate legacy is the transformed lives of women like Justine Babirye.

27. Archdiocese of Kampala, *2006 Report*, 4.

28. Museveni led the National Resistance Army's insurgency against Milton Obote's government between 1981 and 1986, claiming that Obote had stolen the 1980 elections. The violence was especially concentrated in the central Luweero region of Uganda. Obote was eventually toppled in a military coup in 1985, and Museveni and the NRM took Kampala six months later. He remains in power over thirty-five years later.

29. Justine Babirye, interview with author in Kampala, July 5, 2017.

30. Justine Babirye, interview with author in Kampala, July 5, 2017.

## Mrs. Rosalba Ato Oywa: Social Analyst and Peace Activist

### A. Relocating to the Streets:
### The Gulu District as the Epicenter of the Northern Ugandan War

Born in the small village of Anaka in the Gulu district, Rosalba Oywa (née Ato) was the youngest of six children, including four daughters. As a girl, she received a rare opportunity to pursue further education when her father became frustrated with her older brother's poor performance in school.[31] She studied at local Comboni primary schools in the Gulu area before receiving a scholarship to study at one of Uganda's best Catholic girls schools in Namugongo, near Kampala. After secondary school, she completed a bachelor's degree in chemistry and biology at Makerere University in 1977.[32] During the next decade, she worked as a science teacher, got married, and gave birth to three children. Shortly after Museveni took power in 1986, the Acholi prophetess Alice Lakwena sparked what was described as an uprising of the Holy Spirit against the NRM government. This provided the initial impetus for the better-known Lord's Resistance Army (LRA) movement led by Joseph Kony.[33]

One of the first battles of the northern Ugandan war broke out near her school in Pabbo in August 1986. The headmaster was killed, and Rosalba fled for her life. In the process, she lost her home and all of her possessions. "The only thing I could carry was my children and myself and the clothes we were wearing."[34] She and her children journeyed on foot for fifty kilometers to her husband's home village. She describes this displacement as one of the formative experiences of her life. "It was just an experience that impacted so much on me. It shaped my life completely."[35] Her husband's brother, a Catholic priest, gave her and her children a place to live at Lachor Seminary, but she was ultimately displaced by rebels again. After two more years on the run, she settled in Gulu town in 1988. Rosalba's story reminds us that Christian activists do not always need to relocate to the margins—sometimes the margins come to them.

---

31. Rosalba Oywa, interview with author in Gulu, Uganda, November 29, 2018.

32. Rosalba Oywa, interview with author in Gulu, Uganda, July 16, 2017.

33. On Lakwena and the origins of the LRA conflict, see Behrend, *Alice Lakwena and the Holy Spirits.*

34. Rosalba Oywa, interview with author in Gulu, Uganda, July 16, 2017.

35. Rosalba Oywa, interview with author in Gulu, Uganda, July 16, 2017.

## B. Speaking from the Streets and the Camps of Northern Uganda

Rosalba Oywa's experience of deprivation, combined with her recognition of the limited opportunities for uneducated women to restart their lives, led her directly into advocacy work within the local community and church. "When I saw ordinary women, just going through the same process like me, and without any support, without anything, then that itself motivated me to begin doing something toward either ending that war or doing something so that many people don't continue suffering. . . . From that time, I never looked back."[36] She began mobilizing women in the community to stand up to the warring parties and actively work for peace. Toward this end, in 1989 she and the Gulu Women's Development Committee organized hundreds of women in a citywide protest. Women shut down the local market and, invoking a traditional curse, uncovered their breasts to express their anger at the violence. For a time, peace and stability were restored in the city and its environs.[37] In 1992, Rosalba collaborated with the Archdiocese of Gulu and other religious communities in Acholiland to initiate an annual "March for Peace" in Gulu town. In 2005, she worked with Archbishop John Baptist Odama of Gulu and the diocesan Justice and Peace Commission to organize an annual "Peace Week";[38] this Gulu initiative later grew to include the nearby Catholic dioceses of Arua, Nebbi, and Lira, as well as Catholic communities in South Sudan. Peace Week offered extended time for reflection, prayer, and social analysis of the root causes of the conflict and the best means of implementing postwar reconstruction. It also provided invaluable opportunities for participants to express contrition and seek forgiveness on behalf of their compatriots, such as when the South Sudanese bishop of Torit apologized for Sudanese contributions to the war.[39]

In 1988, Rosalba Oywa began working full-time as a social analyst for the UK-based Agency for Cooperation in Research and Development

36. Rosalba Oywa, interview with author in Gulu, Uganda, July 16, 2017.

37. Rosalba Oywa, interview with author in Gulu, Uganda, July 16, 2017; Tinkasiimire, "Women, Peacebuilding, and Reconciliation," 73.

38. On Odama's spiritual vision and own extensive work for peace, see Katongole, *Journey of Reconciliation*, 121–36.

39. Rosalba Oywa, interview with author in Gulu, Uganda, July 16, 2017; Cyprian Ocen P'akec, interview with author in Kampala, July 17, 2017. In the 2000s, Fr. Cyprian Ocen P'akec was the coordinator of the Archdiocese of Gulu's Justice and Peace Commission. At the time of writing, he was a parish priest in an outlying village in Gulu district.

(ACORD).[40] In this work, she focused on understanding the root causes of the conflict, including the destabilizing impact of the collapse of the cotton market and cattle herds on the economic security of men and on overall gender relations.[41] For years, she and her associates fastidiously documented ordinary women's testimonies of their sufferings during the war.[42] Rosalba also worked with a team of researchers to document government abuses in the internally displaced people (IDP) camps established in the region beginning in 1996. Euphemistically named "protected villages," the camps were more akin to "a death trap for the people," according to Rosalba.[43] ACORD published accounts that upwards of 1,000 IDPs were dying each week because of the atrocious conditions in the camps, including the spread of Ebola. Rosalba began receiving death threats, and local political leaders tried to link her to the LRA rebels. She attributes her survival to divine agency. "We were working for the truth. . . . It was now God who intervened, and we put all our hopes in prayer. I think God worked a miracle."[44]

Rosalba Oywa is also known for her extensive work on various dimensions of transitional justice. Having studied the traditional Acholi reconciliation process of *Mato Oput* since 1988, she documented a case of *Mato Oput* in the 1999 film, *Gulu: The Struggle for Peace*, and she ultimately convinced the Belgian government in 2000 to fund the revitalization of this reconciliation process.[45] Since then, *Mato Oput* has played a key role in restorative justice initiatives in northern Uganda.[46] During

40. ACORD was the only international NGO to remain in northern Uganda during the worst years of the war in the late 1980s and early 1990s. For more information about ACORD and its mission, history, and current activities, see their website, http://www.acordinternational.org.

41. To quote one of her early writings: "Men are finding it hard to re-establish their place in post-war society, undermined by the loss of their cattle and the absence of off-farm employment; and social expectations as well as legal rights as regards land, marriage, and women's role are in a state of flux" (Rosalba Oywa and People's Voice for Peace, "PANOS," 92).

42. The PANOS 1994 document includes a sampling of these direct testimonies collected from women during the 1986–94 period.

43. Rosalba Oywa, interview with author in Gulu, Uganda, July 16, 2017.

44. Rosalba Oywa, interview with author in Gulu, Uganda, July 16, 2017.

45. Rosalba Oywa, interview with author in Gulu, Uganda, July 16, 2017. On this point, see Maletta, *Gulu*, 15:13—17:50.

46. For a good overview of *Mato Oput*, see Mpyangu, "Rebuilding Lives and Relationships," 158–63. See also my Creighton colleague John O'Keefe's 2011 film, *Mato Oput*.

the 2006–08 Juba peace talks, Oywa and other women's activists rallied outside the negotiation rooms to lobby both sides to come to terms.[47] In 2009, she worked with twenty-one women's groups to pressure the Ugandan government to better integrate gender perspectives into the post-Juba Peace, Recovery, and Development Plan (PRDP).[48] She has also contributed extensively to the Makerere University-based Refugee Law Project's reparations and restorative justice initiatives in northern Uganda.[49] For Rosalba, it was important to ensure that issues like land reform and victim compensation were framed as questions of justice rather than charity. In her words, "Those are people's rights; they are not a gift."[50]

Rosalba Oywa also speaks out via the airwaves. Every Saturday, she serves as one of three panelists on Gulu radio station Mega-FM's *Teyat*, a program that is meant to simulate the traditional process of Acholi elders addressing social challenges "under the tree."[51] On the program, she addresses issues critical to northern Uganda's full recovery, ranging from government corruption to conflicts over land and mental health. A decade after the war ended and after most NGOs left the region, Rosalba remains a tireless voice for long-term reconstruction.

## C. Transforming the Streets of Gulu

Rosalba Oywa reminds us that, in addition to engaging in charitable works, diplomatic negotiations, and general activism, social analysis is critical to the long-term transformation of the streets of Uganda. In the words of John-Bosco Komakech Aludi, the current director of Caritas Gulu, Rosalba's most important attribute is that "she is very knowledgeable about the situation, and she understands the local context."[52] For Mega-FM host and journalist, Steven Balmoi, "she [Rosalba] is so rich in information . . . she is knowledgeable in almost every area of peace,

47. Rosalba Oywa, interview with author in Gulu, Uganda, November 29, 2018.

48. See Isis-Women's International Cross-Cultural Exchange, "Women's Task Force for a Gender-Responsive PRDP."

49. Chris Dolan, interview with author in Kampala, October 30, 2018. Chris Dolan is the long-time director of the Refugee Law Project, who first collaborated with Rosalba Oywa in the late 1990s. For more background on the RLP, see https://www.refugeelawproject.org.

50. Rosalba Oywa, interview with author in Gulu, Uganda, July 16, 2017.

51. Steven Balmoi, interview with author in Gulu, Uganda, November 25, 2018.

52. John Bosco Komakech Aludi, phone interview with author, July 21, 2017.

governance, health, education, and women's empowerment."[53] Notable
here is the length of time that Rosalba has spent on these issues. In a
region where international activists come and go, she embodies a "rooted
activism,"[54] recognizing that northern Uganda's problems require a long-
term presence and long-term solutions. In sum, if Sr. Rose Muyinza was
an exemplar of the Catholic activist focused on charitable works, Rosalba
Oywa is a model of the analytical social justice activist and grassroots
mobilizer. In her own words, "What are the root causes of the conflict?
And how can we stop the cycle of suffering and handouts?"[55]

Like Sr. Muyinza, Rosalba Oywa has helped transform the streets of
Uganda by empowering vulnerable people. For Rosalba, it is not enough
to "extract" information from locals to further international understanding; instead, researchers need to move among the people to work with
them, give them hope, and collaborate with them to transform their
situation.[56] In this regard, one of her most notable initiatives is People's
Voices for Peace, a network she founded in 1995 to give a platform for
survivors of war, sexual abuse, and land mines. In her work as a community organizer, Oywa envisions her role as "building local capacity,"
particularly through training youth, women, and traditional religious
leaders in mediation and peacebuilding.[57]

Ultimately, however, Rosalba Oywa's call to incarnational solidarity
comes from her heart. Her obvious strengths as a peace-building leader
include intellectual analysis, international networking, and social mo-
bilization, and many associates commented on how she doesn't "wear
religion on her sleeve."[58] When asked about her spiritual motivations,
she spoke of God's tasking her with a mission to "bear witness" to the
suffering around her, on the performance of which God will ultimately
judge her. "Supposing I keep quiet, even when people trust me so much
and give me this information? Then the consequences could be very bad
after my life."[59] In her work to carry out this mission, the Virgin Mary
gives her solace. "When you look at our Mother Mary, then you know the

53. Steven Balmoi, interview with author in Gulu, Uganda, November 25, 2018.

54. Chris Dolan, interview with author in Kampala, October 30, 2018.

55. Rosalba Oywa, interview with author in Gulu, Uganda, July 16, 2017.

56. Rosalba Oywa, interview with author in Gulu, Uganda, November 29, 2018.

57. Rosalba Oywa, interview with author in Gulu, Uganda, July 16, 2017.

58. Chris Dolan, interview with author in Kampala, October 30, 2018; Steven Balmoi, interview with author in Gulu, Uganda, November 25, 2018.

59. Rosalba Oywa, interview with author in Gulu, Uganda, November 29, 2018.

anguish she went through and how she had to deal with all the problems of seeing her own Son suffering."[60] A voice of solidarity on the streets of Gulu, Rosalba Oywa is a model of Catholic compassion leading to Catholic action.

## Ms. Sherry Meyer: Postcolonial Missionary

Sherry Meyer grew up about as far from Uganda as one can imagine, in a small suburb of Indianapolis, Indiana.[61] The oldest of six children, she attended Franciscan Catholic schools from primary school through college. After graduation, she worked as a high school English teacher and later as a Catholic school principal. In her late thirties, she took a new position with the Archdiocese of Chicago and pursued graduate studies in ministry at the Catholic Theological Union. She assumed she would either keep working at the archdiocesan offices or go back to Indiana to work in parish ministry. At the age of forty, however, she began to dream about Africa.

### A. Relocating to the Streets of Uganda

Instead of immediately embracing her romantic dream of missionary life, Meyer resisted. Questions churned in her head. How could she leave her close-knit family? What if she got sick? And perhaps most of all, "What good can a forty-year-old American woman do in Africa?"[62] But over weeks and months of discernment, the call remained persistent. Finally, Meyer decided to join the Volunteer Missionary Movement (VMM), one of the only Catholic agencies exclusively focused on lay ministry and mission. After several months of training in the UK, she arrived in Uganda in October 1991, just in time for the Catholic Church's annual worldwide celebration of Mission Sunday. Despite this momentous feast, the initial auguries were not good. Her roommate came down with hives, and Sherry's asthma kicked in. She had no toilet for the first time in her

60. Rosalba Oywa, interview with author in Gulu, Uganda, July 16, 2017.

61. Sherry Meyer, interview with author in Arua town, Uganda, July 1–2, 2017. Her biographical information is drawn from two days of extended interviews that I conducted with her at her home. Follow-up field work was conducted in October 2018.

62. Sherry Meyer, interview with author in Arua town, Uganda, July 1–2, 2017.

life. "Every day I said, I can't do this, I am going home!"[63] Solidarity with
the people of Uganda meant learning to be totally dependent on others,
a mentality that did not come easily to an oldest child and single woman
who had always prized her personal independence. Even the most basic daily functions had to be learned anew. In Sherry's own recollection,
"How do you take a bath here with a basin and soap? How do you hold a
chicken? How do you prevent it from *^#$% on me?"[64]

Overwhelmed by the challenges, Meyer told herself that she would
complete a year of service and then move back to the US. But a long-
time Italian Comboni missionary, Fr. Tonino Pasolini, had other plans
for her.[65] Recognizing her administrative abilities and passion for lay
ministry, he invited her to help the Combonis develop a new lay ministry
training program. Seeing that this would allow her to make a tangible
contribution to the local church, Meyer developed a renewed sense of
purpose that enabled her to grind through the daily deprivations of her
life in West Nile. Soon she was teaching Scripture to lay catechists, running workshops for priests and laity, and translating the South African
Lumko Institute's pastoral materials into local languages.[66] In fact, 90
percent of the materials for Ugandan Catholic "liturgies in the absence of
a priest" were developed by Meyer, working out of the newly constructed
Christus Center in Arua town. Her overall mission was simple: to help
local people understand that the church was far more than priests and
women religious and that the laity were called to be "participants [in the
church] rather than spectators."[67] Although some of the old-school Italian Comboni priests fretted that she was, in Meyer's words, "one of these
wild American feminist women who go to theology school,"[68] her results
slowly won them over. When her five-year contract with VMM ran out
in the late 1990s, the Combonis accepted her as a lay missionary. She

63. Sherry Meyer, interview with author in Arua town, Uganda, July 1–2, 2017.

64. Sherry Meyer, interview with author in Arua town, Uganda, July 1–2, 2017.

65. Founded by the Italian saint Daniel Comboni in 1867, the Comboni Missionaries of the Heart of Jesus (also known as the Verona Fathers) were the most important
European Catholic missionaries in Sudan and northern Uganda in the late nineteenth
and twentieth centuries. See the website for the Comboni Missionaries at https://www.
combonimissionaries.org.

66. The Lumko Institute had a major impact on formation in Catholic lay ministry in Africa in the post-Vatican II era. See its website at http://sacbcoldsite.org.za/
about-us/associate-bodies/lumko-institute/.

67. Sherry Meyer, interview with author in Arua town, Uganda, July 1–2, 2017.

68. Sherry Meyer, interview with author in Arua town, Uganda, July 1–2, 2017.

stayed in Uganda in part because she offered a different image for the local church: a laywoman engaged in pastoral and liturgical ministry.

## B. Speaking from the Streets through the Airwaves

After a decade working in pastoral ministry, Sherry and Fr. Tonino were asked to help jump-start a new diocesan initiative in mass communications—a local Catholic radio station to be called Radio Pacis (literally, "peace radio"). The name was chosen to distinguish the new station from the community radio model emphasizing political speeches and hip-hop music, and also from the Ugandan Catholic model of Radio Maria. To be sure, Pasolini and Meyer broadcast traditional Catholic programming such as the Mass, liturgical music, catechesis, biblical reflection, and the rosary. For fifteen years, for example, Meyer has aired a weekly radio program called *Scripture Moments*. But Meyer and Pasolini went beyond apolitical devotional programming to also address human rights, health, education, sports, family, gender relations, and civic education. In its holistic approach, Radio Pacis embodies what Meyer calls "gospel values radio."[69] For Meyer, this focus on human lives echoes Jesus' own ministry: "Jesus always preferred the poor, the lame, the sick, and those on the margins, and this entails issues of justice, human rights, courts, corruption, and healthcare access. . . . One of the huge roles here is to raise awareness."[70]

Launched in 2004, Radio Pacis became the most popular radio station in the region over the next decade, and current listenership is estimated at 10 million.[71] Broadcasting in three towns and five languages, it reaches far-flung villages, not just in northern Uganda but across northeastern Congo and South Sudan. In addition, Radio Pacis has crossed not only national borders, but also religious borders—its highest listening percentage is in the overwhelmingly Muslim district of Yumbe. Most impressively, in 2007, Radio Pacis won BBC Radio's inaugural Best New Radio Station in Africa award. On their return to Arua airfield after receiving the award, Sherry, Fr. Tonino, and other station leaders were met

69. Sherry Meyer, interview with author on Radio Pacis in Arua town, Uganda, July 1–2, 2017.

70. Sherry Meyer, interview with author on Radio Pacis in Arua town, Uganda, July 1–2, 2017.

71. Charles Idraku, interview with author, Radio Pacis, Arua, Uganda, 13 May 2019.

by a crowd of thousands who cheered them all the way back to the Radio Pacis headquarters.[72]

Radio Pacis embodies Sherry Meyer's commitment to "speaking from the streets." For Meyer, radio has the potential to be akin to liturgy by creating a sacred space that enables an elevated conversation about important human questions and social challenges, such as domestic violence and child labor. In this vein, Meyer related what an older man said to her in a local supermarket: "I am a Christian of Arua diocese. I just want to tell you that we so appreciate what you've given up for us. Knowing what you left behind to live with us all these years. And the things you say on the radio are really unique—no one else can say that to us!"[73]

The mission of Radio Pacis revolves around bringing "the peace of Christ to all"[74] to help transform the local community. Since 2010, the station has sponsored "community engagement" initiatives in which field reporters go into local villages to inquire into the felt needs of the community. Radio Pacis then hosts a forum in the village that enables ordinary people to voice their concerns directly to their civic leaders. The radio station follows up months later to see whether local leaders have kept their promises (the station's huge listenership provides ample motivation for recalcitrant politicians). Radio Pacis has focused on sensitizing the local population to questions of human dignity like child sexual abuse, alcoholism, and domestic violence.[75] According to Sarah Amviko, Radio Pacis's human resources manager, women are now speaking more openly about domestic violence. "[The radio] has empowered women to stand their ground and to know that they are human beings."[76] In recent years, the station has given a platform to the more than 1 million Sudanese refugees in the region. Radio programs such as those hosted by the Rural Initiative for Community Empowerment (RICE) bring together refugees and local host communities to discuss areas of shared

72. Tonino Pasolini, interview with author on Radio Pacis in Arua, Uganda, July 1, 2017.

73. Sherry Meyer, interview with author on Radio Pacis in Arua town, Uganda, July 1–2, 2017.

74. This phrase is part of the Radio Pacis logo; see the Radio Pacis home page, https://www.radiopacis.org.

75. Paul Aroga, interview with author in Burua village, Arua district, Uganda, October 7, 2018.

76. Sarah Amviko, interview with author on Radio Pacis in Arua town, Uganda, July 3, 2017.

concern and conflict, such as environmental destruction and infrastructural development.[77] For longtime reporter Gabriel Adrapi, this reflects Radio Pacis's mission that "whatever we do, we do for the voiceless of the community."[78]

Radio staff also share narratives of professional and personal transformation. Local staff members have been sent to apprentice with some of the best mass media outlets, including BBC World Service, Uganda Media Development Foundation, Farm Radio International, the Konrad Adenauer Foundation, and Vatican Radio. Many staff members spoke of how much they appreciate Meyer's and Pasolini's consultative leadership style, including a tradition of Friday morning meetings in which staff are given free rein to air their concerns and ideas. Asked what makes Radio Pacis work, station manager Gaetano Apamaku highlighted "decentralization," noting that "in leadership you have to trust other people to do things."[79] In the view of program manager Noel Ayikobua, station leaders "involve everyone in decision-making."[80] For Amviko, the ultimate measure of Meyer, Pasolini, and Radio Pacis is personal growth of the staff rather than a big listening audience. "Radio Pacis has not just inspired people but has made people grow."[81]

## C. Transforming the Streets of West Nile

When asked about her own legacy, Meyer does not use language of "transformation"; rather, she speaks of "competence," "organization," and "planning."[82] Her response reminds us that genuine transformation does not happen instantaneously and dramatically, but instead it is slow, gradual, and decidedly unromantic. In contrast to the methods of Muyinza,

77. Moses Atule, interview with author on Radio Pacis in Arua town, Uganda, October 8, 2018.

78. Gabriel Adrapi, interview with author on Radio Pacis in Arua town, Uganda, October 10, 2018.

79. Gaetano Apamaku, interview with author on Radio Pacis in Arua town, Uganda, July 3, 2017.

80. Noel Ayikobua, interview with author on Radio Pacis in Arua town, Uganda, July 3, 2017.

81. Sarah Amviko, interview with author on Radio Pacis in Arua town, Uganda, July 3, 2017.

82. Sherry Meyer, interview with author on Radio Pacis in Arua town, Uganda, July 1–2, 2017.

Meyer offers an important lesson that creative charisma must be balanced by effective organization. "My legacy is administration; Catholics tend to thrive in building institutions. But many institutions in Africa are failing because of failures in management and administration."[83]

Missionaries have always sought to transform mission territories, and some of their proselytizing efforts in Africa have come in for a deserved postcolonial critique. Rather than being an anachronistic throwback, however, Meyer emerges as a model for the postcolonial missionary who practices a missiology best captured, in John the Baptist's words, at the beginning of John's gospel: "He must increase, and I must decrease" (John 3:30). In this vein, Meyer describes her ministry as one of "empowering the people,"[84] respecting them for who they are and recognizing that God was here long before she or any other Christian missionaries arrived in Uganda. The missionary's gift is, thus, not her introduction of an unknown God but rather her long-term witness of love and solidarity. Or, as Meyer says, "The difference between missionaries and development workers is that missionaries come to stay and live."[85]

Like an "ambassador for Christ" (2 Cor 5:19), Sherry Meyer continues to move between worlds, spending every summer back home in Indianapolis and Chicago. Approaching seventy, and thirty years into what was initially a two-year volunteer contract, Meyer is under no obligation to return to Uganda. Yet every year—even after breast cancer treatment in 2003—she has chosen to make the long safari from Indiana back to Arua. Even though she professes no desire to be a martyr, her commitment to the people of Uganda shines bright. And it does not go unnoticed—in the words of the Ugandan Comboni father Romano Dada, "We are proud of them [Fr. Tonino and Sherry]. I appreciate them so much. They have given their lives to this place. We hope they die here!"[86] It is hard to think of a better tribute to a lived ecclesiology of solidarity in the streets.[87]

83. Sherry Meyer, interview with author on Radio Pacis in Arua town, Uganda, July 1–2, 2017.

84. Sherry Meyer, interview with author on Radio Pacis in Arua town, Uganda, July 1–2, 2017.

85. Sherry Meyer, interview with author on Radio Pacis in Arua town, Uganda, July 1–2, 2017. This is one of the reasons Meyer ultimately affiliated with the Combonis—they are "down-home," "get things done," and "live with the people."

86. Romano Dada, interview with author in Arua, Uganda, July 3, 2017.

87. This chapter draws material from Carney, *For God and My Country*. I am grateful to my interlocutors at DePaul University's 2018 World Catholicism Week conference titled "Daughters of Wisdom" for their critical feedback and encouragement.

## Conclusion

In this essay, I have lifted up three exemplars of an ecclesiology I call "solidarity on the streets." Operating within Uganda's challenging post-colonial context of war, poverty, and political authoritarianism, Sr. Rose Mystica Muyinza, Mrs. Rosalba Ato Oywa, and Ms. Sherry Meyer offer powerful and creative examples of Catholic women's grassroots leadership in the Global South. In particular, they embody Catholic social teaching's call to solidarity in terms of relocating to the streets, speaking from the streets, and transforming the streets. Their voices join those of other Great Lakes Africa luminaries such as Angelina Atyam, Anne-Marie Mukankuranga, and Maggy Barankitse,[88] not to mention the other women's activists and theologians lifted up in this volume. Inspired by such a "great cloud of witnesses" (Heb 12:1), may we discern our own apostolates of incarnational evangelization on the streets of our towns and cities.

## Bibliography

Archdiocese of Kampala. *2006 Report on the Daughters of Charity*. Kampala, Uganda: Archdiocese of Kampala, 2006.

Arrupe, Pedro, SJ. "Men for Others." Speech. Valencia, Spain, 1973. http://onlineministries.creighton.edu/CollaborativeMinistry/men-for-others.html.

Behrend, Heike. *Alice Lakwena and the Holy Spirits: War in Northern Uganda, 1986–97.* Athens: Ohio University Press, 2000.

Carney, J. J. *For God and My Country: Catholic Leadership in Modern Uganda.* Eugene, OR: Cascade, 2020.

————. "A Generation after Genocide: Catholic Reconciliation in Rwanda." *Theological Studies* 76.4 (2015) 785–812.

City Vision University. "CCDA 2006: Dr. John Perkins Sermon: Thursday Morning Bible Study." *YouTube*, 55:25. https://www.youtube.com/watch?v=bU_nZKsg-yM.

Dotzler, Ron. *Out of the Seats and into the Streets*. Omaha, NE: Abide Ministries, 2015.

Fox, Chris, and Roz Combley. *Longman Dictionary of Contemporary English*. 6th ed. Harlow, UK: Pearson Education Limited, 2014.

Francis, Pope. *Evangelii Gaudium. Vatican.va*, 2013. http://www.vatican.va/content/francesco/en/apost_exhortations/documents/papa-francesco_esortazione-ap_20131124_evangelii-gaudium.html.

Isis-Women's International Cross-Cultural Exchange. "Women's Task Force for a Gender-Responsive PRDP: Policy Brief, Recommendations for a Gender-Responsive Peace, Recovery, and Development Plan for North and North Eastern Uganda (PRDP)." Working paper, November 2009.

88. See Katongole, *Sacrifice of Africa*, 148–92; Carney, "Generation after Genocide," 795–97.

John Paul II, Pope. *Sollicitudo Rei Socialis*. Vatican.va, December 30, 1987. http:// www.vatican.va/content/john-paul-ii/en/encyclicals/documents/hf_jp-ii_ enc_30121987_sollicitudo-rei-socialis.html.

Katongole, Emmanuel. *The Journey of Reconciliation: Groaning for a New Creation in Africa*. Maryknoll, NY: Orbis, 2017.

———. *The Sacrifice of Africa: A Political Theology for Africa*. Grand Rapids: Eerdmans, 2011.

Maletta, Robert, dir. *Gulu: The Struggle for Peace*. Film. London: Trojan Horse Productions, 1999. https://vimeo.com/9697961.

Marsh, Charles. *The Beloved Community: How Faith Shapes Social Justice from the Civil Rights Movement to Today*. New York: Basic, 2005.

Mpyangu, Christine Mbabazi. "Rebuilding Lives and Relationships through Forgiveness and Reconciliation in Northern Uganda." In *The Ugandan Churches and the Political Centre: Cooperation, Co-option, and Confrontation*, edited by Paddy Musana et al., 151–70. Cambridge, UK: Ngoma Publishing Consortium and Cambridge Centre for Christianity Worldwide, 2017.

Namuddu, Pauline, and Paul G. D'Arbela. "The Congregation of the Little Sisters of St. Francis of Assisi." In *The Catholic Church in Africa: The Uganda Perspective in the Pontificate of Pope Francis*, edited by Antonia Namuli et al., 110–20. Kisubi, Uganda: Marianum, 2015.

O'Keefe, John, dir. *Mato Oput*. Omaha, NE: Creighton Backpack Journalism Program, Creighton University, 2011. https://vimeo.com/33414929.

Oywa, Rosalba, and People's Voice for Peace. "PANOS—Uganda Briefing." Gulu, Uganda: n.p. 1994.

Pontifical Council of Justice and Peace. *Compendium of the Social Doctrine of the Church*. Washington, DC: Libreria Editrice Vaticana and USCCB, 2004.

Tinkasiimire, Theresa. "Women, Peacebuilding and Reconciliation in East Africa: A Case of Uganda." In *Peacebuilding in East Africa: Exploring the Role of the Churches*, edited by Paddy Musana, 67–79. Nairobi: Paulines Africa, 2013.

Tripp, Aili Marie. *Women and Politics in Uganda*. Madison: University of Wisconsin Press, 2000.

———. *Women and Power in Postconflict Africa*. New York: Cambridge University Press, 2015.

# 7

# Women's Leadership Roles in the Church, the Family of God in Africa: The Example of Rebecca in Genesis 25–27

MarySylvia Nwachukwu, DDL

## 1. Introduction

THIS ARTICLE INVESTIGATES THE nature of women's leadership in the church, the family of God in Africa. Within the context of the African worldview and culture, women's leadership roles are described from a viewpoint read from the figure of Rebecca in Genesis 25–27. The First Special Assembly for Africa of the Synod of Bishops in 1994 used the term "Family of God" as an especially apt description of the church in Africa and as the guiding idea for evangelization in Africa toward the year 2000.[1] The church in Africa is formed by communities of the people of God in various parts of the continent who have accepted the Christian faith and are committed to living the call to discipleship in their African context. The church adapts itself to the set liturgies and theologies of the Roman Catholic tradition, and to its rigid rules and rationalistic Western conceptions, yet it is permeated by the tropical African temperament and by spontaneity, dance, and enthusiasm.

---

1. John Paul II, "Ecclesia in Africa," 63.

Understanding the African cultural context in which the African church carries out its mission of evangelization is essential for understanding the human relationships and roles that characterize it. Despite the ongoing modernization of the continent, Africa is a place where the historical culture continues to determine these relationships and roles. It is important, therefore, to measure the extent to which traditional African beliefs affect relationships between the people of God and the nature of their call to discipleship. Another important determinant of these relationships and roles is the African people's concern for the family. It is noteworthy that the church replicates many aspects of family life. In this church, women fulfill roles that they also fulfill in their families. For this reason, the role of women in the family unit is a good backdrop for understanding their contribution to and roles in the church.

The article unfolds in the next section with a description of the African cultural environment, which sheds light on a later discussion of the changing status of women in contemporary African society. This is followed in section 3 by a description of the negative view of women in the history of the church and of the recent changes to this view. In the fourth section, we use data collected from a survey on two cultural groups, the Igbos of Nigeria and the Akan of Ghana, to draw conclusions on the enormous contributions of present-day African women to both the family and the church, despite the restrictions placed on them by the patriarchy and the hierarchy. In the last section, the roles played by Rebecca, the wife of Isaac, as described in Genesis 25–27, are interpreted and used as a dramatic example of the leadership roles played by women in the African church.

## 2. The African Cultural Context and System of Values

Africa's colonial history, which saw the introduction of Western-oriented Christianity, has affected and continues to affect the lives of Africans and the traditional African culture. The introduction of Islam into Africa has also had these effects. Despite these influences on and interferences in the patterns of life in Africa, and despite the ongoing modernization of African societies, some cultural practices and ideas from precolonial times have remained strong and continue to influence present-day African lifestyles.

Most resilient of these precolonial ideas is the African view that the world is an integrated phenomenon in which divine, human, and terrestrial realities are inextricably joined.[2] Africans see the spiritual and human worlds as being intricately tied together and mutually interrelated—the invisible world manifests itself in the visible, and spiritual beings influence human life positively or negatively.[3]

The African finds the meaning of life in a wider family—the community or "clan." The community is the context for defining the human being's identity and sense of belonging and roles that individuals play. This fact has led to excessive tribalism, which presents problems for contemporary Africa. Socialization into the community is achieved through various rites of passage that are reserved only for men.[4] The community operates traditional rites of socialization of young men into membership of the community and inculcates in them rigid sex-determined roles and customs, which symbolically imply that women are not accorded legal membership and rights, such as status and inheritance.[5]

Most African cultures are patriarchal, even though a few matrilineal societies are found in various places in Africa.[6] However, Vusi Moloi is of the opinion that the powerful female figures of ancient precolonial African cultures represent an inherently matrilineal orientation in African societies, and that this orientation changed with the introduction of Islam, Christianity, and colonial conquest.[7] Even though, generally, matrilineal cultures give women the right to inherit status and property, this does not however translate to female dominance.[8] Principally, matrilineal cultures were founded on the premise of food production which was controlled by women.[9]

2. Cf. Mugambi, *Christianity and African Culture*, 116.

3. Cf. Nnamani, "Ambivalent Impact of Pentecostalism," 246–48.

4. For example, there are rites for men connected with puberty and with marriage (Mugambi, *Christianity and African Culture*, 123–24).

5. Cf. Uchem, *Overcoming Women's Subordination*, 64–66.

6. Narayan, "Matrilineal Society."

7. For instance, Queen Nerfetiti of Egypt, Queen Makeda of Ethiopia, Queen Candace Amanirena of Nubia, the Rain Queen Modjaji, and Queen Manthatisi of South Africa. Cf. Moloi, "Organic Roots of African Matrilineal Society."

8. Narayan, "Matrilineal Society."

9. In precolonial Africa, land was owned by African mothers, for which reason land is referred to as "motherland," in contrast to European culture, where land is called "fatherland." The concept of dowry was also born as compensation for the economic loss incurred from marrying a woman out of a family where she was a food

A case in point is the matrilineal culture of Akan[10] societies, where all property and power are bound within the matrilineal system.[11] Economic matters link wives to their husbands, who provide financial support. Children belong to the family of their mothers even though they bear the father's surname. Leadership functions through the institution of queen motherhood (queenship); queen mothers enjoy considerable influence and prestige in Akan communities and are instrumental in decision-making. Though men are appointed by the queen mother to be the heads of household, women also exert power over and have influence on the decision-making in family matters.

In patriarchal societies among the Igbos of Nigeria, on the other hand, men control property and are the legal guardians of children; they even have the right to restrict their daughters' and wives' public activities. Leadership is a sex-based role associated with men, eldership, and the man's moral integrity.

How do women fit into the cultural world of the patriarchy? A woman's role and place is in the home, where she is a wife, mother, and caregiver. This is the goal toward which the traditional education and upbringing of female children is aimed. Male children are preferred over female children, because males are seen as transmitters of family life and because only males can inherit property.

We must, however, admit that the social status of women has improved, thanks to modernization. While researching on the topic of this paper, I explored popular opinion about the status of women in modern African families.[12] Questionnaires were sent to both Nigerian Igbos, who live in a patrilineal culture, and to the matrilineal Akan people of Ghana. The goal of my assessment was to examine the changes in the status of women which are taking place in modern African societies and their impact on the family.

---

producer (cf. Moloi, "Organic Roots of African Matrilineal Society").

10. In Ghana, all of the matrilineal societies—including the Fante, Nzema, Ashanti, and others—are part of the larger umbrella group called Akan. The Akan group is the largest ethnic group and the only matrilineal group in Ghana.

11. Obiorah, "Facts about Akan People."

12. I distributed 300 questionnaires, and 254 were returned.

2.1 The Changing Status of Women in Contemporary African Society

The family is of preeminent importance for African people, and women play key roles in it as custodians and caregivers. This is the reason that Africans pay particular attention to the traditional domestic formation of the female child. Even as African societies progress and women are more able to escape the confinement of the domestic sphere, a woman who can neither cook nor clean is still not considered to be well-trained.

The responses in my survey seem to indicate that the traditional African view of women has changed tremendously thanks to their involvement in many different spheres of life. Even though more needs to be done, significant improvement has been recorded with respect to women's access to education, health care, and the labor market, and with respect to the variety of the contributions they make to the family. The survey responses point to an increased access for women to what are considered basic human rights (education, health, work), and through the corresponding changes, women are contributing and influencing the family unit. The paragraph below is feedback on my investigation into the educational achievement of women and their ability to contribute to family because they are gainfully employed in the labor market.

*Table 1: Feedback of Respondents on the Academic Achievement and Employment Status of Family Members*

| Employment Status of Parents | Family Members with Higher Academic Degrees |
|---|---|
| Only father is employed = 26 percent | Father = 14 percent |
| Only mother is employed = 11 percent | Mother = 13 percent |
| Both parents are employed = 57 percent | Son(s) = 41 percent |
| Both parents are unemployed = 6 percent | Daughter(s) = 32 percent |

The result of the survey shows that there is a growing number of female components of the family who are gainfully employed in the labor market. In the families of some respondents, only fathers have professional employment (26 percent), and there are families where only mothers are employed (11 percent). More than half of respondents (57 percent) stated that both their mothers and their fathers are gainfully employed, which implies that the era of the father or first son as breadwinner is phasing out.

These numbers reveal that the percentage of women with higher academic degrees is growing, and nothing enhances status and equal opportunities for employment more than education; education is the key that unlocks the door to professions and roles earlier reserved for men. Today, families who have the means typically do not hesitate to provide their daughters with an education that is equal to that received by their sons.

*Table 2: Feedback of Respondents on the Contribution to Family Life*

Another significant area of the survey concerns the dimensions of the contribution of women to the household.

| Contribution of Family Members to the Household | Dimensions of Women's Contribution to the Household |
|---|---|
| Father = 10 percent<br>Mother = 39 percent<br>Son(s) = 20 percent<br>Daughter(s) = 31 percent | Decision-making = 11 percent<br>Education of children = 19 percent<br>Management of finances = 18 percent<br>Domestic chores = 23 percent<br>Care of family members = 29 percent |

The analysis of data collected from respondents reveals that the woman's contribution is more in the allied spheres of domestic chores and care of family members. Even though some cultural roles are still restricted to men—for example, leadership roles, control of property, right to inheritance, and responsibility as legal guardian of children—women now make significant contributions to many different aspects of the life of the family: education of children, management of finances, and even decision-making, in addition to domestic care. Other chores related to caring for the household in general are gradually becoming the work of every member of the family, even though women take on the greater share of this work.

The results of my survey show that, truly, many women have attained an improved educational status and now earn wages, facts that have enhanced their financial independence. Studies have shown that in Ghana, for instance, women have registered considerable improvements in education and in the labor market. Ghana has also seen a significant growth in the number of female business leaders and female entrepreneurship, especially in garment factories. These businesses are enhancing women's self-esteem and providing opportunities and livelihoods for women employees.[13] A common difficulty they experience is how to strike a balance between work and family demands—although many women have attained higher status in society, achievements often reached in the midst of difficult life circumstances, women are not likely to abandon their domestic responsibilities. For the sake of their families, women make more compromises than men, who are not socially predisposed to equally sharing the load of parenting.

When asked if women have leadership roles in the family, 36 percent of the respondents from a patrilineal culture answered in the affirmative, 52 percent said that leadership roles and decision-making are assigned to men, and 12 percent were neutral. On the other hand, respondents stated that, even though men are regarded as family heads, women are more likely to have influence over family members (72 percent) than men (28 percent), because of their domestic responsibilities. Men's roles are more defined in terms of financial contribution and decision-making. On the other hand, there are significant differences in the responses that concerned families from matrilineal cultures, especially in the area of decision-making in the family and within the household, where respondents scored women at 80 percent. The status of women is changing in African society, and I now consider whether a similar change is occurring with the church in Africa.

## 3. Status of Women in the Church

### 3.1 Negative Perceptions of Women in Church History

This subsection of the article begins by placing the question of the church's view of women in historical perspective. It recounts the long history of wrongs done to women and to their personal identities by human cultures, wrongs which were made worse by the influence of patristic and medieval commentary, an influence that is still present in contemporary society and the church. Ancient patristic and scholastic interpretations of the Eden story—for example, those of Tertullian, John Chrysostom,

---

13. Chichester and Pluess, "From Women's Economic Participation."

Ambrose, and Thomas Aquinas—denied the woman theomorphic nature[14] and judged her inferior to man,[15] as well as morally and emotionally weak and dependent. Augustine of Hippo says

> Woman does not possess
> the image of God in herself but only when taken together with the
>     male who is her head, so
> that the whole substance is one image. But when she is assigned the
>     role as helpmate, a
> function that pertains to her alone, then she is not the image of God.
>     But as far as the man is
> concerned, he is by himself alone the image of God just as fully and
>     completely as when he
> and the woman are joined together into one.[16]

According to this way of thinking, she was destined only for the domestic sphere, in which her role was servile and strictly procreative; she was to be redeemed only through child-bearing.[17] The harshest of these ideas about women is found in the works of Tertullian and Aquinas.[18]

The thought of Tertullian, Aquinas, and others must be understood within the context of the prejudices and concerns of their times. Their distorted views of women were partly based on pagan philosophy,[19] rather than Christ's teachings or the Christian Scriptures, and were also the result of the early and medieval church's deep suspicion of sexuality.

These interpretations contributed to the festering wounds of oppression, disregard, and disparagement that women have suffered over the centuries. The perception of women began to change at the end of the

14. Tertullian and John Chrysostom, for instance, read Genesis 1:26 alongside New Testament texts like 1 Corinthians 11:7, Ephesians 5:22–24, and Colossians 3:8 as evidence that the image of God, which is an expression of dominion, is present only in the male human being. Cf. Clark, "Ideology, History, and the Construction of 'Woman,'" 176.

15. Ambrose, *De Institutione Virginis*, 4.25–31; Aquinas, *Summa Theologica*, 1.92.1; 1.99.2; 1.115.3–4.

16. Augustine of Hippo, *On the Trinity*, 7:9–10.

17. Cf. Ambrose, *De Institutione Virginis*, 4.25–31.

18. Tertullian calls woman "the devil's gateway" ("On the Apparel of Women," 4:1), while Aquinas refers to woman's inherent imperfection and calls her a "defective male" (*Summa Theologica*, 1.92, a.1).

19. For instance, Aquinas's ideas about women were influenced by Aristotle's infamous affirmation that "the female is a misbegotten male" (Aristotle, *Generation of Animals*, 2.3).

twentieth century, as a result of certain historical and cultural transformations. Credit for these transformations also lies with the modernization of Western societies,[20] and, to a lesser extent, with the sociocultural changes that arose out of feminist movements. It has become possible for women to study, attend universities, gain the right to individual freedoms, and, little by little, gain access to the professions that previously were restricted to men. In many contemporary cultural environments, no longer only in the Western world, the developments of modernity are leading to the collapse of sex-based roles.

## 3.2 The Church's Changing Perception of Women

A discernible measure of positive change in women's identity is also taking place with respect to the ministries open to women in the church. It must be admitted that the church's progress in this area is the result of broader developments in society. John XXIII described the phenomenon of the sudden entry of women into public life as among the signs of the times.[21] John Paul II appreciated these developments in his letter to women, stating,

> I cannot fail to express my admiration for those women of good will who have devoted their lives to defending the dignity of womanhood by fighting for their basic social, economic, and political rights, demonstrating courageous initiative at a time when this was considered extremely inappropriate, the sign of a lack of femininity, a manifestation of exhibitionism and even a sin![22]

In John Paul II's collection of his reflections from general audiences from 1979 to 1984 known as the "Theology of the Body," there is an understanding of the Adam-Eve relationship in terms of the complementarities of male and female and the completeness of humanity. In this document, he stated that "the presence of the feminine element, alongside the male element and together with it, signifies an enrichment for man in the whole perspective of his history, including the history of salvation."[23]

20. Cf. Scaraffia, "Socio-Cultural Changes," 15.
21. John XXIII, *Pacem in Terris*, 41.
22. John Paul II, "Letter of Pope John Paul II to Women," 6.
23. John Paul II, *Theology of the Body*, 49.

Women are now able to teach theology in universities and other institutions of higher learning,[24] teach catechism, conduct retreats, serve at Mass, participate in pastoral councils and synods, perform the function of lector, expose and repose the Blessed Sacrament, act as communion ministers, and perform baptisms. In some parts of the world—Switzerland, for instance—women also act as parish administrators with a right to employ priests visiting the parish to administer sacraments and perform other priestly duties. Despite all these developments, however, the church continues to reiterate that the ministerial priesthood is the exclusive preserve of men, even though the conversation about the possibility of women's ordination continues.

The church continues to disapprove of the admission of women to the ministerial priesthood based primarily on two arguments: (1) the ministerial priesthood is reserved only to men because the priest operates *in persona Christi*, and Christ was incarnated as a male;[25] and (2) the practice of conferring priestly ordination only to men originates with Jesus, who chose only male apostles. On the basis of this second argument, Paul VI expressed his disapproval of the Anglican Church's decision to admit women to priestly ordination.[26] In 1994, John Paul II added a third reason, saying that, since the Blessed Virgin Mary was neither an apostle nor was admitted to the ministerial priesthood, the church's practice cannot be seen as discriminating against women but is rather part of God's design.[27] The church has not moved from this position.

In 2016, however, Pope Francis set up a commission to study the possibility of admitting women to the office of deacon,[28] even though an

24. This was not possible before 1964. Cf. Garutti Bellenzier, "Identity of Women and Men," 125.

25. On October 26, 2009, Pope Benedict XVI modified canon law to clarify the distinction between deacons and priests, noting that only the latter act "in the person of Christ" and that the diaconate and priesthood are distinct ministries rather than stages in the sacrament of holy orders, thereby putting to an end the argument that women cannot be deacons because they cannot be priests. Nevertheless, the possibility of women deacons is still being debated in the church, as I describe below.

26. Cf. Paul VI, "Rescript to the Letter of His Grace," 599–600. Both reasons were also raised in the declaration *Inter Insigniores*, authored by the Congregation for the Doctrine of the Faith and issued on October 15, 1976.

27. John Paul II, *Ordinatio Sacerdotalis*, 3.

28. The commission was established in August 2016 in order to review the theology and history of the office of deacon and to investigate the roles women deacons have played in the church. Women deacons are mentioned in 1 Corinthians 9:5, Romans 16:1; 1 Timothy 3:11; Clement of Alexandria (*Stromata* 3,6.53.3–4) and Origen

ecclesiastical document has stated that admitting only men to the diaconate is a "holy tradition" that the church would not be willing to change.[29] Speaking to young people on March 19, 2018, Pope Francis told them that they can help the church fight "the logic of 'it's always been done this way,'" which he describes as "poison, a sweet poison that tranquilizes the heart and leaves you anesthetized so you can't walk."[30] The report from the 2016 commission was inconclusive; they were unable to come to agreement regarding the role of women as deacons in the early history of the church. So, in April of 2020, Pope Francis created a completely new commission to study the same topic. Because of modernization and the growing influence of women in human societies, it is clear that this discussion about the place of women and their access to ministerial roles in the church will continue.

## 4. Women and Leadership in the Church in Africa

Considerable change is happening in both the wider church and the African church, although the circumstances of the African church are unique in several ways. The resilience of the male-dominated African culture explains why the church, with its male and hierarchical leadership structure, found a friendly home in Africa. At the beginning of the evangelization of the continent, Africans were certainly very comfortable with an organization run by celibate male priests—in some parts of Africa, traditional priests were required to be celibate. The African preference for male-based systems holds even for matrilineal African cultures, in which women do not exercise leadership roles despite their influence in other areas.

---

(*Commentary on Romans*, 10:17). According to Karen Torjesen, the early Christian arts depict various roles of deaconesses, which included teaching, baptizing, leading community prayers, and physically caring for the needs of the church (*When Women Were Priests*, 10, 16). Cf. the history of the decline of the roles and ordination of women deacons in the Byzantine and Western churches in Wharton, "Ritual and Reconstructed Meaning," 358–75, and Olsen, *One Ministry, Many Roles*, 22–29, 41–60, 70.

29. This Vatican document from 1998, *Basic Norms for the Formation of Permanent Deacons*, from the Congregation for Catholic Education and the Congregation for the Clergy, affirms that the office of deacon is conferred in view of the sacrament of holy orders and that the Holy See does not contemplate allowing women into the diaconate so as to maintain a "holy tradition" (cf. Congregation for Catholic Education and Congregation for the Clergy, "Basic Norms").

30. Wooden, "Pope Francis Talks Tech, Sex, and Tattoos," para. 4.

## 4.1 The Contribution of Women to the Church in Africa

Respondents to my questionnaire list the following as among the contributions that women make to the African church: (1) they provide the largest number of members to the church generally, and specifically to church choirs; (2) they are mothers to the worshipping community through their motherly care and solicitude to priests and seminarians; 3) they are often responsible for organizing church events; (4) they contribute to and supervise charitable activities aimed at the poor, widows, orphans, and the needy; (5) they often initiate or contribute to the implementation of church projects; (6) they are active as lectors, ministers of hospitality, and teachers of catechism; and (7) some dedicate their lives to the church's apostolic work as consecrated women.

Of all my interactions during the process of gathering materials for this paper, a conversation with Barrister Mrs. Celine Ugwu, the president of the Catholic women's organization in Nigeria's Enugu diocese, provided the most interesting description of the role of women in the church. Celine said,

> The church in Nigeria is experienced as family. Family structures are largely replicated in the church. This is epitomized in the structure of the lay council, which contains within its membership every kind of person you find in a family, including men, women, and young people. The chairperson is a member of the Catholic Men's Organization (CMO), the secretary is a member of the Catholic Women's Organization (CWO), and the financial secretary and the treasurer are members of the Catholic Youth Organization of Nigeria (CYON). Within these separate duties performed in the service of a single goal, the family of God meets. Continuity is assured with the presence of young people on the council.[31]

Asked why women in Africa are comfortable with having a man as the leader and chairperson of the lay council, and if she envisions a member of the CWO becoming the chairperson, Celine said that it is a cultural thing: "It would not be out of place to have a woman as the chairperson of the council, but the man must step aside for that to happen," adding that "[w]e do not contest position with men, our husbands. What we strongly contest is any form of injustice, child trafficking, genital mutilation, or

31. Oral interview with Barrister Mrs. Celine Ugwu, the president of Catholic Women's Organization (CWO), Catholic Diocese of Enugu, Nigeria, February 8, 2018.

anything that is against human life." When questioned about her idea of leadership in the church, she said,

> What people expect from leadership is honesty, transparency, and collaboration. Leadership is the ability to carry people along. When this happens, pastoral work is done with more ease; there is support, solidarity, and love. Today, women do not want to be kept in the dark; they want to be part of the process. Any leader who does not carry women along with them is bound to fail. Priests know that they cannot achieve anything without the support of mothers.[32]

Concerning the role and contribution of women to the church, she said,

> The mothers! We are the church! We are the neck that carries the head and the body. We give the church the taste of family. We are connected to every church member; the men are our husbands, the priest is our son, the rest are our children. The church is our own; we carry the church just as we carry our families. It is our church! What women contribute to the church is enormous. We feed priests and seminarians, equip the parish house, encourage our husbands to make contributions to the church, teach indigent children, train priests, organize seminars for couples, and direct building projects, like vocational centers for young girls and primary and secondary schools.[33]

Celine Ugwu's comments represent a firsthand witness to the contributions of women to the Nigerian church. It is important to complete this picture with a description of the contributions of consecrated women to the church in Africa.

According to the Vatican's Statistical Yearbook of 2019, women religious in the church have a total population of 630,099.[34] To date, the enormous work done by women religious worldwide has remained chiefly undocumented. In a recent *Global Sisters Report*, Joyce Meyer says, "There is very little academic research about the thousands of women religious who helped build—and continue to build and rebuild—nations around the globe through education, health care, and social services,

32. Oral interview with Barrister Mrs. Celine Ugwu, the president of Catholic Women's Organization (CWO), Catholic Diocese of Enugu, Nigeria, February 8, 2018.

33. Oral interview with Barrister Mrs. Celine Ugwu, the president of Catholic Women's Organization (CWO), Catholic Diocese of Enugu, Nigeria, February 8, 2018.

34. Wooden, "Vatican's Statistical Yearbook," para. 4.

often with limited resources. I look back in amazement at women from the earliest times of Jesus who have been inspired to carry on his work among God's people. Unfortunately, these women remain a little recognized resource in the Catholic Church, missing from much of its written memory."[35]

Today, most consecrated people have embarked on a variety of challenging missions. They are health care workers; they run schools for both poor and rich and teach in institutions of higher education. They are also educators in faith, reaching out to small Christian communities to share the word of God with the people. In remote villages and cities alike, they live with and share in the daily struggles of the people, promoting their liberty, defending their dignity, and caring for the integrity of creation. Many of these apostolates are sponsored by their religious institutions, which are responsible for taking care of the sisters involved in the work. My own religious congregation, the Daughters of Divine Love, sponsors missionary work in Chad, Haiti, and Cuba.

Despite restrictions imposed by the patriarchy and hierarchy, women continue to serve the church and contribute to its growth. Just as women think about family, they also think about church. Paid, underpaid, or not paid at all, they inspire, motivate, mentor, and direct others, and their enthusiasm for God's church is constant. Very often, they have no access to the church's resources, and because they are not in official positions of leadership in the church, they do not have the authority to command the obedience of anyone, yet the growth and success of local churches largely depend on their contribution. They realize many of their achievements through their undaunted spirit and their efforts to create a sphere of influence within the restraining walls of the patriarchy. A biblical figure that provides a dramatic example for understanding the position of women in and contribution of women to the church is the Rebecca figure of Genesis 25–27.

## 5. Rebecca and the Promise Made to Abraham: Genesis 25–27

In this section, the figure of Rebecca and the role she played in the family of Isaac offer an example for explaining some of the characteristics shown as central in the leadership roles exercised by women in the church in Africa. The patriarchal and monarchic traditions that are part of Israel's

35. Meyer, "Research on Women Religious," para. 2.

history provide important categories for expressing its identity as a nation. However, it is clear that these categories alone are not sufficient to describe all of what sustains the life and identity of a nation. Of similar importance is the genealogical continuity of the nation through its matriarchs. Genesis 11:10—50:26 is the paradigmatic text that highlights Israel's reliance on God's promise, yet this section also pays a surprising amount of attention to the women who provide the legitimacy of genealogical continuity. From a genealogical point of view, what distinguishes Jacob from Esau is the character of their marriages. Esau's marriage was unlawful, because he married foreign Hittite women (Gen 26:34–35), while Jacob married women from within the kindred (Gen 28:1–2), a practice which was considered legitimate (Gen 24:2–4; 27:46; 28:1–2, 8–9). In matters regarding marriage, heirship, and descent in the family of Israelite patriarchs, the position of women in the family unit is central.[36] For this reason, the stories of Sarah, Rebecca, Leah, and Rachel are crucial to the family stories of Genesis, implying that the status of a son is connected to the status of the mother. For instance, in the Sarah-Hagar cycle, since only one son can function as Abraham's heir, the statuses of Ishmael and Isaac are derived from the statuses of their mothers, Hagar and Sarah, respectively.[37]

The story of Rebecca is found in the Isaac cycle of the patriarchal stories (Gen 25:19—35:29). She is the wife of Isaac and the mother of the twin brothers, Esau and Jacob, whose story is laden with conflict from their birth, conflict that is dramatized by their struggle inside Rebecca's womb and by Jacob gripping his elder brother's heel at birth (Gen 25:22, 26). Rebecca is remembered especially for how she contrived God's purpose for Jacob in spite of the restrictions imposed on her by patriarchy.

## 5.1 Rebecca Contrives[38] God's Purpose in a Context of Patriarchy

Rebecca's family was a domestic church on mission. Isaac was heir to the promise made to Abraham; on this promise lay the future of the family and of God's salvific plan for all of creation (Gen 12:1–3). The time came

---

36. Cf. Steinberg, *Kinship and Marriage in Genesis*, 10–11, 45.

37. Hagar was an Egyptian slave, while Sarah shared family ties with Abraham, being Abraham's half-sister (Gen 20:12).

38. A contrived action is devised in the face of pressure, especially in situations in which a normal course of action is considered to be impossible.

for Isaac to bequeath this promise on the elder of his twin sons (Gen 27:1–4), and Isaac was poised to follow convention. The text is silent as to whether he was aware of the oracle's prediction to Rebecca that the "elder shall serve the younger" (Gen 25:23). The biblical author depicts Isaac as a one-dimensional and predictable character, a man in whom there was no guile, who followed tradition and did the will of God. He asked his firstborn son, Esau, to prepare his most cherished food so that he could bless him. To Isaac, that blessing was the final traditional rite before he went to rest with his fathers.

On the other hand, for his wife Rebecca, who had complete control over the family, the bestowing of the blessing given to Abraham was not simply a traditional rite but an event of utmost importance to the future of Abraham's descendants. Rebecca, the mother who knew her sons better than anyone else, foresaw that Jacob—not Esau—was more fit to inherit the blessing.[39] As a woman in a patriarchal family, she could not openly challenge her husband's decisions or change conventional practice, so she contrived to intervene in the workings of tradition. The narrator does not say that the oracle in Genesis 25 was the reason behind her action, probably in order to dissociate God from anything unethical.

Did Rebecca hate Esau? The narrator does not judge Rebecca's actions in any way,[40] so the modern reader is also not allowed to do so, but he or she may question why Rebecca would harm her firstborn son in this way. The story itself provides no answers to this question, and no part of the story of the blessing hints at the presence of any conflict between Rebecca and her son.

However, Isaac's love for Esau and Rebecca's for Jacob (25:28) play some role in the selection of an heir, but they are not determinant. The main considerations are Esau's choice of a non-Hebrew profession and lifestyle (he was "a man of the field"; 25:27) and his lack of concern for his identity as the prospective heir to Abraham's promise. This was demonstrated in his excessive love of food (25:34) and his exogamous marriages, the latter of which made life bitter for his parents (26:34–35). His lack of concern for the fate of the promise discredited him in the eyes of his mother (27:46), but Isaac was only interested in Esau's game (25:28).

39. The reader is also told that Rebecca loved Jacob, while Isaac loved Esau (Gen 25:28).

40. The biblical authors usually do not judge the characters but instead guide the reader toward a focus on the protagonist of the story. Cf. Fokkelman, *Reading Biblical Narrative*, 148–49.

The action of Rebecca in contriving the transfer of the blessing to Jacob is set within the divine plan that the oracle introduces at the beginning of the story (25:23). The oracle establishes a program that goes against tradition and foreshadows the outcome of the story. In spite of her subordinate status as a wife, Rebecca's initiative negates that of Isaac's and actualizes the plan of God. Twice her initiative eclipses those of Isaac and Esau (Gen 27:1–4, 41–46); she is continually present in the scene, physically or not, and her actions ensure that the blessing is given to the son who would preserve it within the family.

## 5.2 Understanding Rebecca in Context

Rebecca's role and actions should be evaluated alongside those of other biblical women—wives and mothers—who played similar roles in their patriarchal families and societies. We first consider Eve and Sarah. These women seemed to have enough power to be able to make decisions about what their families should do at critical times, and the decisions they made corresponded more closely to what God wanted than other alternatives. I will also consider the New Testament's example of the Syro-Phoenician woman who played a key role in Jesus' desire to follow Jewish tradition.

### 5.2.1 Eve

Eve is the most controversial and embattled figure in the Bible. For both professional and lay interpreters of the biblical story, she is a model of disobedience and a deceiver who joined forces with the serpent to release the powers of evil into human history; her action is the source of much of the negative view of the female gender. Many scholars have blamed the role assigned to Eve on the misogynist culture of the biblical writers, but I see these interpretations as a deep misunderstanding of the *literary* role of Eve in the story of the garden. I do not think Eve has been assigned blame because of an intention to discredit and victimize women. Instead, I see a consistent effort by the biblical narrators to show that women of various backgrounds—whether good, evil, wise, foolish, sick, healthy, immoral, or moral—enjoy a special connection to God and his purposes. This view of Eve, whose action had such a negative cosmic effect, results in the conclusion that she is the only character in the Eden story whose dramatic viewpoint represents the mind of God. What the church fathers called the first sin—"the Happy Fall"—is not an accident in the history of salvation. It made necessary the incarnation, which is an integral part of God's plan.[41]

It must be understood that Eve's negative action serves the theological purpose of explaining the journey that created reality must make toward divinity. According to Paul, "God imprisoned all in disobedience that he might show mercy to them all" (Rom 11:32). According to John Paul II, the dominion of man over woman suggested by Genesis 3:16 is an evil that every human being, male and female, must strive to overcome.[42] Eve represents humanity in crisis, while Mary embodies humanity restored, but both are active collaborators with God's purpose for the world.

### 5.2.2 Sarah (Genesis 12–25)

Sarah, the wife of Abraham, remained barren for many years despite God's promise that Abraham would have innumerable descendants. Sarah's barrenness was a setback in the realization of God's promise. When she could not bear the trauma of barrenness, Sarah encouraged Abraham to give her a child by her Egyptian maidservant (Gen 16:2), and Ishmael was born. Ishmael became Abraham's legitimate firstborn son and the heir to the promise. After the birth of Ishmael, Abraham seemed to forget about the prospect of having a son from Sarah. But after receiving God's reassurance that he would establish his everlasting covenant with him through Sarah's son (Gen 17:15–16), and in consideration of Abraham's strong faith in God's promise, Isaac was born. Isaac's birth introduced another conflict into Abraham's family as to who would inherit the promise. According to tradition, Ishmael as the firstborn son had a legitimate claim to it. Sarah decided that Ishmael should be sent away, an opinion that distressed Abraham (Gen 21:8–11). But God tells Abraham, "Whatever Sarah says to you, do as she tells you for it is through Isaac that offspring shall be named for you" (Gen 21:12). In this situation of conflict, Sarah appears unreasonably wicked, oppressive, and unjust, but her point of view corresponds to what God ordained through the promise.

41. The phrase, *O Felix Culpa* (Oh, Happy Fall), was first used by Augustine (*Confessions and Enchiridion*, viii;) and was developed further by Thomas Aquinas in his *Summa*: ". . . For God allows evils to happen in order to bring a greater good there from" (*Summa Theologica* III, q. 1, a. 3, ad. 3).

42. John Paul II, *Mulieris Dignitatem*, 10.

*5.2.3 The Syro-Phoenician Woman (Mark 7:24–30 and Matt 15:21–28)*

The Syro-Phoenician woman's dialogue with Jesus brought about a change in his pastoral strategy. She vehemently challenged Jesus' decision to limit his activities to benefiting Israel alone, and her faith encouraged Jesus to begin a ministry among the gentiles at a time when he did not intend to (Matt 15:28).

All of these women had the ability to devise a plan of successful action in situations of constraint or deprivation. Women were able to do this because of their multidimensional traits. Women are typically more involved in situations of brokenness. They are more flexible and prone to compromise their comfort for the achievement of institutional goals or for their loved ones. Many readers of the biblical texts have judged the actions of these women to be unethical or even wicked. However, their actions must be seen within the bigger picture of what happens at the fringes, or outside the traditions, of human society. In the bigger picture, God often makes human experiences of weakness the preferred backdrop for divine revelation.

## 6. Conclusion

It was my intention in this chapter to draw attention to two important things. The first is the human family, in which women play important roles. At the center of the family is the woman, whose resourcefulness and maternal solicitude accompany the family in its joys and buoy it in its sorrows. A necessary prerequisite to developing a theology of family for the African church is pastoral attention to the daily stories of modern families and the changing face of relationships within the family. As the church, we must allow these stories to open our minds and senses to God's way of embracing human beings. This is especially necessary for believers because family life is replicated in the church.

The second is women's openness to the mystery of God, which I think is intimately connected to their role as mothers and nurturers of life. In the patriarchal narratives of Genesis, the oracle announced God's choice of Jacob to Rebecca while she was pregnant, and Abraham was asked to listen to Sarah when inheritance was at stake. The mystery of the incarnation was announced to Mary and not to Joseph. These examples demonstrate that women's commitment to the purpose of God is unique. This special charism stands out especially in situations in which the achievement of God's purpose might be compromised by adhering to conventional practices or tradition. The Bible does not typically give women a prominent or significant place in official religious institutions or their administration, but the way in which their perspective is uniquely connected to God must not be overlooked. Because of their role in the family, women are more in touch with human misery than men and seem to have a greater grasp of the complexities of human situations and of how the life of each individual fits into the perspective of God.

In the African church, women see themselves as the neck that carries the head and the body. A church that defines itself as the family of God must recognize the crucial role that women play in the family and in the church. The church has yet to reap the fruits of evangelization that could spring from making full use of the numerous gifts and charisms of women. In order to accomplish this, the church must embrace diversity, take stock of the gifts of all of the members of the church, and work out the ways in which all members might be integrated into full participation in the church according to those gifts.

Finally, it is clear that what underpins today's controversies over the role of women in the institutionalized church is the challenges created by the relationship between men and women over the course of human history. The question of the relationship between men and women is a cosmic one, involving very sensitive and complex matters. The book of Proverbs describes it as being among the most difficult and incomprehensible realities in human existence when it says, "Three things are too wonderful for me; four, I do not understand: the way of an eagle in the sky, the way of a snake on a rock, the way of a ship on the high seas, and the way of a man with a girl" (Prov 30:18–19). Most of the mysteries regarding the movement of the eagle, the snake, and the ship have been deciphered by science. The relationship between a man and a woman, however, remains enigmatic, and this article does not pretend to unlock the enigma. As the joke is told, man does not understand woman, because on the day God created her, the man was sleeping.

## Bibliography

Ambrose. *De Institutione Virginis*. Turnhout, Belgium: Brepols, 2010.
Aquinas, Thomas. *Summa Theologica*. Translated by the Fathers of the English Dominican Province. New York: Ave Maria, 1981.

Aristotle. *Generation of Animals*. Translated by Arthur L. Peck. Cambridge, MA: Harvard University Press, 1942.

Augustine of Hippo, and Albert C. Outler. *Confessions and Enchiridion*. Philadelphia: Westminster, 1955.

Augustine of Hippo, et al. *On the Trinity*. Cambridge: Cambridge University Press, 2002.

Chichester, Ouida, and Jessica Davis Pluess. "From Women's Economic Participation to Empowerment: Insights from Ghana." *Our Insights* (*blog*), June 20, 2016. https://www.bsr.org/en/our-insights/blog-view/from-womens-economic-participation-to-empowerment-insights-from-ghana.

Chittister, Joan. *Women, Ministry, and the Church*. New York: Paulist, 1983.

Clark, Elizabeth A. "Ideology, History, and the Construction of 'Woman' in Late Ancient Christianity." *Journal of Early Christian Studies* 2.2 (1994) 155–84.

Clement of Alexandria. "The Stromata, Books 1–3." In *Alexandrian Christianity: Selected Translations of Clement and Origen*, edited by John Ernest Leonard Oulton and Henry Chadwick, 15–93. The Library of Christian Classics 2. Philadelphia: Westminster, 1954.

Congregation for Catholic Education and Congregation for the Clergy. "Basic Norms for the Formation of Permanent Deacons: Directory for the Ministry and Life of Permanent Deacons." *Vatican.va*, March 31, 1998. http://www.vatican.va/roman_curia/congregations/ccatheduc/documents/rc_con_ccatheduc_doc_31031998_directorium-diaconi_en.html.

Diaz de Pfennich, Maria Eugenia. "Participation and Collaboration in the Life of the Church." In *Men and Women: Diversity and Mutual Complementarity*, edited by Pontificium Consilium Pro Laicis, 175–80. Vatican City: Libreria Editrice Vaticana, 2006.

Fokkelman, Jan P. *Reading Biblical Narrative: An Introductory Guide*. Louisville: Westminster John Knox, 1999.

Garutti Bellenzier, Maria Teresa. "The Identity of Women and Men According to the Teaching of the Church." In *Men and Women: Diversity and Mutual Complementarity: Study Seminar, Vatican City, 30–31, January 2004*, edited by Pontificium Consilium Pro Laicis, 101–29. Vatican City: Libreria Editrice Vaticana, 2006.

John XXIII, Pope. *Pacem in Terris*. *Vatican.va*, April 11, 1964. http://www.vatican.va/content/john-xxiii/en/encyclicals/documents/hf_j-xxiii_enc_11041963_pacem.html.

John Paul II, Pope. "Ecclesia in Africa." *Vatican.va*, September 14, 1995. https://www.vatican.va/content/john-paul-ii/en/apost_exhortations/documents/hf_jp-ii_exh_14091995_ecclesia-in-africa.html.

———. "Letter of Pope John Paul II to Women." *Vatican.va*, June 29, 1995. http://www.vatican.va/content/john-paul-ii/en/letters/1995/documents/hf_jp-ii_let_29061995_women.html.

———. *Mulieris Dignitatem*. *Vatican.va*, August 15, 1988. https://www.vatican.va/content/john-paul-ii/en/apost_letters/1988/documents/hf_jp-ii_apl_15081988_mulieris-dignitatem.html.

———. *Ordinatio Sacerdotalis*. *Vatican.va*, May 22, 1994. http://www.vatican.va/content/john-paul-ii/en/apost_letters/1994/documents/hf_jp-ii_apl_19940522_ordinatio-sacerdotalis.html.

———. *The Theology of the Body: Human Love in the Divine Plan.* Boston: Pauline, 1997.

Meyer, Joyce. "Research on Women Religious Identifies Trends, Establishes Framework for Tracking Changes." *Global Sisters Report,* October 16, 2020. https://www.globalsistersreport.org/news/religious-life/blog/research-women-religious-identifies-trends-establishes-framework-tracking.

Moloi, Vusi. "The Organic Roots of African Matrilineal Society." *Africa Unbound* 2 (2008). https://africaunbound.org/index.php/aumagazine/issue-2/item/the-organic-roots-of-the-african-matrilineal-society.html.

Mugambi, Jesse Ndwiga Kanyua. *Christianity and African Culture.* Nairobi: Acton, 2009.

Narayan, Anjana. "Matrilineal Society." *Encyclopedia Britannica.* https://www.britannica.com/topic/matrilineal-society.

Nnamani, Amuluche G. "The Ambivalent Impact of Pentecostalism on Enculturation." In *The New Religious Movements: Pentecostalism in Perspective,* edited by Amuluche G. Nnamani, 235–49. Benin City, Nigeria: Ava, 2007.

Obiorah, Chuka. "Facts about Akan People, Language, Religion, and Culture." *BuzzGhana.com,* 2018. https://buzzghana.com/akan/.

Olsen, Jeannine E. *One Ministry, Many Roles: Deacons and Deaconesses through the Centuries.* St. Louis: Concordia, 1992.

Origen. *Commentary on the Epistle to the Romans, Books 6–10.* Fathers of the Church 104. Translated by Thomas P. Scheck. Washington, DC: Catholic University of America Press, 2002.

Paul VI, Pope. *Lumen Gentium: Dogmatic Constitution on the Church.* In *The Sixteen Documents of Vatican II,* edited by Marianne Lorraine Trouvé, 111–202. Boston: Pauline, 1999.

———. *Perfectae Caritatis: Decree on the Adaptation and Renewal of Religious Life.* In *The Sixteen Documents of Vatican II,* edited by Marianne Lorraine Trouvé, 303–26. Boston: Pauline, 1999.

———. "Rescript to the Letter of His Grace, the Most Reverend Dr. E. D. Cogan, Archbishop of Canterbury, On the Priestly Ministry of Women." *Acta Apostolicae Sedis* 68 (1976) 599–600.

Sacred Congregation for the Doctrine of the Faith. *Inter Insigniores. Vatican.va,* October 15, 1976. http://www.vatican.va/roman_curia/congregations/cfaith/documents/rc_con_cfaith_doc_19761015_inter-insigniores_en.html.

Scaraffia, Lucetta. "Socio-Cultural Changes in Women's Lives." In *Men and Women: Diversity and Mutual Complementarity,* edited by Pontificium Consilium Pro Laicis, 15–22. Vatican City: Libreria Editrice Vaticana, 2006.

Steinberg, Naomi. *Kinship and Marriage in Genesis.* Minneapolis: Fortress, 1993.

Tertullian. "On the Apparel of Women." In *Fathers of the Third Century: Tertullian, Part Fourth; Minucius Felix; Commodian; Origen, Parts First and Second,* edited by Alexander Roberts et al., 14–26. Ante-Nicene Fathers: Translations of the Writings of the Fathers Down to A.D. 325, Vol. 4. 10 vols. Buffalo, NY: Christian Literature, 1885.

Torjesen, Karen. *When Women Were Priests: Women's Leadership in the Early Church and the Scandal of Their Subordination in the Rise of Christianity.* San Francisco: Harper, 1993.

Uchem, Rose N. *Overcoming Women's Subordination in the Igbo African Culture and in the Catholic Church: Envisioning an Inclusive Theology with Reference to Women.* Irvine, CA: Dissertation.com, 2001.

Wharton, Annabel J. "Ritual and Reconstructed Meaning: The Neonian Baptistery in Ravenna." *The Art Bulletin* 69.3 (1987) 358–75.

Wooden, Cindy. "Pope Francis Talks Tech, Sex, and Tattoos with Young Adults." *America*, March 19, 2018. https://www.americamagazine.org/faith/2018/03/19/pope-francis-talks-tech-sex-and-tattoos-young-adults.

———. "The Vatican's Statistical Yearbook Has a List for (Almost) Everything You Need to Know about the Catholic Church." *America,* April 9, 2021. https://www.americamagazine.org/faith/2021/04/09/vatican-statistical-yearbook-catholic-lists-top-five-240422.

# 8

# Catholic Women's Movements in Asia: Redefining Faith for the Twenty-First Century

JEANE CAÑA PERACULLO

## The Continuing Power of Religion in the Face of Secularization

MANY FEMINIST SCHOLARS OF religion and politics have observed that the conceptual categories of women and gender are not really taken seriously in these fields. Elizabeth Pritchard observes that "[f]eminist scholars of religion as well as scholars of gender in multiple disciplines have done careful work sifting through religion's persistence, pointing to its proclivity for producing conservative gender codes and boundaries, as well as its capacity to offer women new leadership roles and political platforms."[1] In the current scholarship, which is often focused on the postcolonial reality of many societies, the study of religion itself is discounted because religion is thought to be part of the experience of colonization; that is, an influence that needs to be overcome. This view considers that resistance and agency cannot take place within religious parameters.[2] The process of secularization also adds to this complex reality. Any attempt by some women to appeal to religion as emancipatory might be seen as suspicious

---

1. Pritchard, "Special Introduction," 5.

2. Auga, "Decolonizing Public Space," 49–68; Giorgi, "Gender, Religion, and Political Agency," 51–72.

because those with secular points of view see religion as a hindrance to social issues such as freedom and justice.

However, a growing body of scholarship has emerged in Europe and North America that has acknowledged that instead of a march toward inevitable secularization and a systematic discounting of the importance of religion, a countervailing movement of sacralization, or making-sacred, is taking place and gaining ground, especially in non-Western contexts. The sociologist Grace Davie has observed that some scholars have already recognized this trend and that it has changed the way they think about modernization and secularization.[3] These scholars have been forced to come to grips with the fact that for most people in most parts of the world, to be religious is an integral part of their modern identity, not a reaction to it.

There are many questions about whether this trend is a good thing. Religion and religious practices often do not appear to have the potential to transform social and political life—on the contrary, religion typically seems to be more aligned with ideological constructs that uphold systemic violence, constructs that manifest themselves in sexism, nationalism, fundamentalism, racism, ethnocentrism, transphobia, and other unwelcome points of view. In this regard, the anthropologist Saba Mahmood, in her groundbreaking work *Politics of Piety: The Islamic Revival and the Feminist Subject*, asks pointed questions about what kinds of religious practices have the potential to transform social and political life.

Many feminists around the world steer clear from or express disdain for religion. One practice that has been the subject of frequent comment is the wearing of the hijab by Muslim women; the requirement that they do so has often been characterized as overly restrictive and controlling. As the Indonesian feminist Diah Ariani Arimbi has observed, "Commonly for many in the West the veil is immediately correlated with 'seclusion' and 'politically charged with connotations of the inferior "other,"' implying and assuming a subordination and inferiority of Muslim women."[4]

Despite this, however, it would seem that many non-Western women have embraced their religious identity, even if by doing so they might be seen by Western feminists to be cowering in submission to patriarchy. How is it that feminism and feminist principles, which originated in

3. Davie, "Thinking Sociologically about Religion," 21.

4. Arimbi, *Reading Contemporary Indonesian Muslim Women Writers*, 36.

the West, can be compatible with religion and its seemingly antiwomen nature?

Mahmood criticizes a Western feminism that emphasizes a certain kind of agency that is anchored in the Enlightenment values of freedom and autonomy. She argues that this agency sharply limits our ability to understand and interrogate the lives of women whose desires, affect, and will have been shaped by nonliberal traditions.[5] Mahmood discusses two cases in making her point. One is the women's mosque movement in Egypt, and the other the women's piety movement in Indonesia. The counterdiscourse offered by these movements led Mahmood to suggest that "we think of agency not as a synonym for resistance to relations of domination, but as a capacity for action that historically specific relations of subordination enable and create."[6]

The women's mosque movement in Egypt involves women and girls studying the Qur'an in a formalized manner in schools, houses, or mosques. Traditionally, lessons in the Qur'an are offered in mosques to males only.[7]

The women's piety movement in Indonesia is known as Tarbiyah Bukan PKS. Many see the Tarbiyah movement as mirroring the radical Islamist movement in the Middle East known as Ikhwanul Muslimin (the Muslim Brotherhood). However, for Indonesian Muslim women, the only "radicalness" expressed in the movement is their radical love for Allah. They see veiling as a manifestation of religious freedom in both the private and public spheres.[8]

The women and girls who have joined these groups do not just study the Qur'an,[9] but are also provided platforms to express their devotion to Islam as they go about navigating the secular world. Mahmood refers to some of the issues that are discussed in these groups, such as what a devout Muslim woman should do if she is sexually harassed on public transportation, what it means to have a sexual dream, how to police one's desires, what is the proper way to relate to a man to whom one is betrothed, and what to do if a woman finds out that her daughter has had an extramarital affair. In these groups, women feel comfortable raising

5. Mahmood, *Politics of Piety*, 23
6. Mahmood, "Feminist Theory, Embodiment, and the Docile Agent," 203.
7. Mahmood, "Feminist Theory, Embodiment, and the Docile Agent," 202.
8. Arimbi, *Reading Contemporary Indonesian Muslim Women Writers*, 64.
9. Mahmood, *Politics of Piety*, 153–88.

queries about matters both private and public that they would not raise elsewhere.

Mahmood highlights the dilemma faced by feminist analysis. In many postreligious, secular societies, women's liberation is achieved when they are able to participate in the political, economic, and social spheres, which have previously been overwhelmingly the domain of men. There is, however, a question about whether women are truly emancipated when, despite the fact that they can assert their presence in spheres previously defined by men, the idioms they use to accomplish this are grounded in discourses that have historically secured their subordination to male authority. This question arises from the fact that women's subordination to feminine virtues like shyness, modesty, and humility, appears to be a necessary condition for enhancing their public role in religious and political life.[10]

Mahmood concluded that when we talk about agency, which is a component of resistance, we need to reconfigure its usual starting points of freedom and autonomy. For Mahmood,

> viewed in this way, what may appear to be a case of deplorable passivity and docility from a progressivist point of view, may actually be a form of agency—but one that can be understood only from within the discourses and structures of subordination that create the conditions of its enactment. In this sense, agentival capacity is entailed not only in those acts that resist norms but also in the multiple ways in which one inhabits norms.[11]

Mahmood underlines that agency may be found not only in resisting dominant discourses, but also in the inhabiting of norms. The consequence of this is that religion can be understood to open up possibilities.

## Redefining the Role of Faith in the Public Sphere in the Twenty-First Century

Jürgen Habermas cautions liberal, secular political philosophers against dismissing the role of religion in political spaces as being no longer relevant or almost extinct. In his article "Religion in the Public Sphere," Habermas describes an important quality present in people whose religion informs their political lives:

10. Mahmood, *Religious Difference in a Secular Age*, 5–6.
11. Mahmood, *Religious Difference in a Secular Age*, 14.

It is their conviction that they ought to strive for wholeness, integrity, integration in their lives: that they ought to allow the Word of God, the teachings of the Torah, the command and example of Jesus, or whatever, to shape their existence as a whole, including them, their social and political existence. Their religion is not, for them, about something other than their social and political existence. Their religiously grounded concept of justice tells them what is politically correct or incorrect; meaning that they are incapable of discerning "any pull" from any secular reasons.[12]

This important article contributes to a growing awareness that the world is gripped in our postsecular times by a renewed interest in the centrality of religion in people's social and political lives. Religion is firmly back in the public sphere.[13]

Faith as expressed in the twenty-first century relates not only to religion as it is lived every day or to particular ways of living that are anchored in belief in a supernatural being or beings but also to how such belief contributes to convictions and resulting actions that extend into the public sphere. Pronouncements about this topic are often found in the mission statements of faith-based movements.

This article examines two important Catholic women's movements/organizations in Asia whose work proceeds from the current understanding of the relationship between faith and matters of public interest, namely, Ecclesia of Women in Asia (EWA) and Wanita Katolik Republik Indonesia (WKRI). EWA is a transnational organization of Asian Catholic women theologians, and WKRI is a women's organization based in Indonesia.

## Asian Catholic Women's Movements

Philosophical literature describes Asia as being largely in the grip of Western epistemological trajectories. Some Westerners may think of Asia as that bunch of countries lying east of the West. The fact that Asia encompasses 30 percent of the earth's total land mass is mostly ignored, and the countries that lie within it are mentally thrown together in one indistinguishable heap by some who are ignorant about geography. In actual fact, the peoples, regions, and countries of Asia are markedly different

12. Habermas, "Religion in the Public Sphere," 8.
13. Davie, *Sociology of Religion*, xvii.

from one another. Asia claims to be the birthplace of many of the world's major religions and spiritual traditions. This fact alone is a testament to the continent's cultural diversity.

For the purposes of this article, it is important to unpack the notion of "Asia" as seamlessly connected in terms of culture and identity. This unpacking is especially necessary to a consideration of gender and religion, as these exist in Asia in order to highlight the participation of women in the life of the church, the peculiarities of church members' lived experiences that shape their participation in faith-based social movements, the catalysts that paved the way for the rise of these movements, and the challenges of redefining faith in postsecular times.

## Ecclesia of Women in Asia: Herstory

EWA is a feminist forum of women doing theology both in the academy and at the grassroots level in Asia. EWA defines its convictions and sense of purpose in its Vision-Mission Statement: "Ecclesia of Women in Asia is committed to the formation of inclusive and just ecclesial communities and societies by doing theology from Asian women's perspectives and by the recognition of Asian Catholic women as equal partners in the life of the Church."[14]

"Ecclesia of Women" is an especially fraught phrase in a Catholic context that is dominated by the church's dogma. The sheer immense physicality of the Vatican announcing the Catholic Church's masculinist and imperialist core, juxtaposed with a community of Asian Catholic women interacting in cyberspace because it does not have a physical office or building or church, presents a stark contrast. Because of its very liminality, the space inhabited by EWA, which is neither geographical nor physical, becomes a place to announce publicly that a church of the marginalized does not have to remain invisible. The resulting visibility is an affirmation that the relationship between religion and faith does not have to be a private matter and is an affirmation that resistance is possible. A further characteristic of the resulting visibility is that feminist theology in Asia should not be understood as only an intellectual discipline or as a mere rational reflection on Christian faith.[15]

14. Ecclesia of Women in Asia, "Constitution and By-laws," para. 2.
15. Pui Lan, *Introducing Asian Feminist Theology*, 32.

The use of "Asia" in the acronym EWA is a deliberate attempt to properly frame the term. It is meant to highlight both a particular and a general way of looking at Asia—particular because of the use of a Catholic, feminist lens, and general because it focuses on the different countries of the region coming together to pursue shared goals. By this act of framing, EWA correctly renders "Asia" a metaphor for the real and imagined spaces that the continent includes and encompasses. A proper use of metaphor produces a flash of insight, making it possible to grasp a continuum that exists between dissimilar events, objects, and situations and to draw similarities between them. The creation of illuminating metaphors also echoes what Sri Lankan theologian R. S. Sugirtharajah deems to be the work of postcolonialism, which essentially involves a "style of inquiry, an insight or a perspective, a catalyst, a new way of life."[16]

The story of EWA began when, at a conference organized by the Asian Federation of Catholic Bishops' Conferences (AFCBC), the four women theologians present, greatly outnumbered, wondered, "Where are the women theologians? Are there more women doing theology in Asia based on the experience of women?" These questions spurred a subsequent conference specifically for women doing theology in Asia. This event is described on EWA's website as "a historic attempt at making Asian Catholic women seen and heard, women theologians from all over Asia gathered . . . [in] Bangkok, Thailand, for a five-day conference held on 24th–29th November 2002 entitled 'Ecclesia of Women in Asia: Gathering the Voices of the Silenced.'"[17] Thirty papers were presented on various themes: women and violence, women and spirituality, women and church structures, ecofeminism and theological method, women and the Bible, and women and world religions. "Ecclesia" was reimagined as a "democratic assembly of free citizens." By 2022, twenty years later, EWA had organized a total of ten conferences.

In 2011, the Congregation for the Doctrine of the Faith initiated a crackdown on the Leadership Conference of Women Religious (LCWR) for their alleged "radical feminism." This move was a flexing of the immense dogmatic muscles of the Catholic Church hierarchy aimed at silencing and ultimately forcing these so-called renegade women to toe the line by appointing bishops to leadership positions within the LCWR. The crackdown had a worldwide chilling effect on religious nuns in general

16. Sugirtharajah, *Postcolonial Criticism and Biblical Interpretation*, 13.

17. Ecclesia of Women in Asia, "EWA's Herstory."

and feminist theologian in particular, even though the loud objections to this censure also reverberated around the world. At the same time as it took this action, the congregation also declared that a book authored by the theologian Margaret Farley, *Just Love: A Framework for Christian Sexual Ethics*, contained "false" theology harmful to the faithful. Critics, however, suspect that this book was singled out because its subject, sexual ethics, made it indecent in the eyes of the clerical vanguard.[18]

So why did EWA convene a conference of Asian feminist theologians in 2004 to speak and write about the body and sexuality? The Filipino feminist theologian Agnes Brazal, who was EWA's coordinator for the 2004 conference and one of the editors of the book *Body and Sexuality: Theological Pastoral Perspectives of Women in Asia*, which collected the papers from the conference, explained in her opening remarks at the conference that the theme was in recognition of EWA's special role in promoting contextual theology rooted in the embodied experiences of women. The theme also highlighted how the seemingly innocent, innocuous words "body" and "sexuality," when framed by religious discourse, could be either demeaning or liberating to women. Brazal noted that women's bodies are at the very center of certain power dynamics that both include and exclude women at the same time. These power dynamics are inclusive in the sense that a spotlight on women's bodies highlights the special power of women that can be a starting point in intercultural theologizing; they are exclusive because the dominant discourses around women's bodies in theology can be essentialist.

EWA engages in a deliberate reclaiming of words like "silenced," "broken," "bent," "erotic," and "queer" in order to destabilize stereotypes of the female body. Stereotyping, according to postcolonial theorist Homi Bhabha, is an attempt to fixate. "Fixity, as the sign of cultural/historical/racial difference in the discourse of colonialism is a paradoxical mode of representation: it connotes rigidity and an unchanging order as well as disorder, degeneracy, and daemonic repetition."[19] In other words, one's identity—though crafted, informed, and motivated by one's colonialist past—transcends it. I am more than what shaped me; the whole is always greater than the sum of all its parts. EWA reimagines and redefines what it means to be a church that is truly inclusive: a deliberate embracing of those who were (and still are) silenced, broken, bent, indecent, and queer.

---

18. Speciale, "Vatican Censors Nun's Book," and Traina, "Just Love," 712–14.

19. Bhabha, *Location of Culture*, 94.

*Body and Sexuality: Knitting Diversity*
*Out of a Convergence of Theological Methods*

The inaugural 2002 EWA conference was a call for Asian Catholic wom-en to come out of invisibility and into the spotlight, and for this reason, the call for papers and participation was broad. Papers were received on topics related to liberation theology, social justice, and feminism, among other topics. Because of the prevailing influence of Latin American theo-logians doing theology of the poor, most Catholic theologians in Asia operate under the paradigm of liberation theology promoted by the Ecumenical Association of Third World Theologians (EATWOT), which has members from Latin America, Africa, and Asia. It is not surprising that women theologians and pastoral workers are heavily geared towards social justice. Most women theologians (as opposed to grassroots work-ers) have been exposed to feminism, especially Western feminism, an exposure that adds an additional dimension to their analysis. For these theologians, gender is an epistemological lens that can be used to do con-textual theology. The content of the papers suggests that they were fully abreast of current feminist discourses.

While there is no chapter in *Body and Sexuality* that contains the term "postcolonialism" in the title or that explicitly identifies it as the conceptual framework being employed, we can glean from the chap-ter titles ("Revisioning Eros," "The Pauline Body as a Metaphor of the Whole Human Being," "Re-imaging Woman and Reshaping her Destiny," "Women Re-living the Eucharist," "Queer Revisions of Christianity," and "Theologizing on Difference") that the methodology of postcolonialism was in fact liberally employed. And while there is no chapter dealing exclusively with a theoretical take on resistance, which is one of the hall-marks of the postcolonial method as outlined by R. S. Sugirtharajah in *Postcolonial Criticism and Biblical Interpretation*, the arguments, themes, and language of the chapters embodies strong resistance.

In *Body and Sexuality*, we see a convergence of feminist, liberation-ist, and postcolonial methodological frameworks. The classic hermeneu-tic circle of "experience-reflection-action" used in liberation theology was expanded and deepened by feminism. The first of these steps ("ex-perience"), which was on display in the contextual feminist theologizing featured in the conference's various workshops, was to identify and char-acterize the experience of contemporary Asian women. As part of this process, women were encouraged to ask why this experience is critical, which religious and cultural beliefs have reinforced dominant perspectives on the experience, who has suffered as a result of these perspectives, what is the nature of this suffering, and who has profited from this suffering. Questions like, "Are there local cultural categories that can help provide a lens for looking at this experience differently?" were asked. The process then proceeded from identification and analysis to the gathering of insights relevant to analyzing the experience culled from the days together at the conference. This second step ("reflection") involved a rereading of scriptural and theological tradition as these relate to body and sexuality. As in the first step, local cultural categories were employed to assist with this rereading. Finally, the third step ("action") is related to concrete pastoral actions that directly affect women's lives—specifically, how a newer and more explicit theology on body and sexuality could help women live better lives, and what deeper theological examinations or pastoral action, or strategizing, everyone could undertake about body and sexuality.

## Body and Sexuality: Feminism Enriched by Postcolonialism

The theological methodology outlined above closely follows the steps of the hermeneutical circle as outlined by Juan Luis Segundo in his book *Liberation of Theology*.[20] Gemma Cruz's essay in *Body and Sexuality*, "Em-body-ing Theology: Theological Reflections on the Experience of Filipina Domestic Workers in Hong Kong," is an example of Segundo's theological method. Cruz presents the case that looking at the particular experiences of women helps uncover multiple levels of oppression that can only be understood by reflecting on the impacts of differences in class, race, and ethnicity on the lives of particular women. These multiple levels of oppression are played out in the bodies of Filipina domestic workers. Culturally, Filipinas are viewed as the primary caregivers of the family—a role in which they have been simultaneously revered and enslaved. Like all other forms of oppression, the oppression inherent in this role has become embedded in their collective consciousness, causing them to define themselves by it. Remittances from overseas domestic workers are the country's main sources of precious US dollars, and yet Filipinas who perform this work are quite vulnerable to the forces of the gendered economy of globalization, as well as the antimigrant domestic

20. Segundo, *Liberation of Theology*, 116.

policies of Hong Kong. "In many ways, the migration of the Filipina DHs [domestic helpers] in Hong Kong is gendered. The stereotyping of women with domestic work alone reflects how the politics of gender is at play, first of all, in the global economy."[21] According to Cruz, a responsive theology is born when the experiences of the most vulnerable are identified and analyzed.

The contributions to *Body and Sexuality* raise questions about the implications of drawing on the resources of one's culture to destabilize the dominant worldview. Does doing so imply a claim that one's cultural tradition is just as good as others, if not better? On the global stage, do all actors get equal billing? What does it take for a former colonial subject to take pride in her own culture—preferably a culture as it existed before the colonial onslaught—and claim legitimacy for it?

In the chapter, "Bodily Representations of Hindu Goddesses," Metti Amirtham argues that worship of female Hindu goddesses is in tension with the actual situations of Indian women. Hindu representations of goddesses are inconsistent with the realities of poor Indian women who are denied access to basic education and property rights. Married women are regarded as the personal property of their husbands, while unmarried women are regarded as such by their fathers. Moreover, for Amirtham, these women are oppressed by the impossibly beautiful representations of Hindu goddesses.[22] She draws from the representations of popular Hindu goddesses (e.g., Lakshmi, Saraswati, Parvati, and Kali) in temples and artworks across India. These goddesses are worshipped because they possess *shakti*,[23] which is missing in male gods. They are the consorts of male gods but are themselves worshipped because their male counterparts would be frankly helpless without them. Amirtham notes that India is one of the few civilizations that has retained goddess worship and presents it as a vital aspect of religious life in India.[24]

It is important to note that first-wave Western feminist theology was preoccupied with reclaiming the female face, aspect, and nature of God. Women's power was strongly present in ancient times, as evidenced in

---

21. Cruz, "Em-body-ing Theology," 61.

22. Amirtham, "Bodily Representations of Hindu Goddesses," 258–61.

23. See Joseph, "Re-visioning Eros for Asian Feminist Theologizing," 38. According to Joseph, *shakti* refers to the primordial force from coiled energy that emanates from the lowest *chakra,* or energy fount, that is located at the base of the spine. *Shakti* is believed to be a source of creative power.

24. Amirtham, "Bodily Representations of Hindu Goddesses," 253.

myth and legend and by archeological discoveries of numerous female images, but the goddess image was slain and replaced by God, a male and father figure.[25] The image of God as father represents a new level of thinking about divinity, but its elements were already present in the Great Goddess, which developed from the image of the Great Mother.

It is in these considerations that we can see how the postcolonial method enriches contextual feminist theologizing. R. S. Sugirtharajah describes the need for "coding" and "decoding"[26] and for doing so with respect to one's own culture, because it has now become imperative that culture becomes a *locus theologicus*, the nature of which, according to Bhabha, is continually defined and redefined, contested, and interrogated by people entering and exiting the culture, who often bring with them the ideas of modernity and liberalism. These ideas are frequently used to interrogate "native" cultures, which in the process of doing so, are often found wanting.[27] On the other hand, the act of interrogating enables Amirtham, a Christian Indian woman, to look even closer at Kali's "black face, disheveled hair, and naked body."[28] Kali's emaciated body and menacing eyes seem to mock other goddesses in temples who are adorned (burdened?) by jewels, flowers, and beautiful saris while she stands outside guarding the gates of villages. Amirtham had not encountered Kali for much of her life, because her strict Catholic upbringing forbade her from entering temples or scrutinizing the faces of Hindu goddesses. But now when she did encounter Kali, she marveled at what Kali represents for village women and how her worship can help feminist theologians articulate a divine that is disruptive, erotic, and no-nonsense.

25. Not, however, in Hinduism, judging by the continuing worship of goddesses in that religion.

26. R. S. Sugirtharajah originally meant these terms to be applied to the scriptures as part of the postcolonial methodology. "Coding" a text means understanding it according to its context and milieu, according to how a particular passage in the text was understood by the people of the time and according to how gender, race, and ethnicity are highlighted or relegated to the background. "Decoding" a text involves being aware of hegemonic discourses: Who is speaking? Who is silent or silenced (Sugirtharajah, *Postcolonial Criticism and Biblical Interpretation*, 74–102)?

27. Bhabha, *Location of Culture*, 175.

28. Amirtham, "Bodily Representations of Hindu Goddesses," 264.

## The WKRI (Wanita Katolik Republik Indonesia) Story

The story of WKRI began in 1924 when the founding members held its First Women's Congress on December 22–25 of that year. Before adopting its present name, the organization was called Catholic Women of Indonesia (Poesara Wanita Katholiek). The historic gathering of Indonesian women took place on June 26, 1924.[29] Even though it is an organization of the Catholic Church and Christianity is a minority religion in Indonesia, WKRI is established firmly in the cultural and political life of the country. Like many women's organizations in the country, whether Islamic or otherwise, WKRI includes within it a variety of cultural and religious elements.[30]

The organization is active in promoting the dignity of women. Its goal is to tackle issues of underdevelopment and gender, and its initiatives include programs for female literacy, sewing classes, and other training courses. WKRI has over 90,000 members all over Indonesia,[31] and only mothers (either married or single) can become members.

### Knitting Diversity through Nation-Building

In her 2017 anniversary speech, WKRI president Justina Rostiawati emphasized that the organization adheres strongly to the Five Principles of Pancasila, a set of philosophical precepts that guide the republic. These are

- belief in the One and Only God (*Ketuhanan Yang Maha Esa*),
- a just and civilized humanity (*Kemanusiaan Yang Adil dan Beradab*),
- a unified Indonesia (*Persatuan Indonesia*),
- democracy, led by the wisdom of the representatives of the people (*Kerakyatan Yang Dipimpin oleh Hikmat Kebijaksanaan, Dalam Permusyawaratan Perwakilan*), and
- social justice for all Indonesians (*Keadilan Sosial bagi seluruh Rakyat Indonesia*).

---

29.  "Presidium DPP Wanita Katolik."
30.  Porter, "Feminism Is a Good Woman," 16.
31.  Lestari, "Indonesia Presents Award."

According to Rostiawati, however, these principles are at present being threatened by radicalism and terrorism. WKRI has for this reason renewed its commitment to the republic by participating in the Indonesian president Jokowi's efforts to revitalize them.

WKRI is seen by many in Indonesia as a group of "old-fashioned, elderly, and ignorant women."[32] This impression is unfortunate, but it might have sprung from the organization's association with the country's conservative political elite. It is worth noting that many social movements in Indonesia are based on some kind of religious belief or piety that aimed to expand Islamic devotion from the private to the public sphere.[33] These social movements took root in the late 1980s, which marked the emergence of such Islamic revival movements as Hizbut Tahrir, Darul Arqam, and Tarbiya (education).[34]

Karel Steenbrink describes the group as being concerned with maintaining the status quo, not reform.[35] According to this view, WKRI is akin to the Catholic Women's League (CWL) in the Philippines. The CWL is chiefly composed of middle- and upper-middle-class women. I would assert, however, that this is where the similarity ends. WKRI sees itself as a major player in the efforts of the state aimed at nation-building.

In recent documents, particularly from 2017 (the year it turned ninety-three years old), WKRI reiterated that it upholds social justice as part of its mission. Social justice is manifested in upholding the value of diversity. And the fact that, as Catholic women in Indonesia, WKRI members are part of a minority religion makes WKRI's work aimed at unity amidst diversity crucial. The Mission-Vision Statement of WKRI describes an intimate connection between the members' religious identity and national identity, with the contours of each blurring into the other seamlessly. In her message for the 97th anniversary of WKRI, chair Justina Rostiawatti reminds the members of the vision and mission of the organization, emphasizing the necessity to "build the Unitary State of the Republic of Indonesia towards a prosperous country, just and full of peace, where many people from different backgrounds live. Let us call out loudly that all differences in the Unitary State of the Republic of

32. Steenbrink, *Catholics in Independent Indonesia*, 169.

33. Arimbi, "Politicizing Piety," 229.

34. Arimbi, *Reading Contemporary Indonesian Muslim Women Writers*, 64.

35. Steenbrink, *Catholics in Independent Indonesia*, 169.

Indonesia will bring goodness and strength to become a great country."[36] The organization's mission highlights the empowerment of Indonesian Catholic women, "starting from the smallest unit; improving the quality of life through living the values of the Gospel and the Church's social teachings; promoting a better life based on social justice; and fighting for gender equality and fairness in all aspects of life."[37]

*Maternal Feminism for Indonesian Catholic Women*

For the Javanese Catholic woman theologian Nunuk Murniati, an "Asian feminist should be a feminist who has gyne-ecological orientation since Asian culture is rich in matriarchal culture, which sees the womb as a micro cosmos which is a continuum of macro cosmos of the universe."[38]

The blue background of the WKRI logo symbolizes the sacred mother,[39] as well as "willingness, [a] mother's loyalty."[40] In a blog entry written by a member on a WKRI-affiliated website, the "mother approach" adopted by the organization resonates with the Javanese community because it speaks to the common people. There is an abundance of terms associated with the mother, such as mom, mommy, *mamak*, *embok*, and many more. The blog entry delves more deeply into the connotations of the Javanese terms *mamak* and *embok*, bringing forth familiar images and pleasant memories of being enveloped in a mother's warm hug:

> Mother = adding spices, adding flavor, comfortable, adding spirit, healthier, stamina, and so on . . . *Embok* = to complement, refine, give or add strength, give spirit, give moral support, and so on.[41]

However, younger generations of women seem to find no use for such images, which conflate motherhood with domesticity. Younger Indonesian women tend to prioritize career over domestic life. In her observations of young Muslim women activists in the Tarbiyah movement, Diah

36. "Saya Mengajak Wanita Katolik"; translation mine.

37. WKRI Sathora, "Visi dan Misi"; translation mine.

38. Murniati, "Another World Is Possible," 125.

39. The WKRI logo was ratified during the Ninth Congress of the WKRI, held August 20–23, 1970. See "Lambang/Logo Wanita Katolik RI" and "Arti Lambang" in "Organisasi."

40. DPP WKRI, "Penataan Warna Lambang"; translation mine.

41. Suhartana, "Hakekat Ibu," paras. 4, 5.

Arimbi notes that they no longer see domesticity as an obligation for women. Domestic conceptions of motherhood are no longer important in shaping their status as women, and they have begun to reject the cultural constraints of *kodrat,* or destiny, which essentially involves a life of domesticity. The writer chides the women for this position, because it devalues the services that mothers perform for others.[42]

WKRI must adapt to these changing attitudes toward motherhood without compromising its core beliefs about the unique capacity of mothers to effect social transformations for the greater good of all Indonesian people. A blog entry written by another member defends WKRI's maternal feminism based on the group's reading of the role of Mary in shaping Jesus' life and actions. The modern Catholic Indonesian woman who is a member of WKRI channels Mary's example through her dedicated efforts to shape her children's physical and mental health and through becoming involved in their education. The idea is that, if mothers were heavily invested in the shaping of their children's values, their children would grow up to become productive citizens of the country.[43]

According to Marilyn Porter, non-Muslim women in Indonesia often frame their worldview based on the existence of strict gender roles. While this complex ideological framing allows for some flexibility, the general effect is to constrain women to traditional roles and stereotypes.[44] WKRI's Mission-Vision Statement and its civic involvements would seem to problematize this reality. However, the social justice impetus that guides the organization's activities is concretized in its addressing gender issues that impact all women, including those living a domestic vocation. For example, a housewife has the same voting rights as other family members. This example crosses the private/public divide that has defined Western feminist discourse, particularly in the seventies and eighties. The fight for the political rights of women in a culture that adheres strictly to traditional gender roles is indicative of a consciousness that values a woman's worth, even if she is a housewife.

The WKRI president's address during the ninety-third anniversary of its founding underscores the proper place of Catholic women in Indonesian society, which is out there in public spaces and responding to calls to action aimed at nation-building. Although it is a government-recognized

42. Arimbi, "Politicizing Piety," 232.

43. "Ibu Dan Budaya Nilai."

44. Porter, "Feminism Is a Good Woman," 16.

mass organization, it is not a political organization or aligned with any political party. WKRI leaders believe it is important to emphasize this fact so that the organization can remain independent. Members of the WKRI are Catholic women from all walks of life, whether married, single mothers, or widows. The organization's emphasis on the members' active engagement in the political life of their respective communities translates into several concrete community actions on health, education, cultural diversity, and care for the environment. For instance, WKRI leader Magdalena Maria Nunung Purwanti led her community in Surakarta to obtain an MOU between the local government and hotel owners to work for water security amidst threats of water scarcity that can severely affect the communities where several hotels were built.[45]

WKRI's understanding of faith is rooted in love, the exemplar of which is a mother's love for her children. This love enables her to guide them toward becoming good citizens of the republic who are able to foster unity in diversity, promote social justice, and defend human dignity. When Catholic mothers work together in unity, the resulting movement is a strong moral force because "Indonesian Catholic women add positive values in the aspect of education, especially character education of the Indonesian nation."[46] The mission, as WKRI puts it, is spreading the gospel message of divine love. Faith is not a private affair but very much a public one and is lived out in actions that benefit not only the immediate community but the entire nation.

## Conclusion

Japanese feminist scholars Noriko Kawahashi, Kayoko Komatsu, and Masako Kuroki write that gender is a critical concept that can reveal discrimination based on sex and on authority structures and can leverage societal reform.[47] These three scholars lament the scarcity of feminist scholarship done in the context of Japanese religion and note the apparent disdain of other Japanese feminists for religion, which they see as extremely patriarchal and relegating women to their biological roles.

My description of two Catholic women's organizations in Asia is not meant to negate feminist observations about the world's religions. It is,

45. Candraningrum, "Threatened Biodiversity and Empty Wombs," paras. 15–16.
46. Rostiawati, "Sambutan Ketua Presidium"; translation mine.
47. Kawahashi et al., "Gendering Religious Studies," 122.

rather, aimed at highlighting the point that these observations often fall prey to the logic of essentialism.[48] They play right into the dichotomies of public/private, sacred/secular, and primitive/modern, dichotomies that support the continued presence of systematic violence in our midst.

This article underscores that, when we go deeper, dig deeper down to the roots (which is, interestingly, the etymological origin of the word "radical"), and listen with great reverence to the small stories of Catholics worldwide, we begin to see things differently. As Auga puts it, a radical theology of life builds on little narratives, particular experiences, and counter or neighboring discourses.[49]

In closing, I offer two important recommendations relevant to the continuing interrogation of world Catholicism:

1. *We need to appreciate female-centered praxis.* "Praxis" means reflection on and action in the world in order to transform it. An intertwining epistemological and ethical stance marks praxis that is oriented toward the poor, the oppressed, and the marginalized. The challenge is to develop a specific response to the current situation in which vulnerable groups in human society are oppressed and subjugated. The contributions of the women of WKRI to discussions about nation-building highlight the need for the increased participation of women in issues that affect them, including the need for better economic opportunities, the elimination of threats of violence when they migrate abroad, and access to universal healthcare, food security, and quality education.

2. *We must not lose sight of the quest for justice.* The quest for justice informs the work of every person. Even amidst the complexities involved in navigating the social structures that we inhabit, it is possible to be in solidarity with one another. The quest for justice has its origin in Jesus' words, "I came that they might have life, and have it abundantly" (John 10:10 NRSV).

WKRI uses the image of a twig attached to a larger tree to describe the component parts of their organization. EWA has created a quilt sewn from small pieces of fabric representing the countries of Asia that participated in its first conference. The quilt travels with EWA members as

---

48. Essentialism refers to the belief that things have essences, understood as fixed properties that define and limit what a thing is, sharply delineating it from what it is not. See Peracullo, "Sally Haslanger," 130–46.

49. Auga, "Decolonizing Public Space," 65.

they travel to the group's various conferences throughout Asia. These symbolic images highlight our solidarity with one another despite our differences; we all want the same thing for everyone in the world—the flourishing of all people as God wishes.

## Bibliography

Amirtham, Metti. "Bodily Representations of Hindu Goddesses." In *Body and Sexuality: Theological Pastoral Perspectives of Women in Asia*, edited by Agnes M. Brazal and Andrea L. Si, 252–72. Quezon City, Philippines: Ateneo de Manila University Press, 2007.

Arimbi, Diah. "Politicizing Piety: Women's Rights and Roles in the *Tarbiyah* Movement in Indonesia." *Religious Studies and Theology* 36 (2017) 227–44.

———. *Reading Contemporary Indonesian Muslim Women Writers: Representation, Identity, and Religion of Muslim Women in Indonesian Fiction*. Amsterdam: Amsterdam University Press, 2009.

Auga, Ulrike. "Decolonizing Public Space: A Challenge of Bonhoeffer's and Spivak's Concepts of Resistance, 'Religion,' and 'Gender.'" *Feminist Theology* 24 (2015) 49–68.

Bhabha, Homi K. *The Location of Culture*. London: Routledge, 1994.

Brazal, Agnes M., and Andrea L. Si, eds. *Body and Sexuality: Theological Pastoral Perspectives of Women in Asia*. Quezon City, Philippines: Ateneo de Manila University Press, 2007.

Candraningrum, Dewi. "Threatened Biodiversity and Empty Wombs: Climate Change and Women's Plight in Central Java." *Heinrich Boll Stiftung: Southeast Asia*, February 26, 2019. https://th.boell.org/en/2019/02/26/threatened-biodiversity-and-empty-wombs-climate-change-and-womens-plight-central-java.

Cruz, Gemma T. "Em-body-ing Theology: Theological Reflections on the Experience of Filipina Domestic Workers in Hong Kong." In *Body and Sexuality: Theological Pastoral Perspectives of Women in Asia*, edited by Agnes M. Brazal and Andrea L. Si, 60–74. Quezon City, Philippines: Ateneo de Manila University Press, 2007.

Davie, Grace. *The Sociology of Religion*. London: Sage, 2007.

———. "Thinking Sociologically about Religion: Context, Concepts, and Clarifications." In *The Centrality of Religion and Social Life: Essays in Honour of James A. Beckford*, edited by Eileen Barker, 15–28. Surrey, UK: Ashgate, 2010.

DPP WKRI (Dewan Pengurus Pusat WKRI [WKRI Central Board of Directors]). "Penataan Warna Lambang" [Color Arrangement of Emblems]. https://dppwkri.org/lambang.

Ecclesia of Women in Asia. "Constitution and By-laws." https://ecclesiaofwomen.com/constitution-by-laws.

———. "EWA's Herstory." May 19, 2017. https://ecclesiaofwomen.com/2017/05/19/ewas-herstory/.

Giorgi, Alberta. "Gender, Religion, and Political Agency: Mapping the Field." *Revista Crítica de Ciências Sociais* 110 (2016) 51–72.

Habermas, Jürgen. "Religion in the Public Sphere." *European Journal of Philosophy* 14 (2006) 1–25.

"Ibu Dan Budaya Nilai" [Motherhood and Cultural Values]. *Wanita Katolik RI*, December 10, 2010. https://wkriungaran.wordpress.com/2010/12.

Joseph, Pushpa. "Re-visioning Eros for Asian Feminist Theologizing." In *Body and Sexuality: Theological Pastoral Perspectives of Women in Asia*, edited by Agnes M. Brazal and Andrea L. Si, 34–59. Quezon City, Philippines: Ateneo de Manila University Press, 2007.

Kamitsuka, Margaret. *Feminist Theology and the Challenge of Difference*. London: Oxford University Press, 2007.

Kawahashi, Noriko, et al. "Gendering Religious Studies: Reconstructing Religion and Gender Studies in Japan." In *Gender, Religion, and Education in a Chaotic Postmodern World*, edited by Zehavit Gross et al., 111–23. Dordrecht, The Netherlands: Springer Science+Business, 2013.

Lestari, Katharina Reny. "Indonesia Presents Award to Catholic Women." *UCANews*, November 8, 2018. https://www.ucanews.com/news/indonesia-presents-award-to-catholic-women/83822#.

Mahmood, Sabah. "Feminist Theory, Embodiment, and the Docile Agent: Some Reflections on the Egyptian Islamic Revival." *Cultural Anthropology* 16 (2001) 202–36.

———. *Politics of Piety: The Islamic Revival and the Feminist Subject*. Princeton: Princeton University Press, 2006.

———. *Religious Difference in a Secular Age: A Minority Report*. Princeton: Princeton University Press, 2015.

Murniati, Nunuk. "Another World Is Possible." *Voices* 32.1 (2016) 119–36. http://eatwot.net/VOICES/VOICES-2016-1.pdf.

"Organisasi." *Wanita Katolik RI*. https://wkriungaran.wordpress.com/organisasi.

Peracullo, Jeane. "Sally Haslanger and Gayatri Chakravorty Spivak on the Possibility of Metaphysics of Resistance and Its Implications for Postcolonial Feminist Theologizing." *Feminist Theology* 28 (2020) 130–46.

Porter, Marilyn. "Feminism Is a Good Woman: Reflections on the Use of Ideas in the Women's Movement in Indonesia." *Asian Journal of Women's Studies* 9 (2003) 7–36.

"Presidium DPP Wanita Katolik: 'Aisyiyah Punya Andil Menggagas NKRI" [Catholic Women's DPP Presidium: 'Aisyiyah Has Contributed to Initiating NKRI]. *Suara Muhammadiyah*, May 19, 2020. https://suaramuhammadiyah.id/2020/05/19/presidium-dpp-wanita-katolik-aisyiyah-punya-andil-menggagas-nkri/.

Pritchard, Elizabeth. "Special Introduction from the Religion and Politics Editor." *Journal of Feminist Studies in Religion* 26.1 (Spring 2010) 1–5.

Pui Lan, Kwok. *Introducing Asian Feminist Theology*. Sheffield, UK: Sheffield University Press, 2000.

———. "Review of *Body and Sexuality: Theological-Pastoral Perspectives of Women in Asia*, edited by Agnes M. Brazal and Andrea L. Si." *Asian Christian Review* 1 (2007) 85–86.

Rostiawati, Justina. "Sambutan Ketua Presidium DPP Dalam Rangka HUT Ke-95 Wanita Katolik RI" [Message of the DPP Chairperson on WKRI's 95th Anniversary]. *Wanita Katolik RI*, August 23, 2019. https://wkriungaran.wordpress.com/2019/08/.

"Saya Mengajak Wanita Katolik Meneguhkan Visi-Misi Membangun NKRI!" ["I Invite Catholic Women to Strengthen the Vision-Mission to Build the Unitary

State of the Republic of Indonesia!"]. *BarometerSulut,* June 29, 2021. http://www. barometersulut.com/2021/06/29/justina-rostiawati-saya-mengajak-wanita-katolik-meneguhkan-visi-misi-membangun-nkri/.

Segundo, Jorge Luis. *Liberation of Theology.* Translated by John Drury. 1976. Reprint, Eugene, OR: Wipf and Stock, 2002.

Speciale, Allesandro. "Vatican Censors Nun's Book on Sexual Ethics, and Some See a Bid to Muzzle Women's Voices." *Religion News Service,* June 4, 2012. https:// religionnews.com/2012/06/04/vatican-censors-nuns-book-on-sexual-ethics-and-some-see-a-bid-to-muzzle-w.

Steenbrink, Karel. *Catholics in Independent Indonesia: 1945–2010.* Leiden: Brill, 2015.

Sugirtharajah, Rasiah S. *Postcolonial Criticism and Biblical Interpretation.* London: Oxford University Press, 2002.

Suhartana, Romo St.K. "Hakekat Ibu." *Wanita Katolik RI,* December 22, 2009. https:// wkriungaran.wordpress.com/2009/12/.

Traina, Cristina, "Just Love: A Framework for Christian Sexual Ethics." *Theological Studies* 68 (2007) 712–14.

WKRI Sathora. "Visi dan Misi" [Vision and Mission]. "Sejarah berdirinya organisasi Wanita Katolik Republik Indonesia" page. https://sites.google.com/site/wkrisathora/home/visi-dan-misi.

# 9

# The Complex and Countercultural Nature of Women's Leadership Roles in Basic Ecclesial Communities (BECs) in Asia

Wendy M. Louis

## Introduction

The leadership exercised by women in Basic Ecclesial Communities (BECs) in Asia mirrors the leadership they provide in the church generally, in parishes, ministries, educational institutions, and administrative roles. The pastoral and ecclesial context of BECs in Asia varies greatly from country to country and even within small geographical areas. BECs took root in a number of places in the 1970s as a response to social injustice and a growing understanding that Jesus should be seen as a liberator from oppression, while others were begun as a result of the emphasis the Second Vatican Council gave to the mission of the laity and to the notion of *communio*. BECs were one of a number of movements that sprang up in the church in this period embodying the conception of a church of small communities focused on renewal of the larger church and on energizing the laity. By the 1990s, the enthusiasm for these models had diminished and the existing communities were very much in need of renewal.

A vision for this renewal was articulated in 1990 by the Federation of Asian Bishops' Conferences (FABC) during its Fifth Plenary Assembly in Bandung, Indonesia. This renewal was promoted and implemented by the Asian bishops in a top-down manner, but the BECs that emerged after the assembly were part of an ecclesiology of communion underpinning the development of a participatory church, a church conceived as a "communion of communities."[1] A key feature of this vision, which was called the "new way of being . . . church"[2] is that all are invited to participate in the common mission of the kingdom. In this vision, the laity are co-responsible co-workers and not simply helpers. As Pope John Paul II said, "Communion and mission are profoundly connected with each other, they interpenetrate and mutually imply each other, to the point that *communion represents both the source and fruit of mission: communion gives rise to mission and mission is accomplished in communion.*"[3]

The bishops' vision for the church in Asia has been implemented within the socioeconomic, geopolitical, and pastoral context of the local churches. The Asian continent extends from Japan in the east to Kazakhstan in the west, and the relevant circumstances vary so greatly from place to place that one needs to use caution when referring to the entire reality as "Asian." In a number of Asian countries, BECs have not developed for geopolitical reasons or because of the absence of religious freedom, or, as for example in Mongolia, because the presence of the church is relatively new. In some, they are a low pastoral priority within the dioceses. Severe poverty, poor infrastructure, overcrowded housing and slums, and the reality of sparse, far-flung communities are among the factors that have had a significant impact on slowing the development of BECs in Asia.

Attitudes toward women and girls in the Asian society and church creates a challenging context for the emergence of women leadership. For example, in the South Asian countries of India, Sri Lanka, Bangladesh, and Pakistan, great strides have been made toward the building of BECs; however, there is a question about how the position of women in these countries impacts the kinds of leadership that they are allowed to exercise within the structures of the church. Women in these countries, as well as in other places in Asia, must contend with both societal and clerical cultures.

---

1. FABC, Fifth Plenary Assembly, *Emerging Challenges to the Church in Asia,* 8.1.1.

2. FABC, Fifth Plenary Assembly, *Emerging Challenges to the Church in Asia,* 8.0.

3. John Paul II, *Christifideles Laici,* 32; italics original.

## Communion Ecclesiology and the BECs

In order to reflect on the implications of women's leadership roles in BECs, it is necessary to understand their nature and mission. The BEC is a very specific type of community. We could say that it is a family of families, a microcosm of the church comprised of the domestic churches present in a particular neighborhood.

The notion of *communio* is based in the communitarian love of the Father, Son, and Holy Spirit. This holy exchange of love is the foundation of communion ecclesiology. In larger communities led by an ordained minister—a parish or mission station—participation in the Trinitarian life is made visible and expressed through the sacramental and liturgical life of the church. However, in the BECs this participation—the living out of the eucharistic sacrifice—is woven into the fabric of daily life through the regular sharing of the gospel of Jesus and through intimate contact with the risen Lord within a community that gathers in loving service in the name of the Lord. The community is gospel-based and Christocentric. An encounter with the person of Jesus and a relationship with God is central to the life and mission of these communities. As John Paul II observed,

> The mystery of God's loving design is made present and active in the community of the men and women who have been buried with Christ by baptism into death, so that as Christ was raised from the dead by the glory of the Father, they might walk in newness of life (cf. Rom 6:4). . . .The Church's first purpose then is to be the sacrament of *the inner union of the human person with God,* and, because people's communion with one another is rooted in that union with God, the Church is also the sacrament of *the unity of the human race.*[4]

The BEC aims at building bonds of unity and friendship at all levels of the church and society through service and outreach beyond the Christian community. The role of the parish and diocesan leadership in supporting, strengthening, and nourishing the unity sought by BECs may be seen in multiple endeavors. Training programs make use of BEC facilitators from every community, enabling them to share their pastoral experiences and providing them a platform for networking and fellowship. BEC members participate in parish projects that require collaboration and prayer and join in the celebration of parish feasts that

---

4. John Paul II, "Ecclesia in Asia," 24; italics original.

involve common worship and liturgy. BEC festivals or "days" allow BEC members and facilitators to showcase their cooking skills or willingness to participate in social projects while enjoying moments of mutual formation and fellowship.

John Paul II noted that the Asian synod fathers,

> drawing on their pastoral experience, . . . underlined the value of *basic ecclesial communities* as an effective way of promoting communion and participation in parishes and Dioceses, and as a genuine force for evangelization. These small groups help the faithful to live as believing, praying and loving communities like the early Christians (cf. Acts 2:44–47; 4:32–35). They aim to help their members to live the Gospel in a spirit of fraternal love and service and are therefore a solid starting point for building a new society, the expression of *a civilization of love*. With the Synod, I encourage the Church in Asia, where possible, to consider these basic communities as a positive feature of the Church's evangelizing activity. At the same time, they will only be truly effective if—as Pope Paul VI wrote—they live in union with the particular and the universal Church, in heartfelt communion with the Church's Pastors and the Magisterium, with a commitment to missionary outreach and without yielding to isolationism or ideological exploitation.[5]

Pope Francis has called all the faithful to become missionary disciples, and the BECs are one important way to activate the lay faithful to this vocation. Pope Francis also often speaks about going to the peripheries. The BEC is the church in the neighborhood, one of the most effective ecclesial forms for reaching into the corners of parishes and for reaching marginalized, usually invisible, people, and walking with them. "Each Christian and every community must discern the path that the Lord points out, but all of us are asked to obey his call to go forth from their own comfort zone in order to reach all the 'peripheries' in need of the light of the Gospel."[6]

## Membership in BECs

BEC members are a diverse group. Membership is for baptized Catholics, but all are welcome to attend the meetings and join in the fellowship and

5. John Paul II, "Ecclesia in Asia," 25; italics original.

6. Francis, *Evangelii Gaudium*, 20.

social outreach projects. Those who would normally feel excluded or embarrassed to go to the Sunday services in the parish due to their poor appearance, addictions, irregular marriage situations, or distance from the parish are welcomed and cared for. Members and nonmembers generally come from the same neighborhood and have regular and frequent contact. The givenness of neighbors is an important factor for members who wish to avoid associating only with friends and like-minded persons— sometimes there is a danger that communities will be too homogeneous; for example, including only older, retired people. The principle at work here is to develop the BEC as a microcosm of the local church so that it does not function as a mere support group, guild, or association for people having the same needs or of the same profession, age, or economic status. People join such groups to satisfy a personal or professional need. This is perfectly legitimate and laudable, but they are not Basic *Ecclesial* Communities.

Couples with young families, youth, working men and women, and those who have to travel for work can be part of the community without attending all the meetings. They are members by virtue of living within a certain area, but in some urban areas where distances are not great and networks are many and varied, the concept of neighborhood may be understood flexibly. While the ideal is that entire families participate together in the BECs, the reality is that often only one or two members from a family are involved, usually the adults.

## BECs versus BHCs

BECs are Christian, church-based units within a parish. They are different from Basic Human Communities (BHCs), a structure common in many Asian societies, especially in tribal villages where there is a very well-developed sense of community. The aims of BHCs are to create greater friendship, harmony, and tolerance among peoples of different faiths living in an area, and/or to work on improving material and social conditions in the area. The BEC belongs within a parish, uses almost exclusively Christian Scriptures, and is motivated by the Gospels and the mission of Christ. In a BHC, all faiths and Scriptures enjoy equal emphasis. Leaders are chosen from among the membership, who come from different faiths or no faith. The dialogue that occurs in BHCs is dialogue with the poor, dialogue about the lives of the people, and interfaith dialogue. BHCs are often thought to be a progressive step forward from BECs, but the most appropriate view of their relationship is that BECs can coexist with BHCs once they have become established and members are confident and well-rooted in their faith and in the word of God.

## The Role of BECs in Parishes

The parish priest or other parish leaders can make use of a BEC present in the parish by either viewing it as a tool for organizing the parish more efficiently and asking its members to implement parish plans or by simply turning over to them operational responsibility for a significant ministry, such as the church canteen, soup kitchen, or parish library. In the second case, there is a risk that people will feel used. Some, despite feeling burdened, will do whatever is asked of them—women in particular are often eager to please—but some will leave the BEC. Occasionally asking BEC members to help with a big parish feast or anniversary will be welcomed, but asking them to take on major operational responsibilities will be resented because such responsibilities take away time from gospel-sharing and other BEC activities. In any event, if responsibility for some task is given, the authority to carry it out should also be given. Having a great deal to do but no say in how it is to be done is disappointing and frustrating for both women and men in leadership.

## Key Characteristics of Leadership in BECs

Leadership in a BEC has a number of key characteristics. It is shared, facilitating, nondominating, and emerging. Firstly, it is a *shared* leadership which takes place through a meaningful distribution of tasks and responsibilities. The accomplishment of tasks and responsibilities needs to be accompanied by an enabling process that includes training, raising awareness of needs and challenges, and practicing required skills. Shared leadership makes it easy for all members to participate according to their gifts and opportunities to do so. What follows are a few examples of the shared roles and responsibilities in a BEC.

Those who organize, convene, or host the regular meetings of the BEC are called "coordinators." Coordinators also function as the contact person for the parish. The coordinator may be thought of as the most important leader in a BEC, and in some parishes, he or she may be tempted to imitate the existing pastoral leadership, taking over many functions and acting as the central decision-maker. However, properly understood, the role of a coordinator is framed by the specific task of coordinating and communicating with and providing information to the parish and the parish pastoral council concerning various projects, events, and proposals. The coordinator often organizes training programs for members after consultation with others.

Another leadership role is the "Gospel-sharing *facilitator*," a person who has been trained to lead gospel sharing during meetings. The authenticity, sustainability, and effectiveness of BECs in living out the mission of Christ in the neighborhood and beyond depends in large part on the members' depth of spirituality, which in turn depends on their personal encounter with the risen Lord in the Scriptures. The simple work of a facilitator of gospel sharing takes on a special importance if one understands the centrality of the word of God in the life of a BEC.

Members called "animators" work in pairs or small teams, and during the BEC meeting each pair or team takes turns leading the discussion. The pair or team then prepares a report on what was discussed and what more is needed.

The leadership of BECs *emerges* from the community in response to the pastoral needs of neighbors and the needs of the local church generally. Leadership is tied to particular ministries or functions; there is no such thing as a single, powerful leader who delegates work to others. Shared, facilitating leadership fosters equality, encourages all members to take ownership of the community, and brings to community life the excitement of being missionaries.

BEC members are considered to be equal to each other and their leadership style is *nondominating*. Decision-making is accomplished by the use of communication and consensus. For example, someone might be in charge of facilitating the gospel sharing for one year together with a partner, but any decision to change the gospel text to be shared at the next meeting must be made with the agreement of the members. The person chosen, elected, or appointed to represent the community in the parish pastoral council (PPC) is not a powerful leader who can tell everyone what to do. He or she reports and communicates to BEC members and takes the views of the community back to the PPC. Nondominating, animating leadership enables the entire community to grow and to take ownership of the community and the mission.

## Women's Leadership in BECs—
## Roles, Characteristics, and Challenges

Women have played a key role in establishing, nurturing, and maintaining BECs across Asia. While leadership at higher levels of the church is usually male, the ecclesial communities at the grassroots have proven to be a very effective locus for women to discover their leadership potential, to participate in the mission of the church, and to gradually develop as collaborators bringing about the reign of God.[7]

It should be said that many women would not call what they do in BECs "leadership." The scholar Joo-Hyun Ro interviewed women about their leadership roles in BECs present in the Diocese of Jeju in South Korea. Ro found that the tendency to see leaders as big and important and often assertive and dominating causes many women to avoid the term "leader"; instead, they self-identify as "helpers" or "animators" or "volunteers."[8] In this regard, Ro observed that

> Some of them sensitively object to describing themselves as "leaders," and their activities . . . as "leadership." These reactions connote that their understanding of the terms . . . are associated with the concept of domination or assertions of superiority distinguishing between those in priority roles as the privileged or the qualified and those in subordinate positions as the passive or the obedient. Therefore, interviewees suggest portraying themselves as partners or companions to SCC [Small Christian Communities, a reality that is similar to BECs] members instead of calling themselves leaders.[9]

Ro supplies terms for the types of leadership exhibited by women, including "accompanying leadership," "embracing leadership," and "interdependent leadership."[10] Unfortunately, there are many obstacles to the exercise of these types of leadership. First, parish leadership often does not provide a good role model of nondominating, listening, and collaborative leadership. Second, the ministries and activities of BECs that

---

7. This is true even if sometimes women gain leadership positions in BECs because of the absence of men or of men who can perform the necessary tasks. The presence of women leadership in BECs is both a strength and a weakness because men tend to withdraw when women step forward.

8. Ro, "Small Christian Communities and Lay Women's Leadership," 68.

9. Ro, "Small Christian Communities and Lay Women's Leadership," 68–69.

10. Ro, "Small Christian Communities and Lay Women's Leadership," 70, 71, 73.

are inspired by the sharing of the word of God are often not acknowledged as important pastoral initiatives. Third, a small number of women leaders are often loaded down with multiple tasks in both the BECs and in parish ministries and organizations.[11] And finally, parishes sometimes operate according to a corporate model characterized by highly centralized authority, which disrupts the shared leadership that women at the grassroots find more enriching and appealing.

Ro also identifies the leadership of women in BECs as "transforming leadership":

> Interviewees agree that the role and responsibility of SCC leaders have encouraged them to strive to be authentic disciples of Jesus. Their experience of SCCs (BECs) has generated changes in their way of thinking and behaviour as well as in leadership. Interviewees say that they seem to have undergone "transformation" from the values of society to the values of the Word of God. Interactive and growing relationships among SCC (BEC) members, the experience of the power of the Word, and the spirit of the community have brought about their transformation.[12]

Despite feeling discouraged by the lack of support and formation, women continue to realize the mission of Christ and the church in the neighborhoods through a moral authority that is based on deep faith and a relationship with Christ. While their service may often appear to be the product of docile compliance, the reality is quite the opposite. There is a firm belief among many women, whether spoken and conscious or not, that the work of bringing about the reign of God cannot be abandoned because of discontent with the church's leadership. It is my conviction that once a proper forum is provided and the leadership is ready to listen, the expertise and dedication of these women can be a source of renewal for the institutional church.

In some countries, particularly in South Asian societies that are still largely patriarchal, women have been subjected to male domination and subservience. The development of Christ-centered ecclesial communities has, however, transformed both parishes and the lives of women. In one situation that I encountered in the Archdiocese of Trivandrum, one BEC leader came to understand her potential to be a change-maker and

11. This is especially the case in places where BEC leaders do not serve for determined periods of time and where the parish is centralized and organized for efficiency (Ro, "Small Christian Communities and Lay Women's Leadership," 132).

12. Ro, "Small Christian Communities and Lay Women's Leadership," 75–76.

was encouraged to stand in local council elections, enabling Christians to nominate a Christian woman candidate. She is not an isolated case, but there is rarely any mechanism in place in Asian societies to ensure that women's leadership is encouraged and enabled. In many of these societies, women are reluctant to act assertively toward a man, and this is not only the case in Asia. The consequence of this is that men often fill the main leadership roles while women lead through the performance of tasks taken up in the SCCs and end up doing most of the work behind the scenes. Where this is happening, it is up to church leadership to recognize and correct it.

I noted previously that women often end up overburdened in parishes, each sometimes leading a number of ministries and performing many other tasks. This is not about gender but about resources. It seems that this happens unintentionally. The women who help out in the parish are those who have time and resources: they often do not work full-time outside the home and typically have the financial resources to pay for their own transportation to and from church activities; sometimes they also have helpers to care for their homes and children, making them able to afford time away from home. This means that these women are often middle-class and wealthier. There are undoubtedly some in the parish who think that the poor lack wisdom and have "failed," so they are not qualified to make contributions to the parish, which means that the "preferential option for the poor" translates into caring for the poor but not seeing them as people who are creative, wise, and diligent.

The BECs have, however, been instrumental in allowing the poorer members of parishes to take on leadership roles and move from the periphery to the center. This can be illustrated by an example involving thirteen women in the Philippines. These women were from a large and poor parish and lived in a densely populated *barangay*, or village, with very poor housing and facilities. The families there mostly worked as pushcart vendors or construction workers. These women looked like they had lived tough lives. They were elderly, generous, and passionate about their communities. Every one of them was a leader in her BEC. They were on the front lines of the church in their area; without them the church would have been absent in the area because the priest finds it impossible to be present to his 55,000 parishioners. The priest was very supportive of these women leaders and provided continuous training and accompaniment. In February 2018, he paid for them to attend a week-long course at an institute of formation.

## Meetings and Community Involvement in BECs

The members of the BEC and parish leaders focus intensely on the weekly or bimonthly meetings of the BEC. Some members may never attend the meetings, but participate in the community's various ministries and activities, like visiting the sick or the catechesis of children or adults—they are considered to be active members of the BEC through their participation in a BEC ministry and by virtue of living within the neighborhood. In fact, every baptized person living within the neighborhood has a right to the pastoral care provided by the BEC and the parish.

Very often, the leadership of BECs emphasizes attendance at the meetings over community involvement, even though the latter is a living expression of communion and mission. There has been a tendency to reduce the BECs to their meetings. In some places, the BECs are lifeless despite the regular meetings and pious activities like praying the rosary and faith formation, because between the meetings there is very little interaction between members and hardly any involvement in projects or services related to the needs of neighbors or society at large. One reason for this is that BECs are sometimes seen as just one more ministry or organization in the parish rather than being an organizing principle for carrying out mission. Before the advent of BECs, parishes were organized according to their ministries and services. With BECs, it is now imperative to decentralize as many services and ministries as possible so that BEC members can be activated for mission in all the various ways that may be inspired by the gospel and by the circumstances of their lives.

The more flexible and practical the BEC is, the greater are women's opportunities to participate in mission and in the life of the neighborhood. There is also a need to develop more activities and ministries suitable for the whole family. An overemphasis on weekday activities and ministries may exclude working men and women who are only free in the evenings or on weekends. This may result in the most active BEC members being retired and elderly people.

## Women and Visibility

The work of women in many Asian traditional societies is to care for children and the home, collect water and firewood, clean and cook, cultivate gardens, work on handlooms, and make marketable clay pots. Their labor shapes, nurtures, and holds together village life. Their own health and education are often neglected and sacrificed for the good of the family, especially for the good of the male members of the family. It is well known that women do the lion's share of the work in the home, especially in rural communities where they perform most of the labor-intensive farming and animal husbandry.

In the church, in both rural and urban settings, despite all the other work women do, they still find time to be catechists, to visit the sick and bereaved, and to take on active leadership roles in BECs. Women are very much at the forefront of the church's mission in the family and the society, but their work is often invisible.

The invisible nature of women in Christian communities is reflected in the story of the feeding of the 5,000 in the Gospel of Mark (6:34–44). Jesus asked the disciples to organize the people into groups before distributing the bread and fish. "And he commanded them to make all to sit down by companies upon the green grass. And they sat down in ranks, by hundreds, and by fifties" (6:39–40 KJV). The total number given is 5,000, but the Gospel of Matthew tells us that this did not include women and children[13] (Matt 14:21)—which means that there were more than 10,000 people present. This is ironic because the word translated as "companies" is actually *symposia* in the original Greek, which means to "drink together"; that is, not only sharing food but also drink, which indicates a feast.[14] This gospel text is a clear command to form communities, to live out community, and to celebrate communities. Three things are noteworthy—that community means women, men, and children in communion, that it is difficult to conceive of communities enjoying food fellowship in the absence of women, and that in the culture of biblical times women were taken for granted and invisible.

By the time of the early church communities described in the Acts of the Apostles and in the letters of St. Paul, we see that the leadership of women was a visible, accepted, and crucial reality. Paul's coworkers in Christ included both women and men. In Romans 16:3, Paul sends greetings to Prisca and Aquila, who host an ecclesial community in their home. He calls them "fellow workers in Christ Jesus, who risked their necks for my life." According to some scholars, Prisca may have been a preacher in the church. In the same chapter of Romans, in verse 1, there

13. Neither the Gospel of Mark nor Luke mentions women and children.
14. See Kang U-Il, "Small Christian Communities," 3.

is mention of "Phoebe, a deaconess." It is clear that women were at this time working and risking their lives for the faith.

Pope Francis has put into the church calendar the feast of Mary, Mother of the Church on the Monday after Pentecost in order to point to the presence of the mother of Jesus in the upper room, accompanying the apostles. Fast-forwarding to the church of today and comparing it to the time of St. Paul, we find that the role of women has regressed, something that causes great concern and shame. Excessive clericalism, which insists on exaggerated links between ordination and leadership and between ordination and orthodoxy, has spelled disaster for the growth of women's leadership in mission. Women do a great deal of the work of the church—*ortho-praxis*—but are excluded from leadership roles because of the emphasis given to *ortho-doxy* and the false notion that women, even women who are highly qualified theologians, are incapable of making sound decisions for the church because they are not ordained. Despite all this, the BECs in many Asian countries have circumvented the need for clerical leadership at the grassroots and given women a place and a voice that they may not otherwise have had.

## The Feminine Nature of BECs

There are some areas of community life in BECs in which women have readily taken the lead. There is usually hesitation in the early stages, but women eventually find themselves in arenas where their personalities and talents have space to grow. These areas are as follows:

- Spontaneous and shared prayer. Spontaneous prayer is encouraged in BECs because it nurtures an individual's personal relationship with Christ. There are still some structured prayers and devotions, but this form of more direct and personal prayer of thanksgiving, praise, petition, etc., is the norm.

- Times of silent and meditative prayer. Many Asian women have a strong affective side because of the way they have been nurtured, so they are able to enter into silent and meditative prayer with ease. There are many male members and leaders who are also good at this, but I am speaking generally.

- Community life centered on the gospel. The way Scriptures are used in BEC gatherings does not require expertise or deep knowledge.

Neither experts nor teachers are needed. The use of Scriptures in BECs is not a "Bible study" or an exegesis. The proclaiming or reading of the word in a BEC has the aim of encountering the person of Jesus and responding to it personally and communally in everyday life. Because of this element of encounter in the reading of the word, the Federation of Asian Bishops' Conferences Bishops of Asia, in their Fifth Plenary Assembly in Bandung in 1990, called the word of God the "quasi-sacramental" sign of the risen Lord.[15] What is encouraged in the BEC is a personal sharing of the connection between the word and life and of the way in which the word comes alive during the week. Women have much less difficulty with this kind of sharing than the men, who have rarely shared their thoughts and feelings about matters of faith, even to members of their immediate families. Men generally have not had the formation or nurturing to be at ease with their personal, affective, and relational side, so they need more time to become accustomed to the *sharing* aspect of gospel sharing.

- Hospitality and the sharing of food and drink. This is very important in all the BECs. Very often the more mature communities try not to offer food and drink at community meetings except for some simple biscuits and water so that they do not burden the poorer members. This has hardly ever worked because the poor cannot be outdone when it comes to hospitality. So even busy urban dwellers, both the well-off and the poor, typically purchase some little snack to share at the meeting. The women take a central role in offering hospitality and welcoming members.

- The work of many BECs which includes visiting neglected children and the elderly, the housebound, and the sick attracts more women than men, who are often more interested in projects relating to education, housing, conflict resolution, and the like.

The theme of a women's meeting in Dhaka, Bangladesh in 2010 was "Living the Eucharist in Our Daily Lives." I presented a short paper from the perspective of BECs. One of the things I said which is relevant here was a response to an oft-heard disparaging remark about BECs that goes like this: "Oh, these BECs are a waste of time. There are just some old

---

15. FABC, Fifth Plenary Assembly, *Emerging Challenges to the Church in Asia*, 8.1.1.

women coming to these meetings." My reflection was about how close the lives of these "old women" are to the sacrifice of Christ and how fruitful their lives are, as seen in their actions and in the many people they care for. Their bodies are broken, their blood poured out. These old women, brimming over with humility and wisdom, were and are willing to do the most menial tasks in order to care for their families and neighbors and truly "break" themselves like the bread broken in the Eucharist. Leading is not about positions and power. It is about the capacity to serve, love, and build up. Women in BECs show what is meant by servant leadership.

## Conclusion

Much is said about the need for more men to participate and lead in BECs. Women's leadership in BECs, on the other hand, seems to be taken for granted. The success or failure of our BECs and the roles that families, single people, the old and the young, male and female will play in BECs are dependent on church leadership and on the context in which the BECs operate. Neglecting the contributions of women leaders because of their gender, lack of education, age, or economic status will be detrimental to the life of the church. We know from Scripture God's preference for the *anawim*, the little ones. The weak, the small, and the marginalized are preferred in the reign of God. A great deal of sensitive listening and creativity is needed in today's pastoral situations to build up the whole community while providing opportunities for those who are often invisible. It is wise to stand humbly before the immensity and complexity of any context and listen very carefully to the language and the meaning behind the words, and also to understand the impact of culture, structures, and tradition on the balance of power and on the roles played and responsibilities given at all levels of church life.

When a woman leads with competence and clearly expresses her opinions, she sometimes attracts resentment and animosity from those who should be providing her with support and guidance. This resentment and animosity can even result in personal attacks on her integrity. This happens in both church and society, and this may be why women are often not willing to sacrifice their friendships, family life, and peace to take on leadership roles that put them in the spotlight. They are ready to do the work but do not want to deal with the negative dynamics that their leadership will create.

If the BECs are our hope for evangelization and communion in mission in the Asian context, we need to examine how we are enabling their leaders, who are mostly women, to become confident and compassionate missionary disciples working on the front lines. Because BECs in many places are populated by numerous older women, there may be a tendency to withhold the necessary training and upscaling of skills, and even to discourage a deepening of faith by allocating little funding to BECs while spending huge sums on other projects and events. Overlooking the missionary heart of the church in this way would be a costly mistake.

## Bibliography

Federation of Asian Bishops' Conferences (FABC), Fifth Plenary Assembly. *The Emerging Challenges to the Church in Asia in the 1990s: A Call to Respond.* Bandung, Indonesia, 1990. https://fabc.org/document/fabc-papers-059/.

Francis, Pope. *Evangelii Gaudium. Vatican.va*, November 24, 2013. http://www.vatican.va/content/francesco/en/apost_exhortations/documents/papa-francesco_esortazione-ap_20131124_evangelii-gaudium.html.

———. *Gaudete et Exsultate. Vatican.va*, March 19, 2018. http://www.vatican.va/content/francesco/en/apost_exhortations/documents/papa-francesco_esortazione-ap_20180319_gaudete-et-exsultate.html.

John Paul II, Pope. *Christifideles Laici. Vatican.va*, December 30, 1988. http://www.vatican.va/content/john-paul-ii/en/apost_exhortations/documents/hf_jp-ii_exh_30121988_christifideles-laici.html.

———. "Ecclesia in Asia." *Vatican.va*, November 6, 1999. http://www.vatican.va/content/john-paul-ii/en/apost_exhortations/documents/hf_jp-ii_exh_06111999_ecclesia-in-asia.html.

Kang U-Il, Peter. "Small Christian Communities, the Fundamental Paradigm of the Church." Talk given during an exposure program for German bishops, April 14–22, 2009, Jeju Diocese, South Korea.

Ro, Joo-Hyun. "Small Christian Communities and Lay Women's Leadership: In the Context of Jeju Diocese in the Roman Catholic Church of Korea." DMin diss., Catholic Theological Union at Chicago, April 2010.

# IO

# Locating Women in Four Catholic Schools of Theology in the Philippines

## NICETA M. VARGAS, OSA

## Introduction

THE PHILIPPINES IS A predominantly Catholic country, with almost 79 percent of the people registered as Catholics as of 2013.[1] Of the 103 college (minor) and theology (major) seminaries in the country that cater to priestly formation, twenty-two have a school of theology offering bachelor's, master's, or doctoral programs.[2] Three of these offer ecclesiastical degrees—the Central Seminary of the Pontifical University of Santo Tomas (UST), the Institute of Consecrated Life in Asia (as part of a consortium with UST), and the Loyola School of Theology of the Ateneo de Manila University. Two schools are not connected with any diocesan seminary or college/university—the Institute of Formation and Religious Studies and the Maryhill School of Theology. De La Salle University offers a graduate program in applied theology.

---

1. Uy, "Filipino Catholic Population Expanding," para. 4.

2. My own count from the list of seminaries and schools of theology published in the 2014–15 Catholic Directory of the Philippines.

Vatican II's call for *aggiornamento* awakened religious women to the need for and importance of theological formation and education.[3] In response to this need, the Association of Major Religious Superiors of Women in the Philippines founded the Sisters Formation Institute (SFI) in 1963 to provide young women religious academic training in theology and spirituality. This was in response to the sparse or complete lack of theological education received by women religious as compared with that of the men preparing for the priesthood prior to Vatican II. SFI's program was patterned after the Jesuit curriculum of study for seminarians at San Jose Seminary. Credits were received from the College of Arts and Sciences of the Ateneo de Manila University. The professors were Jesuits, CICM[4] priests, and religious sisters. For three decades, the students of SFI were largely women, but when religious men and laypeople first began to enroll in the institute in 1995, its name was changed to the Institute of Formation and Religious Studies. Also in the 1990s, women religious began studying in other schools of theology, some enrolling in full-time theology graduate programs.

Now, in the twenty-first century, the Philippines is a privileged place for studying theology and scripture in Asia. There are at least twenty-two Catholic schools of theology in various parts of the country, almost half of which are in Metro Manila.[5] Using data gathered from four of these schools of theology, this article shall endeavor to arrive at a current picture of the theological education received by women in the Philippines. The article will present a profile of the students and faculty members of these four institutions, the curriculum followed, the impact of the presence of women faculty, and the place of women theologians in the theological formation of future priests and ministers of the word.

3. This happened simultaneously in various parts of the world, but especially in the Northern Hemisphere. See Mulackal, "Paradigm Shift in Vatican II," 53: "The council urged the nuns to look back at the founders of their orders and their missions to discover how to adapt [their] assignments to the needs of the modern world. The sisters took it very seriously." See also Schneiders, *Prophets in Their Own Country*, 51–62, for a historical overview of the awakening of religious women to their place and roles in the church.

4. From the Latin name *Congregatio Immaculati Cordis Mariae*.

5. These are the Loyola School of Theology, Maryhill School of Theology, St. Vincent School of Theology, Inter-Congregational Theological Center, University of Santo Tomas Central Seminary, Institute of Formation and Religious Studies, San Carlos Seminary, Don Bosco School of Theology, Divine Word School of Theology, Recollect School of Theology, Institute of Consecrated Life in Asia, and De La Salle University.

## Criteria for Choosing the Four Selected Schools of Theology

The schools of theology included in this research have been chosen based on their offering both: (1) a solid theological curriculum and (2) a program that is "in dialogue with the world" as suggested by the International Theological Commission (ITC). The ITC suggests that a solid theological curriculum includes foremost the study of Sacred Scriptures as the soul of theology, which is a "scientific reflection on the divine revelation which the Church accepts by faith as universal saving truth."[6] Catholic theology is "faith seeking understanding [*fides quaerens intellectum*]" and "as *scientia Dei* . . . aims to understand in a rational and systematic manner the saving truth of God."[7] In addition, Catholic theology is in constant dialogue with the world: "It should help the Church to read the signs of the times illuminated by the light that comes from divine revelation, and to profit from doing so in its life and mission."[8] Thus, Catholic theology is intercultural, contextualized, and inclusive.

We believe that the four schools we have chosen offer a solid theological formation and a program that is in dialogue with the world. They are also, of course, gender-inclusive. These schools, all located in Quezon City within Metro Manila, are the Institute of Formation of Religious Studies, the Loyola School of Theology, the St. Vincent School of Theology, and the Institute of Consecrated Life in Asia.

## Background on the Four Selected Schools of Theology

### 1. Institute of Formation of Religious Studies (IFRS)[9]

As noted above, IFRS was founded as the Sisters Formation Institute (SFI) in 1963 by the Association of Major Religious Superiors of Women in the Philippines, which is composed of twenty-three founding religious congregations and founded as a response to Vatican II's call for an *aggiornamento* of consecrated life. At the outset, SFI did not offer a curriculum of priestly formation, but rather a course of study in Catholic theology for religious men and women and laypeople, whether Catholic or not.

---

6. International Theological Commission, *Theology Today*, 5.
7. International Theological Commission, *Theology Today*, 19.
8. International Theological Commission, *Theology Today*, 58.
9. See www.ifrs.com.ph for more information.

At present, IFRS offers a one-year certificate program, a bachelor's degree in religious studies, and a master of arts in religious studies for men and women religious and laypeople who wish to gain a solid formation in theology. In the master's degree program, the major fields of study include theology, Scripture, women and religion, and Christian spirituality. After graduation, IFRS alumni become, among other things, teachers of religion and theology, ministers of the word, collaborators in parishes or dioceses, school administrators, medical and allied services personnel, community development workers, or leaders of religious congregations. They serve in numerous ministries offered by various religious congregations, not only in the Philippines and in other Asian countries, but also in other parts of the world.

The vision of IFRS is to offer a theological formation that is committed to a contextual, integrated, inclusive, and transformational ministry that witnesses to biblical and gospel imperatives.

## 2. Loyola School of Theology–Ateneo de Manila University (LST)[10]

The theological faculty of LST traces its origin to the Colegio de San Jose founded in 1601 in Manila by the Jesuits. The current institution was established in 1965 and in 1968 was federated with the Ateneo de Manila University. In 1999, the Congregation for Catholic Education established LST as an ecclesiastical faculty.

LST is an institute for theological and pastoral education run by the Jesuits of the Philippine province that is open to lay, religious, or clerical persons who desire to pursue graduate studies in theology. It provides theological preparation for the priesthood. According to its vision-mission statement, the school is dedicated to formative theological education and research within the Catholic tradition, and to responding to contemporary ecclesial and social concerns. It aims at producing graduates who are academically competent, spiritually well grounded, and apostolically motivated for Christian discipleship, renewed evangelization, social transformation, and responsible stewardship of the earth.

LST offers the following academic degrees: a baccalaureate in sacred theology; a master of arts in theological studies, pastoral ministry, and biblical exegesis; a licentiate in sacred theology; a doctorate in sacred theology; a PhD in theology; and a doctorate in ministry. It also offers a

10. See www.lst.edu for more information.

professional diploma in family ministries and certificate programs in the pastoral care of migrants, theological studies, pastoral ministry, and basic pastoral ministry.

## 3. St. Vincent School of Theology (SVST)[11]

SVST was founded in 1985 by the Philippine province of the Congregation of the Mission, a Vincentian religious congregation. It is an institute for theological, pastoral, and missiological formation in the service of the church and society. Its vision-mission statement outlines "a way of doing theology that builds on the religious experience and praxis of the socially excluded and gears toward the evangelization of the poor."[12] The theological starting point or locus of this way of theologizing is the human experience of the margins, the privileged place of God's revelation.

SVST offers the following academic degrees: doctor of philosophy in theology; master's in theology with specializations in systematic studies, moral studies, biblical studies, liturgical studies, and Vincentian studies; and a master's in pastoral ministry. Special nondegree diploma courses are also offered, including Curriculum for Ordained Ministers, Philosophy, Introductory Theological Formation, and Christian Formation for Lay People.

## 4. Institute of Consecrated Life in Asia (ICLA)[13]

The Institute of Consecrated Life in Asia (ICLA) opened its doors as an institute of higher studies in theology and pastoral ministry in 1997. It is "an academic-formative community of higher learning in doing Theology, lived spirituality and mission, and serving a multicultural student population (Religious, Lay leaders and ministers, and Priests) from emergent churches, particularly in Asia."[14] It educates for effective service in the church, promotes a deep sense of vocation and commitment to mission, forms students in gospel values, and fosters ecological stewardship and the transforming power of God through lived spirituality.

11. See www.svst.edu.ph for more information.

12. www.svst.edu.ph/home.

13. See www.icla.org.ph for more information.

14. Institute for Consecrated Life in Asia, "About Us," para. 1.

ICLA confers Master's of Arts degrees in theology, with majors in consecrated life, spirituality, missiology, and biblical ministry. Because of its affiliation with the Faculty of Theology of the Pontifical University of Santo Tomas, ICLA can confer ecclesiastical degrees—namely, the licentiate (STL) and doctoral degree in theology (SThD), both with a specialization in consecrated life.

We now present the curricula and statistical profiles of the students and the faculty in these four institutions.

## Curricula of the Four Selected Schools of Theology

As can be seen from their programs of studies, these four schools of theology offer solid theological formation to seminarians, religious men and women, and laymen and women. The schools give pride of place to the Sacred Scriptures as the soul of theology, and their curricula emphasize courses in the Old and New Testaments. As the ITC noted, this is the mark of Catholic theology: "Theology, in all its diverse traditions, disciplines and methods, is founded on the fundamental act of listening in faith to the revealed Word of God, Christ himself. Listening to God's Word is the definitive principle of Catholic theology; it leads to understanding and speech and to the formation of Christian community."[15]

A number of specialized fields of theology are available to the students at these institutions: systematic, historical, moral, sacramental and sacred liturgy, spiritual-pastoral, and missiology. LST offers courses in spirituality and leadership and migration theology. SVST has academic programs in liturgical studies and Vincentian studies. ICLA has a special offering on consecrated life.

IFRS has a special master's program in women and religion not offered by the other schools. Courses emphasizing feminist thought offered by IRFS include, among others, Women and Gender Studies, Methods of Feminist Research, Methods of Research and Biblical Hermeneutics, Christology from a Feminist Perspective, Feminist Theologies, Feminist Ethics, Women in Church History, Women in Major Religions, and Feminist Spirituality. All students at IRFS acquire knowledge of feminist critiques of society and the church and the reconstruction of gender paradigms.[16]

15. International Theological Commission, "Theology Today," 1:4.
16. I have also mentioned this in a paper I delivered in 2011 to the Circle of Catholic

None of the other three schools offers a thorough feminist orientation. The doctoral programs of SVST and ICLA include the study of feminist and ecofeminist philosophy, respectively. Once in a while, an elective
course like Women and the Scriptures is offered. At these three schools,
feminist theology and related topics are integrated into the lectures of
some professors who have a feminist orientation. A feminist consciousness is also expressed in certain cocurricular activities, like community
building, theological conferences, or modular classes, as well as through
the presence of women speakers at school gatherings. There are, however,
no required offerings in the curriculum for women and religion, gender
sensitivity, or related topics in these three institutions. Hope Antone has
observed that "very few Asian seminaries offer Feminist Theology as a
required course for all its male and female students. A few offer it as an
elective course, attracting some women and occasionally, a few men."[17]
One limitation on the offering of feminist courses is the fact that there
are very few professors in each locality who can be considered feminist
theologians.

## Statistical Profile of Students and Faculty Members
## in the Four Schools of Theology[18]

For the school year 2017–18, a total of 918 students were enrolled in
the four schools of theology, 549 men (60 percent) and 369 women (40
percent). Of the women, 24 percent came from religious congregations.
There were 289 laypersons (32 percent). The majority were Filipino—545
(or 59 percent)—while 373 (or 41 percent) were international students.
The majority of the international students came from other Asian countries, including Vietnam, China, India, Myanmar, Indonesia, and Korea.

There were a total of 182 faculty members in the four schools, with
129 (or 71 percent) men and fifty-three (or 29 percent) women. With
respect to nationality, 120 (or 66 percent) of the faculty members were

---

Women Theologians in Manila, entitled "The Impact of Feminist Theologizing in Five
Catholic Schools of Theology in the Philippines." As of 2018, the academic curricula of
the five schools discussed in the paper (one of which is IFRS) had not changed.

17. Antone, "Mainstreaming Asian Feminism," 121–22.

18. I am grateful to the following deans of the four schools, who generously as-
sisted me in gathering the data: Fr. Rogel Anecito, SJ, of LST; Prof. Miguel Lambino
of IFRS; Fr. Daniel Franklin Pilario, CM, of SVST; and Fr. Samuel Canilang, ClarM,
of ICLA.

Filipino while sixty-two (or 34 percent) belonged to other nationalities. As to educational qualifications, 115 (or 63 percent) had doctoral degrees (84 men and 31 women), while sixty-five (or 36 percent) had master's or licentiate degrees. A total of 120 (or 66 percent) of the faculty members, twenty-seven of whom were women, received theological training in well-known institutions outside the Philippines.

## Summary and Analysis of the Results

An analysis of the vision-mission statements, curricular programs, and statistical profiles of the students and faculty of the four selected schools of theology shows the following. First, the vision and mission of the schools are moving toward a balance between the academic curriculum and the contextual and intercultural aspects of reality. All four schools offer graduate degree programs that lead to master's degrees or licentiates in theology and scripture, pastoral ministry, religious studies, missiology, consecrated life, spirituality, and related fields. LST, SVST, and ICLA offer a doctoral degree in theology.

Second, the student population of these institutions, which in the past was overwhelmingly male, is becoming inclusive, encompassing not only religious men and those who study theology for priestly formation but also religious women seeking a strong theological foundation for church ministry, plus laywomen (and laymen) who are drawn to theology to discover the meaning of life and/or to participate in church ministry. If we compare the total number of male and female students in all four schools, men are still the majority, but at IFRS and ICLA, women are the majority. The total population of women in the four schools is a sizable 40 percent.

Third, the students of the four institutions are no longer only Filipino but have become international, with many Asians and others from different parts of the world.[19] This is the result of the expansion of religious congregations to Asia—especially to Vietnam, Indonesia, and China—the assignment of foreign religious missionaries to take a theological year in the Philippines, and the establishment of intercultural religious formation houses in the Philippines. All of this means that the Philippines is influencing the practice of theology in Asia. The Asian graduates

19. There are also some students from Europe, Africa, South America, and the United States.

of these institutions will do theology in their own culture and context and are future leaders in their own churches.

Fourth, women students are not only enrolled in bachelor's or non-degree certificate programs as a foundation for ministry, but they are also studying at both the master's and doctoral levels. They include Filipino and other Asian women, especially from Vietnam, India, Indonesia, Myanmar, Korea, China, and neighboring countries.

Fifth, the majority of the faculty members at the four schools are male (71 percent), but at IFRS, women comprise almost one-half of the faculty. As noted above, 66 percent of the total faculty are Filipino, and 34 percent are non-Filipino.

Sixth, the faculty in the four institutions are highly qualified experts in their field. Sixty-three percent have doctoral degrees, while 36 percent have master's or licentiate degrees (1 percent have only a bachelor's degree). Seventy-six percent earned their degrees from foreign schools of theology, while 24 percent did so at schools in the Philippines. The students in these institutions are assured of a solid theological formation because of the excellent academic curriculum and the highly qualified faculty with experience in various specialized areas of theology.

Seventh, although there are a total of fifty-three women professors in the four schools, there are only thirty-one women theologians (Filipino and non-Filipino). A number of these teach in two or three schools of theology. Of these thirty-one women theologians, twenty-five (or 81 percent) have doctorates, while six (or 19 percent) have master's or licentiate degrees. Twenty-three of these thirty-one (or 74 percent) women theologians earned their graduate degrees (master's, doctorate, or both) from well-known schools of theology in Europe or the US while nine (or 29 percent) received their degrees in the Philippines. There are also twelve women with graduate degrees who teach in fields related to theological/religious education. There are a number of women theologians teaching in other schools of theology in the country who are not counted here. It is clear that the impetus of Vatican II toward the *aggiornamento* of religious life encouraged religious women to take up graduate studies in theology. Likewise, the involvement of lay Filipino women in the Basic Ecclesial Communities, the dioceses, and the parishes has pushed them to pursue theological studies as an expression of discipleship or as part of their profession.

## Filipino Women in Schools of Theology

Here, we give attention to the thirty-one women theologians at these four institutions. Despite the fact that the administrators of these schools are keen to have women theologians on their faculties, few full-time Filipino women theologians are members of these faculties. Rather, many of them serve on a part-time basis, especially religious women who have other responsibilities in their congregations.

These women theologians come from many different theological and academic backgrounds and thus contribute to the richness and diversity of the country's theological curricula. Of the thirty-one women theologians in the four schools under study, twenty-two (or 71 percent) finished their MAs or PhDs in schools or universities outside the country, either in Europe or the US. Eighteen of the twenty-two women (or 58 percent) have PhDs, while four (or 18 percent) have STL/SSL degrees. Ten (or 32 percent) of the thirty-one women theologians specialized in Sacred Scriptures or biblical studies; six (or 19 percent) in theological studies; two (or 6 percent) in spirituality; two (or 6 percent) in religion and women's studies; and two (or 6 percent) in cognate fields of religion and psychology or anthropology. Of the thirty-one women teachers, nine (or 29 percent) finished their theological or related studies at schools in the Philippines. Seven have a PhD in biblical theology, applied theology, or religious education/pedagogy, while two have MAs in religious studies. There is a good mix of both religious and laywomen theologians and women in related fields, as well as a good mix of scholars in Scripture and other fields of theology.

## The Impact of the Presence of Women Theologians on Both Women and Men Studying Theology

Heather Grennan Gary describes the ways in which important women theologians in the US have influenced the church.[20] She asserts that they have done so by explaining church doctrines and tradition to the people, authoring prayers appropriate for various occasions, making their voices heard in the public forum, not in the Curia, helping to articulate women's insights and inspiring courage, authoring and publishing feminist books, and teaching and working in parishes.

20. Gary, "What Women Theologians Have Done for the Church."

My 2011 paper titled "Impact of Feminist Theologizing in Five Catholic Schools of Theology in the Philippines" showed with clarity that, during the decade from 2001 to 2011, feminist theologizing at IFRS and four other schools of theology stimulated some students, both women and men, to write master's theses on women's issues. This may be the result of the influence of their courses specifically on topics of feminist theology taught by women theologians, or of the integration of feminist ideas in other courses. In 2011, IFRS had produced ten master's theses by women on issues of women and religion; MST had produced eight theses, seven by women; SVST had produced three bachelor's theses in philosophy (all written by men); and LST had produced eleven theses, ten of which were written by women. It can be seen that feminist ideas stimulate the minds and hearts of both women and men and that men are also challenged by women's issues and concerns. Feminist discourse has widened in scope to include various aspects of theology, including biblical hermeneutics, Mariology, ecclesiology, moral theology, pastoral theology, sexuality, religious life, spirituality, and other issues affecting women.

Many Filipino women theologians, especially those who work full-time in this role, deliver papers and publish their research in journals, monographs, and books. Some others do theology at the grassroots and offer papers relating their experiences at theological and biblical conferences. Their research has influenced their teaching and, consequently, the thinking and insights of their students. It has also influenced their readers and those who have heard them speak at conferences and in theological circles.

As part of this research, I prepared a short survey to collect the impressions of twenty theology students (seventeen men and three women) about the impact their women professors had had on their way of doing theology and their growth in personhood and spirituality. The students attended the classes of two to four women theologians. All twenty of the students agreed that their women scripture professors, all of whom had doctoral degrees and employed effective teaching methodologies, had influenced their practice of theology. Below is a summary of some of the things they had to say about their women professors:

- They are confident, well-prepared, skillful in delivering their lessons, devoted, alive, interesting, creative, and offer challenging insights.

- They are masters in their field and offer more details in their lectures and assignments than male professors. They are motherly, more compassionate, show greater care, and teach from the heart.

- They show mature faith from a biblical perspective.

- They are well-read and interested in what they do, unlike male professors, who seem to teach out of obedience to their superiors.

- They have a nonthreatening, yet powerful, presence and are easy to talk with.

- They are as good as any male professors.

With respect to the impact of women professors on the students, they had the following to say:

- Women theologians demonstrate that study is not only about critical thinking but also involves the whole being.

- They are able to smile during class, which male professors do not do.

- They help students to be more creative, patient, and careful about what they are learning and also to approach concepts in a less rigid manner, using a broader perspective.

- They pay attention to details.

- They expose students to a feminist perspective on interpreting the Bible.

- They guide students to deepen their faith and see God in a mature and scholarly way.

- They guide students to a realization that the church is composed of male and female, with a view toward greater inclusivity.

- They inspire us to be gentle and caring for others.

- Their wholehearted way of offering their best in teaching invites students to become authentic witnesses of Christ.

- Through their lessons in the Scripture, students experience conversion.

- They are steady formators of our theological foundations, always encouraging and teaching the skills needed for independent learning.

In my twenty-two years of teaching a course on the New Testament, I have collaborated with six other women Scripture scholars, who are my fellow alumni, students, friends, and colleagues. We all teach in the same schools of theology and have seen that many of our students have gone on to specialize in scriptural studies in their master's and doctoral programs. In fact, the dean of theology at LST informed me when we began the second term in January of 2018 that 50 percent of the graduate students were specializing in Sacred Scriptures. This was delightful news—I realized that, in one way or another, the women members of the faculty of Sacred Scriptures have influenced their students to love the study of Scripture and to find fullness of joy in their close encounters with the Jesus of the Gospels.

## What Is the Future of Women Theologians in the Philippines (and in Asia)?

My survey of the profile of students of the four selected institutions revealed a population of 222 young religious women and 289 laywomen and men, or 56 percent of the total number of students. They come from the Philippines and other Asian countries and take bachelor's and graduate courses in theology and scripture. If they endure the rigors of theological education and formation, they have the potential—say, over the course of the next ten years—to become the teachers of these subjects in our schools of theology in the Philippines and in Asia. They need our encouragement and support as we mentor them in their chosen disciplines and witness to them the Christian way of life. In the same way that we who are ahead of them have been given our rightful place and respect as scholars in the fields of theology and scripture at this moment in the history of theological education in the Philippines (though not without struggles), so too will they enjoy these privileges. Future women theologians in the Philippines will have even greater opportunities, because the schools of theology in the country are now searching for qualified women to emphasize the feminine aspect of reality as part of the formation of deacons and priests.

Agnes Brazal's research into what theologians see as significant opportunities for theological development in Asia emphasized that "the more dialogical approach of Pope Francis is an opportunity for Asian women theologians to push for a greater recognition of their role in the Church."[21] She observes that, in the Philippines "those with theologi-

21. Brazal, "Professional Women Theologians in Asia," para. 7.

cal degrees can be employed full time, teaching mostly undergraduate students in many Catholic universities" but that "only a handful of women are employed full-time in seminaries/theological institutions."[22] She also notes that there are at least 110 Asian Catholic women with doctoral degrees from India, the Philippines, Korea, and neighboring countries.[23]

Recent statements by the Congregation for the Clergy in an instruction titled *The Gift of the Priestly Vocation* recognize the important role of consecrated persons and laypeople in the theological formation of seminarians and priests and in theological education generally:

> The presence of the laity and of consecrated persons in the Seminary is an important point of reference in the formative journey of the candidates. Seminarians should be formed in a proper appreciation of the various charisms to be found in the diocesan community. The priest, in fact, is called to foster a diversity of charisms within the Church. Consecrated life is an eloquent and attractive sign of the radical nature of the Gospel and of availability for service. For their part, the lay faithful cooperate in the evangelizing mission of Christ, and offer an edifying witness to consistency and to life choices according to the Gospel.[24]

The instruction also affirms the significant role played by women:

> The presence of women in the Seminary journey of formation has its own formative significance. They can be found as specialists, on the teaching staff, within the apostolate, within families, and in service to the community. Their presence also helps to instill a recognition of how men and women complement one another. Often, women are numerically greater among those whom the priest will serve, and with whom he will work in the pastoral ministry. They offer an edifying example of humility, generosity, and selfless service.[25]

Thus, the instruction encourages women to participate in theological education as a ministry. The instruction also states that religious and laymen and women can be partners in the theological formation of the priesthood:

22. Brazal, "Professional Women Theologians in Asia," para. 8.
23. Brazal, "Professional Women Theologians in Asia," para. 1.
24. Congregation for the Clergy, *Gift of the Priestly Vocation*, 150.
25. Congregation for the Clergy, *Gift of the Priestly Vocation*, 151.

The contribution of members of Institutes of Consecrated Life and Societies of Apostolic Life, and also of the lay faithful, can be of value in certain circumstances. Through the diversity of vocations, each professor should be able to present the seminarians with a knowledge of his or her own charism, demonstrate the significance of his or her particular contribution to the life of the Church, and offer a coherent witness to the life of the Gospel.[26]

It should be noted in this regard that Pope Francis, in *Veritatis Gaudium,* his apostolic constitution on ecclesiastical universities and faculties, did not draw any distinction based on gender or status concerning teachers hired in ecclesiastical faculties. This also provides an opening for religious women and laymen and women to become teachers of theology.

With the openness of Pope Francis and other church leaders to the presence of women and laypersons as agents in the priestly formation of seminarians, there seems to be a bright future for women religious and laywomen and men to realize their missionary dream of becoming professors of Scripture and theology—preachers and teachers of the word and witnesses for students of theology of a joyful encounter with the person of Jesus Christ.

But this is dependent on these would-be teachers undergoing a thorough theological formation. *The Gift of the Priestly Vocation* states that "professors must have obtained the requisite academic degrees: a licentiate, or its equivalent, is required as a minimum to teach philosophy and the sacred sciences. . . . Professors should be experienced and have the ability to teach, and are expected to have sufficient knowledge of the disciplines related to those that they teach.[27]

The necessity of thorough educational preparation is also emphasized in *Veritatis Gaudium,* which states that permanent teachers

> must 1) be distinguished by wealth of knowledge, witness of Christian and ecclesial life, and a sense of responsibility; 2) have a suitable Doctorate or equivalent title or exceptional and singular scientific accomplishment; 3) show documentary proof of suitability for doing scientific research, especially by a published dissertation; [and] 4) demonstrate teaching ability.[28]

---

26. Congregation for the Clergy, *Gift of the Priestly Vocation,* 143.

27. Congregation for the Clergy, *Gift of the Priestly Vocation,* 144.

28. Francis, *Veritatis Gaudium,* art. 25, sec. 1.

These requirements also hold true "in proportionate measure" for non-permanent teachers.[29] Moreover, teachers must be persons of "upright life, integrity of doctrine, and devotion to duty."[30]

It is noteworthy that some laywomen and men in the Philippines have earned licentiate and doctoral degrees in theology and scripture and become professional theologians. They are capable of full-time work and can acquire permanent status as teachers in ecclesiastical faculties. As noted above, *The Gift of the Priestly Vocation* underlines the value of lay theologians' presence on ecclesiastical faculties.

In contrast to what is required of the clergy, religious congregations of women in the Philippines do not generally require a graduate theological degree for church ministry. The common practice is to have religious sisters enroll in a one-year certificate course in theology and scripture to prepare them for their ministries and to enhance their personal growth in spirituality. And this is the sum total of the theological formation they receive for a whole life of service in the church![31]

A few congregations, however, have allowed sisters who have a desire to engage in graduate studies in theology to undergo the rigors of full-time study, but only when a scholarship is available. As a result, at this point in time in the Filipino church, there are few highly qualified religious women theologians in the four institutions studied. But even religious sisters who manage to become theologians often cannot become permanent teachers in schools of theology or ecclesiastical faculties, because their first responsibility is to their congregational mission. Hence, they end up becoming nonpermanent teachers even if they have been teaching for decades. As nonpermanent teachers, they can never be promoted to the highest ranks of their profession even if they are excellent teachers, involved in research, publish scientific works, and exhibit commitment to their theological tasks. Adding to these obstacles to their professional development, they will never receive a declaration of *nihil*

29. Francis, *Veritatis Gaudium*, art. 25, sec. 2.

30. Francis, *Veritatis Gaudium*, art. 26, sec. 1.

31. It's worth pointing out that, because religious sisters manage Catholic schools, hospitals, homes for children and the elderly, social and pastoral centers, retreat houses, and work with the poor and oppressed in the peripheries, they are often required to engage in further studies to support their work in these ministries in fields like teaching, school management, social work, hospital administration, healthcare, community development, accountancy and business education, architecture and engineering, and others. For more on this, see Schneiders, *Prophets in Their Own Country*, 60.

*obstat* from the Holy See,[32] which may, in the end, disqualify them from teaching theology in an ecclesiastical faculty, especially if the administration is able to hire permanent teachers.

Sr. Mary Luke Tobin has observed that one of the impacts of Vatican II on women has been the emergence of a number of outstanding theologians and biblical scholars.[33] While she is speaking from her experience in the US, this is also true in the Philippines. There are, however, only a few women congregations present in the Philippines—all of which have roots in the US and Europe—that have ventured to assign a sister or two to a full-time ministry of theological or scriptural education (two examples are the Maryknoll Missionaries and the Religious of the Sacred Heart of Jesus). The majority of religious women who have finished the licentiate or doctorate in theology have instead been given administrative work in their congregations, hindering them from engaging in a full-time ministry in academic theology.

Religious congregations of women in the Philippines need to modify their perspective of their communities' mission to include the full-time teaching of theology and scripture, on equal footing with the management of schools, hospitals, social centers, and prayer houses, as well as working with the poor in both rural and urban places for justice, peace, and the integrity of creation. By adopting this vision, the congregations could positively contribute to the theological education of both men and women, especially those being formed in a priestly or religious vocation.

## Conclusion

There is hope for women practicing theology in the Philippines. The presence of women theologians as professors in schools of theology is encouraging many more young women, both religious and lay, to embark on a ministry or career of theological education. Because the country has institutions that offer theological degrees to both women and men, there are many opportunities for women to undertake graduate theological education. As theology and scripture professors, spiritual directors, liturgists, canon lawyers, religious educators, etc., women with graduate degrees in theology will have many possibilities to collaborate in the discipleship formation of priests, religious, and laity.

32. Francis, *Veritatis Gaudium*, art. 27, sec. 2.
33. See Tobin, "Women in the Church Since Vatican II."

In the not-so-distant future, the theological faculty in these schools will be the home of the religious women and laywomen (and men) whom we now-active theologians are training and developing. With the increasing number of non-Filipinos (both Asian and non-Asian) studying in our schools of theology, there may be a motivation for Filipino and other Asian women to enhance an intercultural theological education of future ministers of the word, a ministry that is a missionary task of the church.

Recent instruction from church leadership, including Pope Francis, has clearly recognized the role of consecrated women and laypeople in priestly formation. The further development of this role will vary according to the understanding and readiness of administrators of schools of theology. This article has discussed how, in four schools of theology in the Philippines' capital city, religious women and laywomen (and men) are already participating in the formation of the future clergy and ministers of the word, both men and women. These four institutions are searching for qualified and well-trained women professors to become part of their faculties on a full-time basis.

Religious congregations of women should come to see theological education as a formal ministry of their communities. This shift in perspective would have a positive influence on not only the formation of the clergy of the future but also on the communities' initial and continuing formation programs for their members.

## Bibliography

Antone, Hope. "Mainstreaming Asian Feminism in Theological Education in Asia." In *Charting the Future of Theology and Theological Education in Asian Contexts*, edited by David Kwang-sun Suh et al., 114–22. New Delhi: ISPCK, 2004.

Brazal, Agnes. "Professional Women Theologians in Asia: Opportunities and Challenges." *INSeCT*, August 13, 2014. https://insecttheology.wordpress.com/2014/08/13/reports-from-asia-pacific-theologians/.

Catholic Directory of the Philippines. *The 2014–15 Catholic Directory of the Philippines*. Quezon City: CBCP and Claretian, 2014.

Congregation for the Clergy. *The Gift of the Priestly Vocation*. London: Catholic Truth Society, 2017.

Francis, Pope. *Veritatis Gaudium: Apostolic Constitution on Ecclesiastical Universities and Faculties*. Vatican City: Libreria Editrice Vaticana, 2018.

Gary, Heather Grennan. "What Women Theologians Have Done for the Church." *U.S. Catholic*, December 11, 2012. http://www.uscatholic.org/articles/201211/what-women-theologians-have-done-church-26587.

Institute for Consecrated Life in Asia. "About Us." https://www.icla.org.ph/about-us

International Theological Commission. "Theology Today: Perspectives, Principles, and Criteria." https://www.vatican.va/roman_curia/congregations/cfaith/cti_documents/rc_cti_doc_20111129_teologia-oggi_en.html#CHAPTER_1.

Mulackal, Shalini. "Paradigm Shift in Vatican II and Its Impact on Women." In *Women as Equal Disciples: Unfinished Task of the Church*, edited by Virginia Saldanha et al., 41–59. Pune, India: Streevani, 2016.

Schneiders, Sandra. *Prophets in Their Own Country: Women Religious Bearing Witness to the Gospel in a Troubled Church.* Quezon City: Claretian, 2011.

Tobin, Mary Luke. "Women in the Church Since Vatican II." *America*, November 1, 1986. www.americamagazine.org/issue/100/women-Church-vatican-ii.

Uy, Jocelyn R. "Filipino Catholic Population Expanding, Say Church Officials." *Philippine Daily Inquirer*, August 11, 2013. https://newsinfo.inquirer.net/463377/filipino-catholic-population-expanding-say-church-officials.

Vargas, Niceta. "The Impact of Feminist Theologizing in Five Catholic Schools of Theology in the Philippines." Paper delivered at the initial meeting of the Circle of Women Theologians of the Philippines in Manila, May 28, 2011.

# Conclusion

## AHIDA CALDERÓN PILARSKI

MELINDA ROPER, THE KEYNOTE speaker at the 2018 conference[1] organized by DePaul University—out of which this book emerged—shared a powerful insight. The wisdom surfacing from her many decades of missionary service revealed to her that in order to advance a person's (or an institution's) understanding of the multiple and diverse ways in which women have been exercising their leadership in the church, one must be attentive to the divine *ruah*, "the breath of God present, creative, moving, evolving" (see page 8). Furthermore, addressing the incommensurability of this divine breath's horizons—especially when seeing the challenges that women had to face throughout history—Roper cites Jesus' words in the Gospel of John which say that this *ruah* "blows wherever it wishes; you hear the sound it makes, but you do not know where it comes from or where it is going" (3:8).

All the essays presented in this volume elucidate the many ways in which this *ruah*—the breath of God—has inspired women, the daughters of wisdom, in their "walking together" (synodality)[2] in hope, despite their challenging journeys (individual and collective). One cannot help but to see in these women's diverse leadership roles the *ruah* that animates their tireless efforts to live up to their call to participate in advancing the mission of the Church in their faith communities, in academia, and in many other spaces in society (locally and globally).

1. Her presentation is included as the first essay in this volume.
2. See the book's introduction.

As described in the introduction, all of the essays in this volume are addressing contexts from the Southern Hemisphere (Latin America, Africa, and Asia). Recently, some academic and theological circles have begun referring to the geographical Southern Hemisphere as the Global South. However, the distinctiveness of this term/concept—Global South—deserves some attention here. Despite the fact that, in reading the essays in this volume, one may find that women's leadership models and/or the challenges they face in their own countries located in the Southern Hemisphere are comparable to those in the Northern Hemisphere, it is important to note that the geopolitical history of the southern continents has been deeply impacted by colonialism. This is a significant difference, and its continuous impact can be observed at many levels. Walter Mignolo explains that the Global South "is not simply a line below the equator . . . [but it] is an ideological concept highlighting the economic, political, and epistemic dependence and unequal relations in the global world order, from a subaltern perspective."[3] When focusing on women's leadership in the contexts of the Global South,[4] it is critical to understand that there are (and continue to be) many additional layers of oppression and suffering. In fact, the term "Global South" is aimed at focusing on "the places on the planet that endured the experience of coloniality—that suffered, and still suffer, the consequences of the colonial wound (e.g., humiliation, racism, genderism; in brief, the indignity of being considered lesser humans),"[5] so that this critical awareness prevents the perpetuation of violence (physical, mental, epistemological, spiritual) by restoring the dignity and value of every person. As the contours of the Global North have been (and continue to be) developed, these contours tend to consider subaltern knowledges as secondary or marginal, and hence it is no surprise that marginalization appears in a more visible manner through the very limited opportunities for the praxis of women's leadership in the Global South.

In sharp contrast to the old geopolitical paradigm in the background of the differentiation between the Global North and the Global South, Pope Francis proposes an alternative geopolitical vision, one that

3. Mignolo, "Global South and World Dis/Order," 166.

4. It is important to note here that, in many cases of migration from the Southern Hemisphere to countries in the Northern Hemisphere, a person's existence might still revolve around the realities of the Global South.

5. Mignolo, "Global South and World Dis/Order," 185. See also Mignolo, "Geopolitics of Knowledge," 57–96.

allows for the consideration of the term "global" in a different manner. His geopolitical vision is based on a sociocultural model. Rafael Luciani points out that, originally, the ideology behind the term "geopolitics"— coined by Rudolf Kjellen in 1899—was aimed at explaining "the need to occupy territories for the sake of the development of the inhabitants and the political projections of nations . . . [and so] the paradigm of occupation and expansion has driven the world political model."[6] This old geopolitical paradigm to some degree describes also the mindset behind many territorial occupations done by ancient, modern, and contemporary empires. Pope Francis proposes instead a new geopolitical model where "the peripheries [are to] be placed at the center, in a multiform and intercultural relationship."[7] It is an alternative geopolitical vision focused on the pursuit of the common good. This vision is based on four criteria of discernment:

> (1) "the whole before the part" (EG 234–36), (2) "reality before the idea" (EG 231–33), (3) "unity over conflict" (EG 217–37, Lumen Fidei [LF] 55.57), and (4) "time over space" (EG 217–37, LF 55.57). The interrelationship of these four principles gives shape to the Bergoglian image of the "polyhedron" as creative unity within diversity, where each . . . contributes its own reality as part of the whole.[8]

It is in this light that one can see that, despite the realities experienced by people in the Global South, through diverse leadership roles, women (unknowingly or oriented by the ruah) have been already paving some of the paths toward this geopolitical vision—focused on the pursuit of the common good—in the Southern Hemisphere.

The essays in this volume, across the southern continents, bring to the fore three important areas where women have tried to exercise their leadership despite the fact that their work and subaltern knowledges[9] have been considered secondary or marginal. By no means are these areas meant to determine the scope of women's leadership praxis in these continents, nor are they aimed at generalizing any of their practices as universal descriptions of their localities. Women's diverse leadership praxis constitutes a part of the whole in the Bergoglian image of the polyhedron.

6. Luciani, Pope Francis and the Theology of the People, 108.

7. Luciani, Pope Francis and the Theology of the People, 115.

8. Luciani, Pope Francis and the Theology of the People, 109–10.

9. To learn more about this term, see Mignolo, Local Histories/Global Designs.

The three areas are academia, basic ecclesial communities/faith-based groups, and grassroots social organizations or movements. As each of these areas are briefly described, this conclusion also includes some of the authors' recommendations for the future in each of the corresponding areas.

In the academic arena, one can see important cross-continental pathways shown in the essays of Calderón Pilarski, Reid, DeAnda (Latin America), and Vargas (Asia). Their contributions highlight two important trends. One focuses on the gradual and increased presence of women occupying teaching positions at theological schools and universities, especially in the last five decades. The other trend relates to how this presence has also signified the opening of other opportunities to advance the field of theology, epistemologically and methodologically (i.e., moving beyond the dominant practice of having women as objects/subjects of study to that of having women fully present as subjects studying and doing theology). DeAnda even calls for the importance of retrieving the earlier theological work done by women like Sor María Anna Águeda de San Ignacio (1695–1750) whose writings remain relevant for Latinx studies today.

These are some of the contributors' observations to continue advancing the work and leadership of women in this area:

- In considering women's leadership in the global church, Ahida Calderón Pilarski calls for prioritizing "deep thinking," which is at the heart of every paradigm shift or reframing of a problematic situation. The church must apply deep thinking using concepts such as the theology of the people and synodality to reflect on its mission. Deep thinking can assist in reenvisioning the mindset or framework that has influenced and shaped the past and current academic, ecclesial, and social structures and practices—especially those that discriminate against women.

- Barbara Reid highlights the ways in which feminist biblical scholars (professional exegetes) have already developed and continue to develop feminist critical methods. Reading the Scriptures with the mind, eyes, and heart of a woman is a life-enhancing endeavor that has brought—and continues to bring—life and new insights into the way people are reading and interpreting biblical stories.

- Neomi DeAnda observes that the writings of women theologians throughout the history of the church, especially those from the

Global South, remain relevant today as their writings may continue to inform current scholarship and ministry by allowing for some braiding of cultures. Interculturality happens not only across contemporary contexts, but it can be found also across time.

- Niceta Vargas shows the very positive impact caused by the presence of women theologians at academic institutions. Just their presence is encouraging many more young women, both religious and lay, to embark on a ministry or career in theological education. Women trained at these theological institutions can collaborate professionally as teachers, spiritual directors, guidance counselors, liturgists, and in many other roles.

The next arena where women's leadership has been exercised is the Basic Ecclesial Communities (BECs) and other faith-based activities/ practices, as in the case of the Marian devotion at sanctuaries (María del Pilar Silveria). The BECs are "domestic churches" (*LG*, 11), forming a family of families (Wendy Louis). These organizations have created an organic platform for women to take on more leadership roles, even if their work in ministry at the BECs remains underestimated. MarySylvia Nwachukwu emphasizes the importance of knowing that, historically in the African contexts, culture has remained essential to understanding family relationships and women's leadership roles in faith communities; it determines many of the roles in these settings. Also connected to the understanding of family and culture, Silveira shows that women have played a key role in keeping, as a family tradition, a Marian devotion at many sanctuaries in Latin America. These spaces are a hidden treasure of women's leadership.

Regarding this area, the authors offer the following observations:

- Louis highlights the importance of understanding the impact of culture, structures, and traditions in gaining a balance of power when it comes to the roles played and responsibilities given to women. She says that, in the Asian context, the BECs represent a hope for evangelization because they provide a key platform for ministry. However, the institutional church has to provide more funding and resources, and it must examine how women leaders can be enabled to become more confident in the roles they are already performing. Building capacity in this area to expand this key platform, especially by offering more leadership training for women, can make a big difference in advancing the mission of the church.

- Nwachukwu calls for more attention to the importance of family culture in African contexts, because she believes that major positive changes connected to women's leadership roles are happening already within the family setting, and these changes are now being reflected in church settings as well. These are clear opportunities to advance and improve women's leadership roles in the church; however, these roles must be identified and supported.

- Silveira calls for the institutional church to offer more resources to study, interpret, and understand the richness of Marian faith experiences. She says that it is necessary to approach these realities with adequate research tools so that the interpretation can be more appropriate and authentic.

The third arena, focusing on grassroots social organizations or movements, has seen fewer institutional/ecclesial constraints for women to exercise their leadership in response to their call, as children of God, to advance the mission of the church. Working through NGOs, orphanages, schools, social media, research or government projects in Uganda (Jay Carney)—or through larger associations like EWA or WKRI in Asia (Jeane Peracullo)—has provided broader and unexpected opportunities for women to develop their leadership potential. Yet, as in the previous areas, there needs to be more intentional and strategic efforts to acknowledge, support, and build increased capacity in those spaces where women have been exercising their leadership already.

The contributors offer the following recommendations in this area:

- Carney believes that the kind of leadership work done by women in diverse organizations truly embodies Catholic social teaching's call to solidarity. As he illustrates, these exemplary ways of being church in the challenging contexts of war, poverty, and political authoritarianism should serve as a call for the church to reexamine and discern the richness of incarnational evangelization on the streets of our own towns and cities.

- Peracullo points to the relevance of the continuing interrogation of world Catholicism to maintain a living tradition. She calls especially for the appreciation of female-centered praxis, because it reflects an intertwining epistemological and ethical stance that is oriented toward the poor, the oppressed, and the marginalized—seeking the common good. She also observes that we must not lose sight of the quest for justice, because it should inform the work of every person.

As Melinda Roper perceptively points out in the conclusion of her own essay, "[s]cience is offering us inspirational organizational principles. . . . From microbiology to astrophysics, dynamic structures of life and the universe are being discovered. . . . It seems to me that the church, as a living sacrament of God present, should be in the forefront of discovering new organizational models for and with the human community" (see page 11).

The church of the Third Millennium must respond to its call to remain faithful to its mission, and this requires being attentive to the "signs of the times" (*GS*, 4), especially in this unprecedented new era. The changes that we are experiencing around the world are different from the past. As Pope Francis, before becoming pope, explained to a group in Buenos Aires: "What is characteristic of the 'change of epoch' [that we are experiencing] is that things are no longer in their place. What previously served for explaining the world, relationships, good and evil, doesn't seem to work anymore."[10] Women's presence and strong adaptive leadership remain a hidden treasure that has been always there at the service of the church's mission despite the many challenges they had and continue to face. Perhaps the kind of reflection that the church needs to do now truly requires deep thinking and strategic thinking.

World Catholicism, using Roper's words, is "being invited to a new moment of creativity and integrity as our living structures reflect more faithfully those of the planet Earth and those of the Gospel. Both Earth and Gospel are alive. Changing structures is risky but so exciting and so necessary" (see page 11).

## Bibliography

Bergoglio, J. M. "Palabras del Arzobispo, Cardenal Jorge Bergoglio, en la primera reunión del Consejo Presbiteral 2008." April 15, 2008. https://www.arzbaires.org.ar/inicio/homilias/homilias2008.htm#consejo_presbiteral.

Luciani, Rafael. *Pope Francis and the Theology of the People*. Maryknoll, NY: Orbis, 2017.

Mignolo, Walter D. "The Geopolitics of Knowledge and the Colonial Difference." *The South Atlantic Quarterly* 101 (2002) 57–96.

10. Bergoglio, "Palabras de Arzobispo," para. 11.

————. "The Global South and World Dis/Order." *Journal of Anthropological Research* 67.2 (2011) 165–88.

————. *Local Histories/Global Designs: Coloniality, Subaltern Knowledges, and Border Thinking.* Princeton: Princeton University Press, 2000.

# Subject Index

Made in the USA
Thornton, CO
07/20/23 15:16:31

d0eff26c-2b69-4f20-936c-cae2029df295R01